Performance Tuning and Optimizing ASP.NET Applications

JEFFREY HASAN WITH KENNETH TU

Performance Tuning and Optimizing ASP.NET Applications
Copyright ©2003 by Jeffrey Hasan with Kenneth Tu

ISBN (pbk): 1-59059-072-4

Printed and bound in the United States of America 12345678910

Technical Reviewer: Michael Machowski
Editorial Directors: Dan Appleman, Gary Cornell, Simon Hayes, Karen Watterson, John Zukowski
Managing Editor: Grace Wong
Project Manager: Sofia Marchant
Copy Editor: Kim Wimpsett
Compositor: Impressions Book and Journal Services, Inc.
Indexer: Rebecca Plunkett
Cover Designer: Kurt Krames
Production Manager: Kari Brooks
Manufacturing Manager: Tom Debolski

Distributed to the book trade in the United States by Springer-Verlag New York, Inc., 175 Fifth Avenue, New York, NY, 10010 and outside the United States by Springer-Verlag GmbH & Co. KG, Tiergartenstr. 17, 69112 Heidelberg, Germany.

In the United States, phone 1-800-SPRINGER, email orders@springer-ny.com, or visit http://www.springer-ny.com.

Outside the United States, fax +49 6221 345229, email orders@springer.de, or visit http://www.springer.de.

For information on translations, please contact Apress directly at 2560 9th Street, Suite 219, Berkeley, CA 94710.

Phone 510-549-5930, fax: 510-549-5939, email info@apress.com, or visit http://www.apress.com.

The source code for this book is available to readers at http://www.apress.com in the Downloads section.

Jeffrey Hasan would like to dedicate this book to his family and loved ones whose support makes everything possible.

Kenneth Tu would like to dedicate this book to Grandma, family, and friends.

Contents at a Glance

Contents

About the Authors

 **Jeffrey Hasan** is a technical architect and software developer specializing in Microsoft technology at InfoQuest Systems (http://www.infoquest.tv), a leading provider of business intelligence applications and services for the telecommunications and broadband industries. He has coauthored numerous books and articles on .NET and Web development topics and has extensive experience developing enterprise applications. Jeff has a master's degree from Duke University and is a Microsoft Certified Solution Developer (MCSD). When he is not working, Jeff likes to travel to far-flung corners of the world. His most recent travels have taken him from the rainforests of Costa Rica to the Karakoram Mountains of northern Pakistan, followed by a tour through the beaches and towns of southern Spain. JHasan85@hotmail.com.

Kenneth Tu is a software developer specializing in Microsoft technology and is currently developing enterprise Web applications at InfoQuest Systems (http://www.infoquest.tv), a leading provider of business intelligence applications and services for the telecommunications and broadband industries. He has extensive experience developing both Windows and Web-based applications. Ken has a degree in Electrical Engineering from the University of California, Irvine. He currently lives in Southern California and spends his free time cycling (road and mountain), listening to music by the Dave Matthews Band, and waiting for the Kings to win the Stanley Cup. KennethTu@hotmail.com.

About the Technical Reviewer

Michael Machowski is a senior consultant with Microsoft Consulting Services. Michael provides architectural guidance and develops solutions for businesses adopting advanced Microsoft technologies.

Acknowledgments

THE BOOK YOU HOLD IN your hands is the culmination of months of hard work and a passionate desire to create a high-quality, informative text on ASP.NET application performance. Like all major projects, it would not have been possible without the support and hard work of a great many people. First and foremost I would like to thank the team at Apress: Dan Appleman, Gary Cornell, Sofia Marchant, Kari Brooks, Kim Wimpsett, Grace Wong, Doris Wong, Beth Christmas, and all of the editorial and production staff who worked on this book. I would also like to thank my coauthor, Kenneth Tu, for his dedication and hours of hard work during what was a very challenging year. Finally, I would like to thank our technical reviewer, Michael Machowski, for his exhaustive reviews of our work and for his admirable expertise and commitment to excellence.

—Jeffrey Hasan

First, I would like to acknowledge the work of Microsoft in creating this fantastic new .NET Framework.

More specifically, I am grateful to Jeffrey Hasan for inviting me to participate in this project and for his guidance and patience throughout the project.

I would also like to thank my family and friends, who made it a point to keep me up-to-date on the many experiences I missed during the lifecycle of this project.

Thanks to the musicians from the Dave Matthews Band, U2, and Radiohead, whose music was greatly appreciated during the time I spent writing and rewriting the material for this book.

And, finally, I want to acknowledge my wife, Yovy. We have shared seven years, and although there have been some bad times, I wouldn't trade them for the world.

—Kenneth Tu

Introduction

THE INTERNET HAS DEVELOPED at an astonishing pace over the past several years. Until quite recently, most Web sites consisted of a collection of static pages linked in a web of hyperlinks and anchor tags. From these humble origins, a typical Web site today is a rich, graphically intense experience that interacts with the user. Currently, Web sites are more feature-rich than ever before, and developers face the dual challenges of delivering rich features and delivering good performance. The best Web site in the world will impress no one if the pages will not load quickly and the user is kept waiting. At best, you risk annoying the user and having them leave your site, never to return. At worst, you can lose revenue if the site in question is a high-volume e-commerce site that must perform quickly and reliably for a large number of users.

Today's sophisticated Web users demand functionality *and* performance, and they are unsympathetic to any tradeoff between the two. As a developer, and as a reader of this book, you need to know the tools and techniques to provide users with both. A Web application is simply a collection of display elements and business components that collaborate to provide a workspace for accomplishing tasks. They are, of course, built on an Internet technology substrate, which includes by-now familiar technologies such as Hypertext Markup Language (HTML) for rendering content and protocols such as Extensible Markup Language (XML), Simple Object Access Protocol (SOAP), Hypertext Transfer Protocol (HTTP), and Transmission Control Protocol/Internet Protocol (TCP/IP) for delivering the content across the wire. You can serve up Web applications on the public Internet or simply on a private Intranet. Whichever is the case matters little from a purely development perspective because the technical challenges are similar for the developer. The deployment and security challenges certainly are not, but that is a topic for another book.

This book focuses on building high-performance Web applications using Microsoft's ASP.NET technology. Pure and simple. The technical book market today is being flooded with a slew of titles on how to build applications with .NET technology, and many are undoubtedly very good. But the majority of these titles simply take a "how-to" approach on how to program with the .NET Framework. They often pay little more than cursory attention to the real-world issues and challenges that developers face. The learning curve for .NET clearly starts with understanding the Common Language Runtime (CLR) and the new Class Framework because they enable you to actually build your application. But from there, the learning curve shifts toward more complex and less neat issues such as design decisions and the relative performance of one technical approach over another. At this level, it is no longer a question of *how* you implement a feature.

It becomes a question of what is the *optimal* way to implement the feature to ensure elegant, bug-free code *and* excellent performance.

Who This Book Is For

The target audience for this book is intermediate to advanced developers who have some experience working with .NET technology in general and ASP.NET technology in particular. The ideal reader falls in the gray area between the two learning curves described in the previous section. In other words, this reader is past the stage where they need to read another language-focused, how-to book; instead, they need a book that tackles real-world issues and challenges with ASP.NET applications. There is clearly no substitute to grinding through the discovery process of how to code with .NET. But once you get past these initial stages, you are ready to start asking the tough questions, such as the following:

- Which data access method gives me the best performance for the kind of data with which I am working?

- My Web application uses Session variables: Is this still taboo?

- What are my options for caching sections of my Web application?

- I cannot get enough of using view state: Is this a good thing?

- How do I monitor the performance of my application?

- How scalable is my application? Will it break under pressure?

- How do I manage state on a server farm?

If this list does not get you sweating, then nothing else will!

The Goal of This Book

This book gives you the tools and techniques for building high-performance Web applications with ASP.NET. In particular, it focuses on the often-neglected topics of performance monitoring and Web stress testing. Web applications are required to perform well under highly variable load levels. If you are lucky—and live on a distant planet in a galaxy far, far away—then your Web application will be overpowered for the actual load it experiences and the application performance will be outstanding from Day 1 on. But if you are like the rest of us, then your Web application will experience variable loads and frequent overexertion, and you will need to work through the painful process of tuning and optimizing the application to perform well under its target load.

To this end, we pay particular attention to the tools available to developers to quantify and monitor performance issues and to diagnose performance problems more quickly. As noted earlier, today's sophisticated Web users *expect* high performance and will quickly turn hostile to an application (and a developer!) that cannot provide the high performance they demand.

We also pay attention to design decisions, meaning the technology choices you make when you have several options from which to choose. For example, when you choose to use a DataSet over a DataReader for accessing data, you are making a specific design decision, whether you realize it or not. With the former, you are choosing an object that enables you to manipulate a disconnected DataSet. With the latter, you are choosing an object that provides a lightweight, read-only data stream. The implications of this design decision can be profound, both on performance and on the code's complexity.

A more complex scenario is how to persist application-level information so that it is available to multiple requests from multiple users. Do you use the standard Application object? Do you use the new cache object? What is the difference between them, and how do you choose the best technology for this scenario? In other words, what is the most appropriate design decision?

We spend the entire book reviewing these questions in one form or another. But at a high level, making a design decision is a two-step process. First, you have to be familiar with how to implement each of the options. Second, you have to understand the implications of choosing one option over another. Many books cover the first step well by showing you how to code with various objects and how to implement certain approaches. But few books provide an in-depth discussion on the implications of one approach over another. This book digs deep into ASP.NET technology. By understanding advanced features, you will realize new, more optimal ways to write your ASP.NET applications.

The bottom line is that you have to be happy with your design decisions because you will have to live with all of the implications, even those you have not yet considered.

This is the perfect lead-in to restating the goal of this book before moving on to the good stuff. Simply put, this book helps you build high-performance ASP.NET Web applications. The way this book gets you there is by the following:

- Educating you about the tools and techniques for programming high-performance ASP.NET applications

- Educating you about the tools and techniques available for you to monitor and optimize the performance of your ASP.NET application

- Providing you the in-depth information you need to better understand ASP.NET technology and thereby make optimal design decisions

NOTE   *ASP.NET provides superior performance compared to classic ASP. Furthermore, the latest independent performance benchmark numbers show that ASP.NET performs significantly better than equivalent Java 2 Enterprise Edition (J2EE) applications written in Java. For more information on this benchmark study, see ".NET Wins New Benchmarks" on MSDN at* http://msdn.microsoft.com/library/default.asp?url=/library/enus/dnbda/html/bdasamppet.asp.

The Organization of This Book

This book addresses ASP.NET application performance tuning and optimization from a developer's perspective. Broadly speaking, this book addresses the following areas:

- Programming optimizations, including data access, state management, and caching technologies, including a chapter devoted to Web services

- Performance testing using Microsoft Application Center Test (ACT), including how to run tests, how to customize tests, and how to interpret the results

- Debugging and tracing tools for troubleshooting and tuning your application

The breakdown of chapters is as follows:

Chapter 1, "Introducing Performance Tuning and Optimization": This chapter contains an overview of the goals of this book and introduces important concepts that affect the optimization of ASP.NET applications.

Chapter 2, "Introducing ASP.NET Applications": This chapter provides an overview of how ASP.NET applications are structured and how they compile and run in the .NET-managed environment. This aim of this chapter is to give readers a common understanding of what comprises an ASP.NET application and to get them thinking of an application in terms of design rather than just code. This chapter starts the process of focusing you on those aspects of an application that most impact overall performance.

Chapter 3, "Writing Optimized Data Access Code": This chapter discusses how to write optimal data access code and highlights issues such as connection pooling, conducting XML-specific optimizations, and choosing the appropriate data access object. It also provides a decision flow diagram and a detailed discussion on how to handle different data access scenarios.

Chapter 4, "Optimizing Application and Session State Management": This chapter discusses how to manage application and session state in ASP.NET applications, including in a server farm.

Chapter 5, "Caching ASP.NET Applications": This chapter covers the numerous options for caching in ASP.NET applications. ASP.NET makes caching quick and easy to implement, but this same simplicity can lull you into making the wrong caching choice. The aim of this chapter is to clearly outline the details of each caching option, including giving examples of when a specific caching option applies best.

Chapter 6, "Writing Optimized Web Services": Web services are a specialized type of ASP.NET application. Web services require unique performance considerations given that they interoperate using SOAP calls. This chapter reviews specific performance considerations for developing optimal Web services.

Chapter 7, "Stress Testing and Monitoring ASP.NET Applications": This chapter discusses the Microsoft ACT testing tool, which is used for stress testing ASP.NET applications. Performance tuning and stress testing is a critical aspect of developing and launching a high-performance Web application.

Chapter 8, "Debugging and Tracing ASP.NET Applications": This chapter reviews tools and techniques for debugging ASP.NET applications and for setting traces. Debugging tools help pinpoint the locations and causes of application exceptions. Tracing tools provide a profile of how long it takes for a Web page to execute and render, thereby helping to pinpoint poorly performing areas in an application.

Each chapter is accompanied by a sample project that illustrates the concepts the chapter covers. Every code sample presented in the book comes from the sample projects. The code samples are never oversimplified and are designed to be useful for addressing real-world scenarios. Each sample project contains a starting page called menu.aspx, which provides a summary of all pages and modules in the project as well as hyperlinks to all of the pages. We have spent a lot of time making the sample projects both informative and interesting, and we hope you will recognize many productivity gains by following the code in these samples.

Finally, please note that this edition provides all code samples in Visual Basic .NET (VB .NET). We think it is more effective to present all code in one language, rather than to switch between different languages, especially given that most developers use one language exclusively. In the near future we want to publish this book in other language-specific editions, including C#.

What This Book Does Not Cover

Many factors affect application performance that are beyond the scope of this book. In the interest of full disclosure, we want to point these out:

Database tuning: A relational database management system (RDBMS) requires a skilled database administrator (DBA) to ensure that the system is running optimally. This includes defining the configuration parameters of a database, including its growth parameters and the dimensions of its data pages. It also includes setting indexes on tables and ensuring that information can be retrieved from the database as fast as possible using efficient stored procedures. Finally, it includes making decisions on whether to cluster multiple database servers for optimum availability. These are complex topics that require specialized discussions, and they are not discussed in this book.

Web-specific infrastructure/architecture: Web applications often run on a cluster of multiple servers, known as a *server farm* or *Web farm*. Load balancers are also frequently used for routing client requests so that the same server handles them. This book does not discuss how to set up these architectures. However, because Web farm architecture is so prevalent in many production systems, we frequently address optimization approaches that are specific to this architecture.

Hardware (general): Clearly, hardware has a significant influence on the performance of the applications that it runs. Servers must be configured optimally to provide the right amount of processing power to its resident applications. Web applications and RDBMS systems alike run best on servers with strong processing power and high available memory. Hardware optimizations require a specialized focus and illustrations of real-world challenges that are not covered in this book.

Network configuration: Web servers must obviously be networked in a way that makes them available to Internet-based clients. This requires skilled network administrators who can ensure that the Web server is installed where it can pipe high-bandwidth data to the outside world. At the same time, Web-based systems represent high-risk, vulnerable targets to hackers who want to penetrate the network or the Web application itself. This requires additional measures, such as the installation of firewalls and perimeter networks (also known as *demilitarized zones* or DMZs). These measures may indirectly impact the performance of a Web application, or they may influence its behavior (for example, by effectively placing a proxy between the Web server and its clients). Networking issues are not discussed in this book.

What You Need To Use This Book

This book provides generous amounts of sample source code. The complete source code files are available for download from the Apress Web site (http://www.apress.com). For your convenience we provide two versions of the source code. One version is compatible with .NET 1.0, and the other version is compatible with .NET 1.1. The discussions in this book are based on .NET 1.1, although we make every effort to point out features that are specific to .NET 1.1.

Download the source code as soon as you can. It is an integral part of this book, and you will find it to be an excellent learning tool and a useful reference in your own applications. One of the biggest complaints you hear from developers is that the sample code they have to work with is too simplistic to be useful. The source code for this book is highly relevant and useful for tackling the real-life challenges that you face every day as an ASP.NET developer. Take advantage of it!

This book is intended for intermediate to advanced ASP.NET developers who want to learn more about optimizing their applications for optimum performance. The concepts presented in this book are relevant to all ASP.NET developers, regardless of the programming language in which you work. The source code is currently written and presented in Visual Basic .NET only. However, we expect that C#, J#, and other developers alike will find the concepts and the code to be highly readable and equally useful. We anticipate that a C# edition of this book will be published in the near future.

We have put months of hard work and effort into this book and have infused it with our collective experiences, gathered from years of building high-performance Web applications. We have attempted to write the kind of book that intermediate to advanced developers will want to keep on their shelves for a long time. Our efforts have been well complemented by the fine staff at Apress, whose emphasis on quality is second to none in the industry.

And now, once more into the breach, dear friends, once more. . . .

CHAPTER 1

Introducing Performance Tuning and Optimization

THE PURPOSE OF THIS CHAPTER is to provide you with a primer on the concepts and terminology of application performance and optimization. For many of you, these are concepts that are familiar, but with which you are not necessarily comfortable. Application performance issues are often paid little attention in smaller Web applications with low hit counts. However, these issues start to feel more important as your application starts experiencing higher hit counts and heavier loads. It is an unfortunate reality that application performance behaves in a nonlinear way. To borrow a phrase from the stock market, this means that current (application) performance is not an indicator of future results.

Loosely speaking, *performance* refers to an application's ability to service user requests under varying load conditions. Performance is measured by multiple kinds of metrics, including throughput and response time, to name a few. Performance benchmarks describe the goal you are trying to achieve. Important benchmark indicators include scalability and availability. *Optimization* refers to fine-tuning an application for performance, based on your goals and the expected load on the application. Optimization is generally an iterative process where you apply your knowledge of the technology to address bottlenecks in performance. The iterative aspect of the process comes about through a cycle of testing and tweaking until you have achieved your performance goals for the application. We cover all of these topics in detail, both later in this chapter as well as throughout this book.

Application performance issues are often ignored until the last minute, precisely when the application may already be experiencing heavy loads. Applications should be designed for optimum performance as a forethought, not as an afterthought. Optimization, by its nature, is a process that applies to a completed application. It is also an ongoing process that does not stop once the application is in production. So, there are different aspects of designing for performance. This book aims to help you with all of these aspects. Our discussion begins with a brief overview of ASP.NET application architecture. Next, we cover performance concepts in greater detail.

Introducing ASP.NET Application Architecture

You build ASP.NET applications using a set of specialized classes within the .NET Class Framework, including (but not limited to) the System.Web namespace for Web form and control classes and the System.Data namespace for data access classes. Figure 1-1 shows a simplified ASP.NET Web application architecture. ASP.NET applications are hosted by Internet Information Server (IIS), which accepts requests from clients and optionally authenticates them before passing the requests on to the Web application.

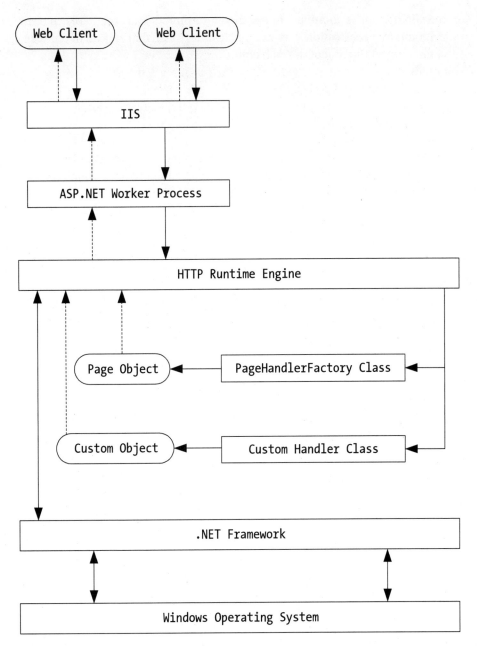

Figure 1-1. ASP.NET application architecture

ASP.NET applications are different from their ASP predecessors in several important respects:

ASP.NET code is compiled, rather than interpreted. The executable content for the Web application lives in a single binary DLL that resides in the \bin directory at the root of the Web application.

You write ASP.NET code using managed code such as VB .NET or C# .NET. Managed code is compliant with the CLR type specification and is more robust and thread-safe than unmanaged code.

ASP.NET supports strong typing and early-bound component calls. ASP supports only weak typing and late-bound component calls, which results in more unstable code and lower performance.

You can break ASP.NET pages into separate user controls that can be compiled into separate files and can be cached separately from the overall page.

ASP.NET supports a wide range of output caching options, from page-level caching to fragment caching. This enables you to fine-tune the execution and the cacheability of a page at a highly granular level. ASP.NET also supports a Data Cache engine and application programming interface (API) that enables developers to cache objects and other items between page requests.

ASP.NET provides expanded support for state management. The available modes include in-process sessions, out-of-process sessions, and database support for session management. ASP.NET state management is more flexible and performs better than its ASP predecessor.

An interesting theme emerges from this list. Namely, ASP.NET intrinsically improves on the performance of its predecessor, ASP. The features that make ASP.NET distinctive from ASP are the same features that inherently perform better. The clearest example of this is the first point: Compiled code is always faster than interpreted code.

Defining Application Performance with Metrics

Let's start with a provocative question: What do we actually mean by *performance*? There is no single answer to this question because what we think of as good performance vs. bad performance is actually the synergistic effect of a number of "performance factors." These factors can be quantified as *performance metrics*. This synergistic effect translates into responsiveness. A high-performance Web application will come up quickly in the user's browser and will respond quickly to their keystrokes and form submissions. A low-performance Web application may crack under the pressure of a few simultaneous requests, creating an unresponsive and generally poor user experience.

Some of the more important performance metrics are the following:

Throughput: Throughput is the number of requests that a Web application can serve in a specified time. Throughput is typically measured in requests per second and is a key indicator of application performance. The throughput rate is controlled by at least three factors: the available server resources, the current server load, and the page execution time. The server load is the number of page requests being processed by the server. The page execution time is the length of time it takes for the application to process a request. In short, the throughput metric is influenced by the currently available server resources and the resources that are required to process additional page requests.

Response time: This is the length of time between the client posting a request and the client receiving the first byte of information back from the server.

Request bytes out total: This is the total size in bytes of the response that is returned to the client, excluding the standard response HTTP headers.

Using Performance Monitor

The Performance Monitor utility allows you to monitor many of these metrics using specialized counters. The previous metric list highlights ones that are easily perceived by users as they work with the application. But an equal number of metrics can cause the *perception* of lowered performance. You need to monitor these counters to have a complete picture of how well your application is performing.

Performance Monitor provides several monitoring objects, each of which provides a set of counters. To access Performance Monitor, select the Windows 2000 Administrative Tools ➢ Performance menu. To monitor a particular counter, you need to select the appropriate Performance object and then select the counters from a multiselect list box. For example, ASP.NET provides the monitoring object ASP.NET Apps v1.0.3705.0. This object includes a Requests Bytes Out Total counter, which is the size of the response being sent to a client. Larger responses take longer to deliver and may result in perceived lower performance, especially over slow Internet connections. Another example is that the Processor Performance Monitor object provides the % Processor Time counter, which is the percentage of time that the processor is working on non-idle threads. If the application resides on a server that is being pegged by another intensive process, then your application users will experience a performance drop that is very real yet is not being caused by the application. Of course, you would probably design your system to avoid pegging your Web servers with non-application-intensive processes.

Figure 1-2 shows the Performance Monitor selection screen. Here, we are selecting the Requests/Sec counter from the ASP.NET Performance object.

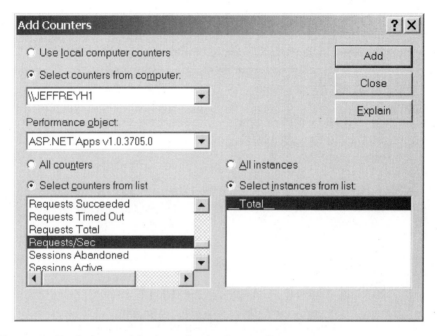

Figure 1-2. Performance Monitor selection screen for counters

Once you have added a few counters and closed the selection window, you return to the graphical view of the Performance Monitor. Figure 1-3 shows one possible view.

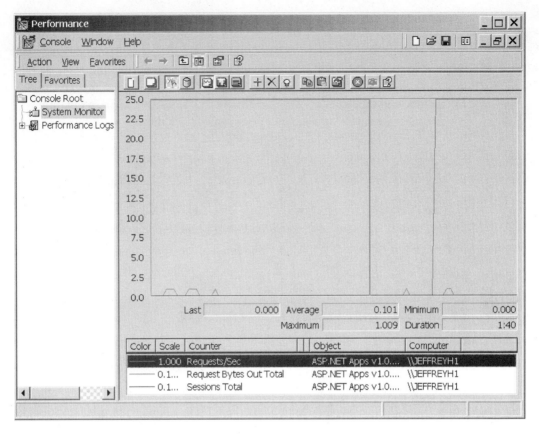

Figure 1-3. Performance Monitor graphs

We discuss Performance Monitor in more detail in Chapter 7, "Stress Testing and Monitoring ASP.NET Applications," and we cover each of the performance counters available for monitoring the overall performance of an ASP.NET application.

Setting Performance Benchmarks

We have established that *performance* refers to several factors that combine to provide the user with a level of responsiveness from the Web application. If you have done your job right as a developer, and as a system architect, then that level of responsiveness will fall within an acceptable range for the user. If you have been especially diligent, then the responsiveness will exceed the users' expectations, and they will proceed to tell all of their friends, family, and pets what a great thing they have going.

Good performance is as much a subjective feeling as it is a quantifiable fact; however, it is the metrics with which this book is concerned. We have presented a number of quantifiable performance metrics you can use to describe how responsive your application is. It is always a good idea to publish unambiguous performance standards in terms of one or more of these metrics. This gives you a benchmark against which you can compare the Web application in the future.

This is one example of a statement on benchmark numbers:

The Web application runs on a server farm of three single-processor Pentium 700MHz Web servers with 512MB of RAM each. The operating system for each machine is Windows 2000 Advanced Server SP2. In addition, the Web application interfaces with a clustered SQL Server 2000 database solution. The Web application supports up to 45 requests per second under a user load of 50–75 concurrent users.

Measuring Application Performance

We have discussed specific performance metrics, but in more general terms, you can measure application performance by three broad measures:

- **Throughput**: Throughput is the number of requests that a Web application can serve in a specified unit of time. Throughput is typically specified in requests per second.

- **Availability**: Availability is the percentage of time a Web application is responsive to client requests.

- **Scalability**: Scalability is the ability of a Web application to maintain or improve performance as the user load increases. Scalability also refers to the ability of an application to recognize performance benefits as server resources increase.

Throughput was already discussed, so let's explore the additional measures, availability and scalability, in more detail.

Assessing Availability

Of course, performance is not the only metric that matters for ASP.NET applications. Application *availability* is equally important and is defined as the percentage of time that an application is functional. Availability is in many ways a harder metric to quantify, compared to performance, because hardware issues factor into the equation more than software issues do.

The factors that affect application availability include the following:

Hardware: Web servers and database servers obviously have to remain running for the hosted Web application to stay available. Multiserver Web architectures are designed for fault tolerance, usually by providing redundancy and backup drives both for the application files and for the database files.

Load: Overtaxed systems are susceptible to failure if the user load exceeds what either the hardware or the software was designed to accommodate. Load can be anticipated through capacity planning and designed for at the software and the hardware levels.

Network latency: This factor refers to delays in the transmission of a request or a response on the network. Latency may result from congestion on the network. Alternatively, it may result from an inefficient network—one that requires too many jumps between the sender and the receiver. Network latency is controllable on a local area network (LAN) or a virtual private network (VPN), but it is out of your control over a public Internet connection.

Connection bandwidth: Application users on the public Internet may not have the same amount of connection bandwidth; for example, broadband users have "a lot," and dial-up users have "very little." It is hard to say much about this factor, given that it is typically out of the developer's control for a Web application on the public Internet. About the only good thing to say about this factor is that users tend to adjust their expectations in proportion to the type of connection they are using. In other words, dial-up users expect to wait longer, and cable modem users do not.

Software: Software issues typically affect the performance of an application, rather than its availability. However, code that causes an application to become unstable and crash is an important factor in application availability. In general, code that is thread-safe is stable and unlikely to crash. Thread-safe code is much easier to write with .NET because the managed runtime environment enforces both a common type system and a range of rules that promote thread safety. Keep in mind, though, that calling COM+ components from .NET code is potentially unstable because COM+ components execute outside of the managed execution environment.

The most common way to quantify availability is by *uptime*, which is the percentage of time that an application is responsive and functional. There is no typical acceptable uptime percentage for an application. The acceptable number is the one that all parties agree is reasonable and can be committed to in a legal contract. Companies typically like to see more than 99-percent uptime, excluding scheduled downtime. On an annual basis, this number is not as unreasonable as it might appear to be. For example, 99-percent uptime translates to a whopping 88 hours, or roughly two standard work weeks per year of downtime. In economic terms, a high-traffic e-commerce Web application can lose a lot of revenue in this time period, particularly if it falls around a heavy shopping period such as Christmas. Figure 1-4 illustrates a sampling of downtime in hours, based on percentage uptimes.

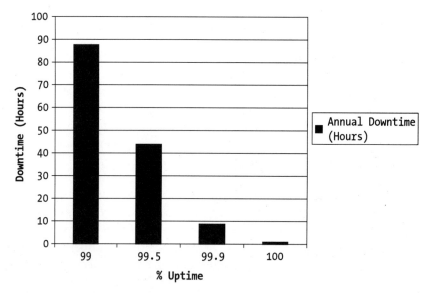

Figure 1-4. Application availability

Assessing Scalability

The third of the big three metrics, after throughput and availability, is scalability. Many people confuse this factor with performance. The two are related, but they are not the same. *Scalability* is the ability of the application to perform under ever-increasing loads. A Web application is considered non-scalable if its performance falls below established standards once the load starts to increase.

Scalability also has a lesser-known definition, which is of particular importance to developers. Namely, scalability is the ability of an application to fully utilize the full processing power of a machine as it increases the number of processors. By this definition, an application that performs well on a two-processor machine is considered non-scalable if a four-processor machine fails to improve application performance by any significant amount.

This definition speaks to a number of low-level issues, such as the ability of both the application and the machine to work effectively using multiple threads. The .NET Framework provides sophisticated thread management capabilities and makes it easier than before to write thread-safe code. However, you may not achieve scalability simply by using the Framework's out-of-the-box thread management abilities. The schematic chart shown in Figure 1-5 illustrates two applications deployed on machines with increasing numbers of processors (X-axis). The Y-axis indicates the requests per second that the applications are able to process. In this example, the number of users, or the *load*, is assumed to remain the same. The chart illustrates that Application #1 experiences much smaller performance gains than Application #2 as the number of processors increases. This implies that Application #2 is more scalable than Application #1. Even so, neither application experiences any performance improvements in moving from a four-processor to an eight-processor machine. Scalability is clearly a parameter that is relative rather than absolute. Application #2 is more scalable than Application #1 as long as the number of processors remains fewer than eight. Application #2 may perform better than Application #1 on an eight-processor machine; however, it is no more scalable than Application #1 at this number of processors.

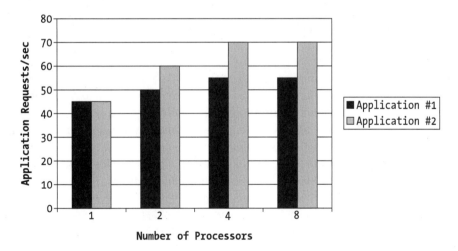

Figure 1-5. Application scalability

The .NET Framework provides other out-of-the-box features that may enhance scalability as an application experiences increasing loads. For example, the ADO.NET managed data providers implement connection pooling for database connections, which at face value would appear to always be a good thing.

This is not so if your application uses dynamic connection strings, where pooling may actually hinder performance for a specific connection even while helping performance on others. So, although the .NET Framework provides the tools for enhancing scalability, you need the smarts of a developer to take full advantage of them. Keep in mind that scalability works in two dimensions: up and out. Traditional scalability actually refers to *scaling up*, meaning that your application must accommodate increasing load on a fixed set of servers. In this model, the processing is distributed across the same set of servers regardless of whether the load is high or low. *Scaling out* refers to applications designed to run across a server farm, where multiple servers collaborate to share the burden of increasing load. In this model, when the application load is low, just a few of the available servers handle the processing. As the load increases, additional servers take on the burden, which effectively increases the available capacity of the system. Thus, architects and developers have a two-fold challenge in designing for scalability: designing their applications to both scale up and scale out. ASP.NET facilitates this effort by making certain management features less dependent on specific servers. For example, you can easily configure state management to run across several servers in a farm. In addition, XML-based configuration files make it easier to point applications to distributed resources.

One final note on the topic of scalability: Throwing hardware at an application usually buys you performance gains, but this approach should complement other measures, not replace them. For example, doubling the memory on a Web server will certainly result in immediate performance gains for many kinds of Web applications, but this will do nothing to address bottlenecks that may exist at the processor level or at the database level. The database server is, after all, an equally important partner to the Web server in terms of its influence on scalability. Similarly, scaling out with additional Web servers will buy you perceived performance gains because more servers are now available to share the processing load. But, again, this approach will not address processor-level bottlenecks. Worse yet, if your application is experiencing memory leaks, then by scaling out additional servers you have essentially increased your problem by transferring an existing issue from a small number of servers to a larger number of servers.

Hardware considerations are an important aspect of designing a high-performance Web application. The hardware configuration is critical for maintaining high reliability and availability for an application. Basically, do not focus on hardware considerations at the expense of application-level issues because in the long-term, scalability will not benefit, even if short-term scalability does.

Profiling ASP.NET Application Performance

Performance profiling is a complicated process that requires developers to run through repeated iterations of profiling and optimization. There are a number of factors affecting performance that operate independently and so must be tackled independently, often by different groups of people. Developers must tackle application coding issues by identifying the offending code blocks and then rewriting or optimizing them. System administrators must tackle server resource problems by examining the full set of tasks that the server is handling. Performance profiling has to be a cooperative task between different groups of people because at the end of the day, a user who experiences slow performance will be unhappy with the experience, regardless of whose piece of the puzzle is causing the issue. Performance profiling affects everyone on the technical team, and so it must engage everyone as well.

Performance profiling is a time-dependent activity because application performance changes over time. Performance may change periodically throughout the day or as the load on the application fluctuates. Alternatively, application performance may experience degradation over a long period of time, particularly as the database grows. Performance profiling must begin with a *baseline*, which is a set of metrics that define the performance at a specific time, under a specific set of conditions. The baseline is the measure against which future performance will be compared. A baseline may also be referred to as a *benchmark*, and earlier in the chapter you saw an example. A baseline includes a description of both hardware and software, and it typically includes a range of performance numbers that were derived without changing the hardware configuration.

This is an example of a baseline description:

The Web application runs on a single, dual-processor 400MHz server with 512MB of RAM. The application was subjected to an increasing load of 10 to 100 concurrent users with five threads. The application serves between 18 and 45 requests per second, diminishing with an increasing number of concurrent users. Response times for 10 concurrent users varied between 0.8 and 3.5 seconds, depending on the page. The Home page, which is cached, responds in 0.8 seconds, and more intensive screens take longer to deliver to the client.

Figure 1-6 shows the baseline application performance's throughput, and Figure 1-7 shows the baseline application performance's response time.

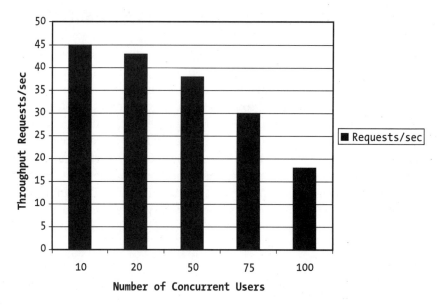

Figure 1-6. Baseline application performance—throughput

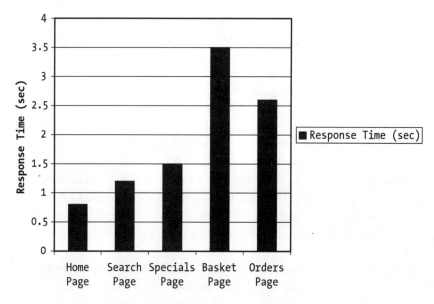

Figure 1-7. Baseline application performance—response time

These graphs focus on just two metrics—namely, throughput and response time. A complete baseline should contain data for several metrics but should always include basic metrics such as throughput and response time because these most directly affect the user's experience with the application.

Monitoring Performance

We have established that performance monitoring does not just begin in a vacuum. It begins once the developers and system architects have released the first version of an application and have collected initial performance measurements. Presumably the team has also established its performance expectations for the Web application and already has a sense of whether additional optimization will be required. The initial baseline is a collection of measurements on specific performance factors. These factors combine to produce the overall responsiveness of the application on a specific hardware platform, and under a specific load.

Performance profiling involves three important steps:

- **Monitoring**: Monitoring includes setting up the counters and traces to collect performance data and picking a sampling period.

- **Analysis**: The monitoring data must be collected, analyzed for problems, and compared against the baseline data.

- **Loading, or *stress testing***: This involves a forceful ramping up of load on the Web application to observe how the performance metrics change in response. Monitoring by itself can be a passive activity where measurements are collected and analyzed, but the system is allowed to operate without interference by the development team.

Once performance profile reports have been generated and analyzed, the technical team may choose to optimize a specific area of the application or the system. Once the optimization has been implemented, the iterative cycle of profiling and optimization begins again for as long as it takes to bring the application performance within an acceptable range. Optimization is never really completed. It continues for as long as necessary, or for as long as the team thinks that further performance improvements are possible. Ultimately, the goal is to bring performance to a level where the users are satisfied and to have the technical team feel satisfied they have delivered an application whose performance meets everyone's expectations.

The following section reviews some of the tools available to accomplish performance profiling and optimization. These tools will be covered in much more detail later in the book, so for now basic introductions will suffice.

Monitoring and Analyzing Performance Using Performance Monitor

Introduced earlier, Performance Monitor provides a wide range of counters that you can add to the Performance Monitor graph and analyze visually. Performance Monitor, or *PerfMon* for short, will also dump measurements to a file for later analysis. The ASP.NET Apps Performance object provides a number of counters for monitoring requests, responses, and sessions for a specific application. If your Web server is running multiple Web applications, then you will need to select a specific application instance from an available list on the selection screen. Table 1-1 summarizes several of these counters.

Table 1-1. ASP.NET Apps Performance Counters

COUNTER	DESCRIPTION
Anonymous Requests	The number of requests utilizing anonymous authentication
Request Bytes In Total	The total size, in bytes, of all requests
Request Bytes Out Total	The total size, in bytes, of responses sent to a client, excluding the standard HTTP Response headers
Requests Executing	The number of requests currently executing
Requests Timed Out	The number of requests that timed out
Requests/Sec	The number of requests executed per second
Output Cache Entries	The current number of entries in the output cache
Cache API Entries	The total number of entries within the cache added by the user

Note that these counters are specifically for the ASP.NET Apps v1.0.3705.0 Performance object, where the version number refers to the .NET Framework. ASP.NET installs another Performance object called ASP.NET v1.0.3705.0, which contains counters for monitoring ASP.NET performance overall, instead of for a specific application. These counters are useful when your Web server is hosting multiple Web applications and you suspect that one Web application is adversely affecting the performance of another by taking up too many resources. Table 1-2 summarizes several of these counters.

Table 1-2. ASP.NET Performance Counters

COUNTER	DESCRIPTION
Applications Running	The number of currently running applications
Requests Queued	The number of requests waiting to be processed
State Server Sessions Active	The number of sessions currently active

As noted earlier, the ASP.NET counters are not the only ones that indicate the overall performance of the system. There are several Performance objects for the server, including the Processor object, which provides counters that monitor how hard the machine processor is working. Performance Monitor is an excellent tool for monitoring the performance and health of a server, as well as an application. It also allows you to save a collection of counters so you can consistently generate graphs and reports as needed.

Performance Testing Using Microsoft Application Center Test

The ACT tool is for stress testing ASP.NET applications and for analyzing performance and scalability problems. ACT ships with Visual Studio .NET Enterprise and Architect editions. The tool allows you to observe the behavior of your application under various loads and to watch how performance metrics change as the application comes under increasing stress. ACT provides the following useful features:

- **Simulation**: The tool simulates a large number of concurrent users each making multiple requests.

- **Support for authentication schemes**: The tool supports several different authentication schemes and the Secure Sockets Layer (SSL) protocol, making it applicable to a wide range of ASP.NET applications.

- **Integrates with Performance Monitor**: The tool allows you to select monitoring counters from the same set of Performance objects used by the Performance Monitor utility.

- **Scripts**: The tool allows you to create and record scripts that simulate a user's behavior on an application. The scripts are generated in VBScript, and ACT provides an API for customizing existing test scripts.

- **Reports:** The tool generates reports showing the progress of the test, including running values of the selected performance counters and graphs.

Figure 1-8 shows the ACT tool interface with the results of a recent performance test.

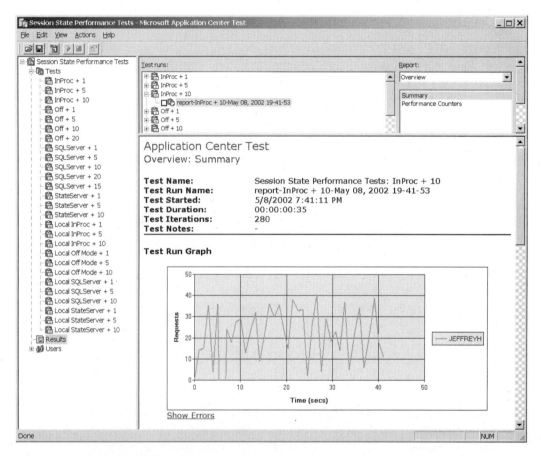

Figure 1-8. The ACT user interface

Chapter 8, "Debugging and Tracing ASP.NET Applications," discusses the ACT tool in detail. It discusses how to configure the tool for testing an application, plus how to generate reports and interpret the results. For now, understand that the ACT tool is an important part of the iterative cycle of testing and optimization that your ASP.NET application needs to undergo before it can be released to users.

Summary

We covered the following topics in this chapter:

- Performance is determined by several factors, including application throughput, response time, and load. A developer's responsibility is to optimize the performance factors over which they have control.

- You achieve optimum performance through an iterative cycle of testing and optimization.

- ASP.NET provides intrinsic performance advantages over classic ASP.

- Windows 2000 provides Performance Monitor for monitoring a wide range of performance counters.

- Microsoft ACT enables you to simulate heavy user load on your application and to monitor performance metrics under changing load conditions.

CHAPTER 2

Introducing ASP.NET Applications

Tнıs снартеr provides a tour through ASP.NET application architecture and reviews the more interesting features of ASP.NET applications. The larger purpose of this chapter is to give all readers a common understanding of the important features and issues in ASP.NET and to lay the groundwork for the rest of the book. Advanced readers, fear not! This chapter does not regurgitate basic ASP.NET 101 by repeating what you may have read in half a dozen other books. Instead, this chapter digs deeper into selected topics ranging from configuring ASP.NET to using view state. It also tackles underserved topics, such as how to customize configuration settings and how to write your own HttpHandler classes for low-level processing of HTTP requests. Finally, the topics covered are pertinent to discussions throughout the book.

Overview of ASP.NET Applications

An ASP.NET application is a collection of files, handler classes, and executable code that reside in a common virtual directory on a Web server. Valid ASP.NET files include the following:

> **Web forms**: A Web form (`*.aspx`) provides a programming model for building user interface pages for a Web application. You construct Web forms using standard Hypertext Markup Language (HTML) mixed with server-side HTML, Web, and custom user controls. Web forms provide *code-behind files,* which include programmatic access to a Page handler object. You can code behind the Page object's lifecycle events using any standard .NET-compliant language. The filename suffix of the code-behind file reflects the language the code is written in—for example, `*.aspx.vb` for Visual Basic .NET (VB .NET) code or `*.aspx.cs` for C# code. In addition, ASP.NET continues to support the classic ASP usage of inline server-side code mixed with HTML. However, this approach is not recommended for ASP.NET applications because it does not cleanly separate client-side and server-side codebases.

Web services: These are components that can be invoked remotely by client applications or other Web services, using Extensible Markup Language (XML) over Hypertext Transfer Protocol (HTTP) formatted in Simple Object Access Protocol (SOAP) envelopes. Web services are based on industry-standard specifications and can be consumed by heterogeneous clients on different platforms. Web services consist of an `*.asmx` file containing basic directives, plus a code-behind file that contains the methods and logic for the Web service. Visual Studio .NET is a powerful tool for creating XML Web services because it handles complex compilation details for you.

User controls: You can save Web forms as reusable components called *user controls*, which resemble Web forms in almost every way except that the file type uses an `.ascx` extension. You can drop user controls onto Web forms much like you can a standard server control, or you can dynamically load them onto the Web form at runtime. User controls provide a sophisticated way to reuse code and allow shared code to be maintained in a single location. User controls are also useful for implementing fragment caching in a Web form.

Code modules: These are stand-alone code module files that contain application-scope functions; any Web form, or module, in the application can call them. You can partition a single code module into several classes within one or more namespaces. Additionally, you can compile the code modules directly into the application executable, or you can move them to separate projects and compile them as stand-alone .NET components. You can write code modules in any .NET-compliant language, including VB .NET and C#.

Client-side scripts: For all of the server-side power of ASP.NET, client-side scripting still plays an important role. ASP.NET makes it easy to delegate a control's client-side events to server-side functions. But sometimes it is most efficient to handle the event on the client, using JavaScript or a similar scripting language. ASP.NET allows you to add client-side scripts to a project. Visual Studio .NET provides limited IntelliSense for JavaScript, as well as the ability to debug client-side scripts.

Web.config: This XML-based file stores configuration settings for ASP.NET applications and is discussed in great detail later in this chapter.

Global.asax: This file is the successor to the `global.asa` file from classic ASP. It provides programmatic access to application and session lifecycle events.

Visual Studio .NET is an excellent development tool for constructing Web applications. The most convenient aspect of the ASP.NET project type is that a single project can include all of the disparate executable content you need, even if that content resides in separate projects. For example, let's say your Web application requires Web forms, a Web service, and a set of .NET components. You could add three independent projects to the solution file to accommodate each of the different project types. Alternatively, you could include all of the executable source files in one project. This step saves you time and makes it somewhat easier to work on several parts of the project simultaneously. However, keep in mind the tradeoff to this approach, which is that all of the content will be compiled into a single, large DLL assembly that resides in the application's \bin directory. For production purposes, you should compile the parts of the application into separate DLLs or assemblies so that you can load them independently or deploy them to separate servers. Of course, separate assemblies are also useful because other applications can use them.

Benefits of ASP.NET

ASP.NET provides many truly impressive benefits over classic ASP, mainly because it is built into the managed environment of the .NET Framework. ASP.NET applications are compiled, rather than interpreted, and they benefit from a sophisticated Class Framework that provides a powerful, extensible application programming interface (API).

At the risk of rehashing what others have already said, the benefits of ASP.NET are as follows:

> ASP.NET applications are developed using compiled code and can be written using any .NET-compliant language, including VB .NET, C# .NET, and J# .NET. ASP.NET is built into the .NET Class Framework, so it benefits from an extensive API as well as all the benefits of the .NET managed environment, including type safety, multilanguage support, optimized memory management, and a just-in-time (JIT) compilation model that optimizes the availability and performance of the application at runtime.

> ASP.NET provides an extensible architecture that you can easily customize. For example, every Web form can be programmatically accessed using the Page handler object. This object not only encapsulates the Web form, but it also provides direct access to the context objects, including the HttpRequest, HttpApplication, and HttpSessionState objects.

The ASP.NET runtime engine architecture is also designed for optimal performance and extensibility. The runtime engine executes in a separate process from Internet Information Server (IIS), and it delegates HTTP requests across a range of handler classes. These classes can be customized or even dropped from an application if they do not provide any benefit. Custom HTTP handlers process HTTP requests at the level of the ASP.NET runtime engine. You can write custom HTTP handlers using a greatly simplified API that avoids the complexity of traditional ISAPI modules.

ASP.NET provides several ways to cache page content, including full-page caching and partial-page caching (fragment caching). In addition, ASP.NET provides a Cache API for even more granular control over cached content.

ASP.NET provides sophisticated debugging and tracing abilities that make application troubleshooting easier than before. The .NET-compliant languages provide structured error handling and a large set of detailed exception classes. Errors will still occur in ASP.NET, of course, but you now benefit from more detailed exception reporting than when using classic ASP.

ASP.NET provides several methods for authenticating clients, including Windows authentication, Forms-based authentication, Passport-based authentication, and standard IIS authentication (impersonation).

Understanding the ASP.NET Architecture

ASP.NET is built with an extensible architecture that provides excellent performance and a logical approach to servicing client requests. The ASP.NET runtime engine delegates client requests to a wide variety of handler classes. Client requests are not serviced by a monolithic process but are instead routed to targeted classes designed to service a specific kind of request. For example, when a client calls up an *.aspx page in their browser, the request gets routed from the ASP.NET runtime engine to a specialized factory class that receives the request and returns a Page object. This object can be manipulated on the server as needed before it is rendered on the browser as HTML. Like a corporate chief executive officer (CEO), the HttpRuntime instance is ultimately accountable for servicing a client request, but it does so by delegating the work to handler classes.

Figure 2-1 provides a schematic view of ASP.NET architecture. The role of IIS is relatively diminished in ASP.NET compared to classic ASP. Specifically, the role of IIS (in ASP.NET) is primarily relegated to that of a request/response broker. IIS is the point of first contact for incoming client requests, and it will run authentication checks before allowing requests to proceed. At a minimum, IIS simply accepts an anonymous client request and assigns it to the default local machine account that has been created for IIS (IUSR_[Machine Name]). Alternatively, you can configure the Web site to use Windows-based authentication, in which case IIS will demand specific credentials from the client. Either way, once IIS has performed its authentication checks, it forwards the client request to a dedicated process called the *ASP.NET worker process* (aspnet_wp.exe). This process executes a number of steps that culminate in passing the client request to the ASP.NET runtime engine.

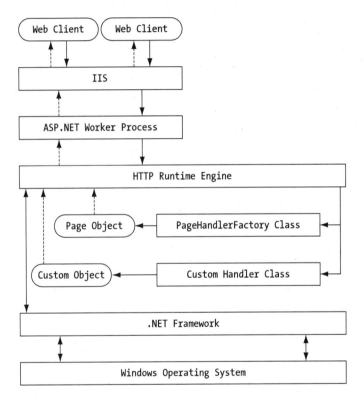

Figure 2-1. ASP.NET Web site architecture

The ASP.NET runtime engine contains a set of classes for handling client requests and serving responses. These classes provide the basic infrastructure and the core capabilities for supporting Web applications. The gateway to the runtime engine is the HttpRuntime class. This class initially accepts a client request and then delegates it to any number of HTTP handler classes, depending on the nature of the request. Figure 2-1 depicts incoming HTTP requests from Web clients that get filtered down to the HTTP runtime engine (shown as solid lines). The HTTP request then gets delegated to several HTTP handler classes, including the PageHandlerFactory class, which is responsible for generating a Page object. The Page object receives a reference to the HTTP request object and begins processing the request. Finally, the Page object renders an HTML response that gets filtered back to the Web clients (shown as dashed lines). The figure also represents the close ties between the HTTP runtime engine and the underlying .NET Framework on which it is built.

HTTP Handlers

HTTP handlers implement a common interface called IHttpHandler (a member of the System.Web namespace). There are two kinds of handler classes:

- **Handler processing classes**: These are classes that implement the interface (IHttpHandler) that allows them to process HTTP requests. For example, the Page class is a handler that represents an *.aspx Web page.

- **Handler factory classes**: These are classes that dynamically manufacture new handler classes. These classes implement the IHttpHandlerFactory interface. For example, the PageHandlerFactory class generates a Page handler class for every HTTP request that calls an *.aspx Web page.

The IHttpHandler interface defines a method called ProcessRequest(), which accepts an HttpContext instance as its argument. The interface also provides a Boolean property called IsReusable(), which dictates whether an HTTP handler can pass a request to another handler:

```
Sub ProcessRequest(ByVal context As HttpContext)
ReadOnly Property IsReusable As Boolean
```

The HttpContext object encapsulates all of the HTTP-specific details for an individual HTTP request. Clearly, the ProcessRequest() method provides a clean way of passing a client's request details between different objects on the Web server.

HTTP handlers must be registered in the ASP.NET configuration files (either Machine.config or Web.config). This is an excerpt from the Machine.config file:

```
<httpHandlers>
    <add verb="*" path="trace.axd" type="System.Web.Handlers.TraceHandler"/>
    <add verb="*" path="*.aspx" type="System.Web.UI.PageHandlerFactory"/>
</httpHandlers>
```

The `<httpHandlers>` section registers HTTP handlers on the server using `<add>` child elements. A handler class can process an individual Uniform Resource Identifier (URI) or a group of URIs that share a common file extension. The `Machine.config` file excerpt shown previously illustrates both options. The attributes for the `<add>` element are as follows:

- **Verb**: This is a comma-separated list of HTTP verbs, including GET, POST, PUT, or the wildcard asterisk (*).

- **Path**: This is a single URI path or a wildcard path, for example, `*.aspx`.

- **Type**: This is a class/assembly combination that contains the handler class. The excerpt only shows the class name, but you can append the assembly name as well, separated by a comma.

We discuss ASP.NET configuration files in greater detail in the "Understanding the ASP.NET Configuration System" section.

By now you can begin to appreciate how extensible the ASP.NET runtime engine is. You can route HTTP requests to any handler you set up. Few readers will ever need to create a custom handler because you can almost always tackle a specific HTTP request through the Page object (discussed next). But in other cases, HTTP handlers are the most efficient way to handle an HTTP request because they can service a request without going to the expense of loading up a Page object.

Let's look at an interesting example. Consider a Web application that logs the Internet Protocol (IP) address and a timestamp of all clients when they first access the application. Let's say that the application provides an entry page, called `ap_gateway.aspx`, that provides no user interface but that records the client's IP address with a timestamp and then redirects the client on to a formal login page. You could create a standard `*.aspx` Web page that performs this function, but this approach unnecessarily creates an instance of the Page object (assuming you have not altered the standard HTTP handler for `.aspx` pages). A better approach would be to create a custom HTTP handler that processes the `ap_gateway.aspx` page directly. If you want even more distinction, you could create a custom file extension, such as `.xyz`, for the gateway page.

Listing 2-1 contains the code for this custom HTTP handler.

Listing 2-1. A Custom HTTP Handler

```
Namespace Apress
    Public Class apXYZHandler
        Implements IHttpHandler

        Public Sub ProcessRequest(ByVal context As System.Web.HttpContext) _
            Implements System.Web.IHttpHandler.ProcessRequest
            ' Instance an EventLog object
            Dim objEvt As EventLog = New EventLog()
            Try
            ' Write the client's IP address to the event log, with a timestamp
            Dim strClientIP As String = context.Request.UserHostAddress
            objEvt.Source = "ASP.NET 1.0.3705.0" ' Event source is ASP.NET
            objEvt.WriteEntry("Client IP: " & strClientIP & " logged at: " & Now)
            ' Redirect the client to the login page
            context.Response.Redirect("ap_login.aspx")
            Catch err As Exception
            ' No action taken. Prevents unhandled errors if .WriteEntry fails.
            End Try
        End Sub

        Public ReadOnly Property IsReusable() As Boolean Implements _
            System.Web.IHttpHandler.IsReusable
            Get
                Return (True)
            End Get
        End Property
    End Class
```

Listing 2-1 is very simple. The client's IP address is extracted using the Request object's UserHostAddress property. Next, the handler writes a record into the system event log. Finally, the handler redirects the user to the formal login page, called ap_login.aspx. Clearly, the HttpContext object is critical for an HTTP handler class to work!

Notice that Listing 2-1 includes exception handling around the WriteEntry() method in case this method fails. The exception handler does not do anything *per se* in that it does not take a specific action when an exception occurs. However, it does prevent unhandled exceptions, which could potentially bring down the Web site. This may happen if the site administrator fails to reconfigure the event logs from the default *overwrite after 7 days* to *overwrite as needed*. If the event logs fill up completely, then a write failure will cause an exception in the code, with potentially adverse effects. This is of particular concern in high-volume sites that write a lot of information to the event logs.

Next, you must register the HTTP handler class in the Web.config (or Machine.config) file:

```
<httpHandlers>
        <add verb="*" path="ap_gateway.aspx"
            type="AspNetChap2.Apress.apXYZHandler, AspNetChap2"/>
</httpHandlers>
```

The syntax for the class name and the assembly is important to get right; otherwise the Web application will generate runtime errors when you attempt to load it in the browser.

We have compiled the HTTP handler class directly into the AspNetChap2 sample project for this chapter. In this case, AspNetChap2 is equivalent to the assembly name, so you see it included in the type description. We experimented with omitting the assembly name from the type definition, but the Web application failed to load.

NOTE *You can download the source code for the sample projects from the Downloads section of the Apress Web site at* www.apress.com. *The sample projects are an integral part of this book and an excellent learning and reference tool.*

Finally, you can test the HTTP handler by opening a new browser and typing the path to the gateway page—in this case, http://localhost/AspNetChap2/ap_gateway.aspx. The page will load, then after a couple of seconds you should be redirected to the ap_login.aspx page. Open the application log in the Event Viewer, and you will see a recent information record with something like the following contents:

```
Client IP: 127.0.0.1 signed in at: 4/15/2002 7:19:45 PM.
```

The most interesting aspect of this example is that the page ap_gateway.aspx does not exist. We never added one to the ASP.NET project, nor do we need to add one. The HTTP handler recognizes the path name and takes that as an indication to start working. The actual page does not need to exist, and this is what makes HTTP handler classes so efficient under certain circumstances.

The Page Class

A Page object is instanced every time an *.aspx page is requested. The Page object is responsible for processing a client request and rendering HTML in response. The Page object provides programmatic access to a Web form, plus access to the HTTP intrinsic objects such as HttpRequest and HttpResponse. Every *.aspx page is associated with an instance of the Page class. Specifically, the Web page inherits from a code-behind class, which in turn inherits from the Page class. For example, the ap_login.aspx page contains the following directive at the top of the file:

```
<%@ Page Language="vb" Codebehind="ap_login.aspx.vb"
    Inherits="AspNetChap2.ap_login"%>
```

Then, when you switch to the code-behind file, you see the following:

```
Public Class ap_login
    Inherits System.Web.UI.Page
    Private Sub Page_Load(ByVal sender As System.Object, _
        ByVal e As System.EventArgs) Handles MyBase.Load
        ' Code goes here
    End Sub
End Class
```

Note that the Codebehind attribute simply indicates the location of the code-behind file. The Inherits attribute is what actually binds the Web form to a specific class. The @ Page directive supports a long list of attributes that control the Web form's behavior at runtime. Several of these attributes override application-level settings in the Web.config file. For example, if the Web application has session state enabled, you can prevent an individual page from participating by setting its EnableSessionState directive to "False."

The @ Page Directive

The @ Page directive provides the three required attributes shown in the previous listing: Language, Codebehind, and Inherits. In addition, many others are set to "True" by default, which means they apply to the page even if they are missing from the @ Page directive. So, the @ Page directive is as much about disabling what you *do not* want as it is about enabling what you need. You should always explicitly set three attributes:

AutoEventWireUp: This is a Boolean attribute that indicates whether Page events are wired into specific delegate functions ("True") or whether they can be wired into user-defined functions ("False"). If the attribute value is "True" (or, by default, if the attribute is missing), then the Page_Init() and Page_Load() event handlers will always be called, and they must be declared in a standard way. If the attribute value is "False," then the events are handled only if the user chooses, and they can be delegated to any function that supports the right interface for the event. Remember, Page events will always raise, but this does not mean you have to devote code and processing time to responding to the events. We always set this attribute value to "False."

EnableViewState: View state allows server controls to persist their contents and selected values between postings. View state is enabled by default for an entire page, but because it can have performance implications, you should set the Boolean attribute explicitly, even if you plan to keep view state enabled ("True"). View state is convenient, but it is not always needed. Typically, it is most convenient to keep view state intact for the overall page and disable it for individual controls. The "View State" section discusses this in further detail.

EnableViewStateMac: This Boolean attribute indicates whether the view state contents should be encrypted and whether the server should inspect them for evidence of tampering on the client. The *Mac* portion of the attribute name stands for Machine Authentication Check. Many users (ourselves included) have run into page loading problems when this attribute is omitted (which sets the attribute to "True," by default). Many users set this attribute value to "False." Microsoft hastens to point out that MAC encryption is not a replacement for a certificate-based encryption system such as Secure Socket Layer (SSL). If tampering is an issue for you, consider implementing a certificate-based encryption system rather than relying on MAC encoding.

Page Class Members

The Page class members roughly fall into three groups. The first group includes the properties and methods that manipulate the Web form controls. The second group includes properties that access the ASP Intrinsic objects. The third group includes the Page lifecycle events (which are discussed in the next section). Table 2-1 describes important members of the Page class that fall into the first two groups.

Table 2-1. The Page Class Members

CLASS MEMBER	DESCRIPTION
Controls	[Property] A collection of Control objects hosted on the page. You can iterate through the collection using for-each-next syntax. For example, to print out control type details, use this code: ``` Dim objItem As Control For Each objItem In Page.Controls Console.WriteLine(objItem.GetType) Next ```
FindControl	[Method] Retrieves an object reference for a specific control on the page, using its ID. For example: ``` Dim MyCtl As TextBox = Page.FindControl("ap_txt1") ```
HasControls	[Method] Determines if a server control contains child controls. For example, a DataGrid control may contain embedded (child) controls, such as textboxes and buttons.
IsPostBack	[Property] A Boolean value that indicates whether the current GET or POST request results from the current page posting back to itself. This property is typically checked in the Page_Load() event. If view state is enabled, this property often indicates that the page should be processed but not re-rendered. Because view state preserves the original contents of the Page controls, you will get duplicate items in the controls if they are re-rendered without first clearing the existing items. (This generalization may not apply to your page.)
Request	[Property] Gets a reference to the current HttpRequest instance, which encapsulates the client's request details.
Response	[Property] Gets a reference to the current HttpResponse instance, which encapsulates the server response details.
Application	[Property] Gets a reference to the Application object for the current request (which wraps the HttpApplicationState class). This class enables global application information to be shared across multiple requests and sessions.
Session	[Property] Gets a reference to the Session object for the current request (which wraps the HttpSessionState class). This class provides access to session-specific settings and values. ASP.NET provides several modes for storing session state.

Page Lifecycle Events

Recall that the Page object is responsible for processing a client request and rendering HTML in response. The Page object runs through a specific set of lifecycle stages as it fulfills its responsibilities. Several of these stages are associated with events that you can capture and code behind.

The Page class itself inherits from the Control and TemplateControl classes, both of which are members of the System.Web.UI namespace. The Control class provides a common set of properties, methods, and events that are shared by all server controls. The TemplateControl class provides additional base functionality for the Page class. Together, these two classes provide the base events that the Page class raises, as well as base methods that the Page class can override.

Table 2-2 summarizes the more important lifecycle stages and their associated events, or the methods that can be overridden, for adding code to specific stages.

Table 2-2. The Page Lifecycle Stages

STAGE	DESCRIPTION	EVENT OR METHOD?
Initialize	Initializes settings.	The Page_Init event
Load View State	Loads view state information from the _VIEWSTATE hidden form field and assigns the contents to a StateBag object. This object is exposed by the Page object's ViewState property.	The LoadViewState() method
Load Post Data	Process incoming form data. If state changes occur between postbacks, the RaisePostDataChangedEvent() method will be raised immediately following the _Load() event.	The LoadPostData() method
Load	Performs actions for all requests, including initializing server controls and restoring theirstate. The Page object provides an .Is PostBack property that will fire for posts (value is "False") and reposts (value is "True"). The .IsPostBack property allows you to set up conditional logic in the Load() event handler for handling the first post vs. subsequent reposts. You can check for postback data and can view state information for the Page's child controls.	The Page_Load() event

(continued)

Table 2-2. The Page Lifecycle Stages (continued)

STAGE	DESCRIPTION	EVENT OR METHOD?
Handle Postback Events	Handles the client-side events that trigger a postback to the server. For example, the _Click() event of a Button server control or the _OnPageIndexChanged() event of a DataGrid with paging enabled.	The RaisePostBackEvent() method
Pre-Render	The stage where remaining updates are performed prior to saving view state and rendering the form. You can add custom values to view state at this stage.	The Page_PreRender() event
Save View State	The stage where view state information is persisted to a hidden field on the form.	The SaveViewState() method
Render	Generates HTML output to send to the client.	The Render() method
Dispose	Releases resources and performs final cleanup, prior to unloading the Page object.	The Page_Disposed() event
Unload	This stage is where the Page object is unloaded from server memory. You can perform cleanupand release resources in this stage, butdevelopers generally perform these tasks in the Page_Disposed() event.	The Page_Unload() event

The descriptions in Table 2-2 are specific to the Page object, but many of the events and methods apply equally to any server control. This should be of no surprise, given that the Page class inherits from the Control class, which is common to all server controls. In addition, the Page object acts as a container for a collection of server controls, all of which run through their own processing stages. There is a complicated interplay between the controls' execution orders and the Page execution order. This sequencing is of particular concern when you are developing a custom server control that handles postbacks and participates in view state.

View State

View state is an ASP.NET feature that allows a Web page to retain all of its state values between requests to the Web server. In classic ASP, developers are forced to handle this task manually, which is a tedious and time-consuming process. Consider one example, where the user fills out a form with several HTML input text controls. Once the form is submitted to the server, the ASP engine retrieves the control contents from the HTTP headers and processes the business logic. When the page returns to the client, the control values (including user input) are not retained, unless the developer has manually rehydrated the control values using embedded server-side code within the HTML form. This issue is a regular headache for form-based applications because the server commonly needs to return control values to the client for a second look—for example, if the user input fails server-side validation.

Input controls represent one of the simpler problems. Drop-down list controls pose a more complicated problem because they contain multiple values and include a user-selected value. Typically, drop-down lists need to be hydrated just once, and they must then retain the same values and user selections. Classic ASP requires you to manually repopulate the select box contents between postings to the server. This requirement is not just tedious for the developer, but it can also be expensive for the server, especially if additional database lookups are required.

View state enables all controls on a Web page to retain their state values between successive postbacks to the server. Furthermore, view state preserves a control's properties between postbacks. For example, if a control's Visible property is set to "False," then the control will remain invisible between successive postbacks. In short, view state saves developers time by reducing the amount of coding they have to do. In addition, view state improves application performance by eliminating the database calls that would otherwise be needed to rehydrate controls between postbacks.

How View State Works

View state is stored using encoded key-value pairs within a hidden form field. Every control on the page is represented using one or more pairs. For view state to work, a Web page must contain a server-side form (with the runat=server attribute) so that a hidden _VIEWSTATE field may be added directly below the opening <Form> tag. (A server-side form is provided by default when you create a new Web page). View state only works for server-side controls contained within the server-side form. In fact, server-side controls will generate compilation errors if they are added to a page outside of their server-side form.

For a Web page with view state enabled, the view state process works as follows:

1. The client requests a Web page.

2. The server renders the page, including a _VIEWSTATE hidden field that contains encoded key-value pairs for the properties and values of every control on the page.

3. The client enters information into the rendered HTML controls and then posts the page back to the server.

4. The server initializes the page and then tracks the client's changes to control state. The server executes the business logic on the page and then renders the page. The server controls get rehydrated using the latest values stored in the _VIEWSTATE hidden field, which is updated to include the new, client-specified values and selections.

You manage view state using the StateBag class, which is a member of the System.Web.UI namespace. The Page object provides access to a StateBag object through its ViewState property. The StateBag class implements a number of interfaces, including the IDictionary and IEnumerable interfaces, which allow you to enumerate and modify the view state contents. Table 2-3 describes important members of the StateBag class.

Table 2-3. The StateBag Class Members

CLASS MEMBER	DESCRIPTION
Add	This method adds a new StateItem object to the StateBag object or updates an existing StateItem object value if it is already included in the StateBag class. The StateItem object represents a view state name-value pair.
Remove	This method removes an object from the StateBag object.
Keys	This property gets a collection of (enumerable) keys that represent the items in the StateBag object.
Item	This property gets or sets the value of an object in the StateBag object.

You can add or modify view state items from the Web form code-behind file up until the Pre-Render stage of the page's lifecycle, which is just before the page starts rendering HTML. For example, you can append custom view state values that are distinct from any of the page controls:

```
Private Sub Page_PreRender(ByVal sender As Object, _
    ByVal e As System.EventArgs) Handles MyBase.PreRender
    ' Store custom ViewState values
    ViewState("Key1") = "MyValue1"
    ViewState.Item("Key2") = "MyValue2" ' Alternate notation
End Sub
```

In fact, you can add any object to view state, as long as it supports binary serialization. *Serialization* is the process by which binary data is converted into a stream of bytes in order to be saved to a storage medium. Serializable objects, such as the DataView object, implement the `ISerializable` interface. Non-serializable objects, such as the ListItem object, do not implement this interface. As you can see, you can add serializable objects to view state easily:

```
' ViewState will store any serializable object
Dim sqlDV As DataView
ViewState.Add("MyDataView", sqlDV)
```

Retrieving objects from view state is just as simple:

```
If Page.IsPostBack Then
    ' Retrieve the DataView object from ViewState
    sqlDV = ViewState.Item("MyDataView")
End If
```

Persisting View State Across Multiple Pages

In special cases, view state may persist values across multiple pages, not just across postbacks for the same page. Consider an application with two Web pages, where each page contains a TextBox server control named TextBox1. If Page 1 submits to Page 2, then the TextBox control on Page 2 will pick up the view state for the Page 1 TextBox control. You can use this behavior to your advantage if you want to persist common information across multiple pages, as long as the Web application uses posting between pages, rather than hyperlinks. For example, consider an application where every page contains a Label server control for persisting the client's login name. This is the design view for Page 1:

```
<form id="Form1" method="post" runat="server">
        <asp:Label id="lblUserName" runat="server" Width="126px"
                Height="28px"></asp:Label>
</form>
```

In the code-behind file, you would assign the login name to the Label control:

```
Public Class ap_ViewState
    Inherits System.Web.UI.Page
    Protected lblUserName As System.Web.UI.WebControls.Label
```

```
    Sub Page_Load([Arguments]) Handles MyBase.Load
        If Not Page.IsPostBack Then
            ' Assign Username to label (Username is hardcoded for demo purposes)
            lblUserName.Text = "AEinstein"
        End If
    End Sub
End Class
```

Then on subsequent Pages 2, 3, and so forth, you can automatically pick up the Label value from view state by doing just two things:

1. Add a Label server control named "lblUserName."

2. Add a variable declaration for the label in the code-behind file for the server control.

The only "coding" you need to do is to ensure that every page declares the server control variable:

```
Protected lblUserName As System.Web.UI.WebControls.Label
```

The inverse behavior also applies: The view state will clear for all server controls that are not repeated between pages. Custom view state values will only persist for as long as the client continues to post back the same page.

Disabling View State

ASP.NET server controls have their view state enabled by default, but you can disable it for those controls that do not need to retain their values between postbacks. For example, DataGrid controls that are rehydrated on every postback do not need to retain their view state.

You can disable view state for a server control in two ways:

*   At design-time, by setting its EnableViewState attribute equal to "False":

```
<asp:Label id="lblUserName" runat="server" EnableViewState=False></asp:Label>
```

- At runtime, although make sure you do so the first time the page loads:

```
lblUserName.EnableViewState = False
```

You can also disable view state for an entire page using the @ Page directive:

```
<%@ Page Language="vb" EnableViewState="false" Codebehind="[Page].aspx.vb"
    Inherits="AspNetChap2.[Page]" %>
```

Finally, you can disable view state for an entire application using the Web.config configuration file. To do so, simply modify the <pages> configuration element's enableViewState attribute value:

```
<pages buffer="true" enableViewState="false">
```

Keep in mind that when view state is completely disabled, you will have to do a lot of work to manage state manually.

Performance Considerations with View State

View state always comes with a performance price for three reasons:

View state can add a significant number of bytes to the overall page size, depending on the amount and complexity of the persisted data. Larger pages take longer to render, and they deliver more slowly back to the client.

View state is only optimized to work with a small set of simple object types, including strings, integers, Booleans, ArrayLists, arrays, and Hashtable objects. All other objects (including server controls) are less efficient to serialize. They take longer to serialize because they generate larger byte streams.

Server control states must be deserialized from view state (or *rehydrated*) every time the server renders a reposted page back to the client. It is expensive and time-consuming to deserialize pages that contain rich server controls (for example, DataGrids) or controls that hold large numbers of values (for example, DropDownList controls).

You cannot modify how a control's view state is persisted, so as the developer, you have no way to optimize the process. A server control will always be entered into the _VIEWSTATE hidden field, even if the control is empty. For all of these reasons, you should always disable view state for controls that do not require it. Also, not all browsers are equally capable of handling view state. For example, a Web application that targets the Pocket PC can only persist a limited amount of information in the _VIEWSTATE hidden field before the contents become corrupted.

Typically, you will want to keep view state enabled for the overall page and then selectively disable view state for certain controls. However, you can disable view state at the page level if you are sure the page will only be reposted once. For example, Figure 2-2 shows a voluntary sign-in page, which reposts to itself and appends the sign-in name to a redirect URL to another page.

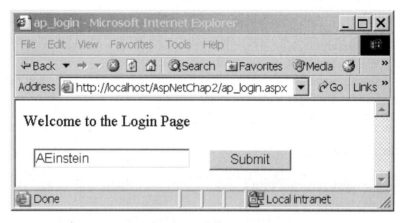

Figure 2-2. The ap_login screen

Listing 2-2 shows the code-behind file for the page.

Listing 2-2. The Code-Behind File for `ap_login.aspx`

```
Public Class ap_login
    Inherits System.Web.UI.Page
    Protected TextBox1 As System.Web.UI.WebControls.TextBox
    Protected WithEvents Button1 As System.Web.UI.WebControls.Button

    Private Sub Page_Load(ByVal sender As Object, _
        ByVal e As System.EventArgs) Handles MyBase.Load
        If Not Page.IsPostBack Then
            ' Initialize the Textbox
            Me.TextBox1.Text = "AEinstein"
        End If
    End Sub
```

```
    Private Sub Button1_Click(ByVal sender As System.Object, _
        ByVal e As System.EventArgs) Handles Button1.Click
        Page.Response.Redirect("ap_ViewState.aspx?User=AEinstein")
    End Sub
End Class
```

Let's assume that any input is acceptable, including blank inputs, so no errors will arise that need to be reported back to the user. This kind of page does not require view state, so it should be disabled at the page level.

Finally, you can always disable view state for a specific control under four scenarios:

- The control contains no dynamic values, only hard-coded values or fixed properties in the *.aspx file. (An example is a Label control with fixed dimensions and font properties.)

- The control contains dynamic values that are rebound on every page request.

- The control does not raise custom-handled events. For example, if a page contains a simple DataGrid, then you can disable view state. But if the DataGrid provides paging, then you cannot disable view state because the code-behind file needs to handle the OnPageIndexChanged() event.

- The control's host page will not be reposted to the server. In this case, avoid the cost of saving and retrieving view state that will never actually be used by the server.

Measuring View State Performance Cost

View state management always exacts a performance price, but as we noted earlier, it can also reduce the need for redundant database calls. View state management may be faster and more secure than manually handling control state on your own. Without view state, a Select box will need to be repopulated from the database on every postback. With view state, the Select box only needs to be populated once, when the page first loads. The cost of view state is measured by the extra bytes it adds to the page, plus the processing cost of serializing the server control (including encryption and decryption). On the other hand, the cost of no view state is the processing cost of making multiple, redundant database calls, as well as the performance and productivity cost of having to create your own state management solution if required.

The point is that you often do not know, *a priori*, whether view state is a good thing for your application. You will have better insight as you become more experienced with using view state. However, barring this, the only way to know is to test your application both with view state and without it, and then you can decide. Without view state, you may be forced to make redundant database calls to rehydrate a posted page. If you implement caching, then redundant database calls no longer become an issue, and view state may lose out on the performance measure. But it may still win over on the convenience measure because you will not need to invest time in creating code to manage state manually. You will have to decide whether you want to support the more complex code that is required for manually persisting server control states. You will also have to determine, through testing and experimenting, whether the manual code will even perform better than view state.

Finally, you will also want to evaluate how many additional bytes view state adds to your pages and whether they are becoming unreasonably large compared to your target page sizes. Visual Studio .NET provides a trace log that will tell you the view state size, in bytes, for every control on a form. To enable tracing on a page, set the @ Page directive's Trace attribute to "True":

```
<%@ Page Language="vb" Trace="True" AutoEventWireup="false"
    Codebehind="ap_ViewState.aspx.vb" Inherits="AspNetChap2.ap_ViewState" %>
```

Figure 2-3 shows a simple application that provides two server controls, a submit button, and a label that displays a timestamp for when the button was clicked.

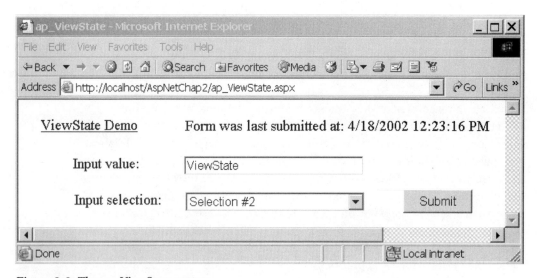

Figure 2-3. The ap_ViewState screen

The Trace log for this screen includes a Control Tree section, which summarizes the render sizes and the view state sizes of the server controls in the page, as shown in Figure 2-4.

Control Id	Type	Render Size Bytes (including children)	Viewstate Size Bytes (excluding children)
__PAGE	ASP.ap_ViewState_aspx	2101	20
_ctl0	System.Web.UI.ResourceBasedLiteralControl	440	0
Form1	System.Web.UI.HtmlControls.HtmlForm	1640	0
_ctl1	System.Web.UI.LiteralControl	5	0
TextBox1	System.Web.UI.WebControls.TextBox	146	0
_ctl2	System.Web.UI.LiteralControl	5	0
lbl2	System.Web.UI.WebControls.Label	128	0
_ctl3	System.Web.UI.LiteralControl	5	0
lblTimestamp	System.Web.UI.WebControls.Label	168	92
_ctl4	System.Web.UI.LiteralControl	5	0
lblTitle	System.Web.UI.WebControls.Label	155	0
_ctl5	System.Web.UI.LiteralControl	5	0
Button1	System.Web.UI.WebControls.Button	155	0
_ctl6	System.Web.UI.LiteralControl	5	0
lbl1	System.Web.UI.WebControls.Label	123	0
_ctl7	System.Web.UI.LiteralControl	5	0
DropDownList1	System.Web.UI.WebControls.DropDownList	277	112
_ctl8	System.Web.UI.LiteralControl	4	0
_ctl9	System.Web.UI.LiteralControl	21	0

Figure 2-4. Trace log for the ap_ViewState screen

In summary, view state management exacts a performance price that may be acceptable if it reduces database calls and code complexity.

Security Considerations with View State

The __VIEWSTATE hidden field is essentially a long, encoded text string that provides no protection for sensitive information such as connection strings or credit card numbers. Encoding is not the same as encryption. View state uses what's called a *base64-encoded string*, which simply means the string will remain unaltered by whatever HTTP encoding scheme the application uses for transmitting bytes during requests and responses between the client and the Web server.

View state contents may be encrypted directly from ASP.NET using machine key-based encryption. However, be aware that this step will add to the view state processing time. You can add view state encryption in two steps:

1. Set the @ Page directive's EnableViewStateMac attribute value to "True":

    ```
    <%@ Page EnableViewStateMAC="True" %>
    ```

2. Open the Web.config configuration file and set the <machineKey> element as follows:

    ```
    <machineKey validationKey="AutoGenerate" decryptionKey="AutoGenerate"
            validation="3DES"/>
    ```

ASP.NET supports other encryption algorithms, but view state only works with the Triple DES encryption algorithm.

The @ Page directive's EnableViewStateMac attribute appends a hashcode to the end of the __VIEWSTATE hidden field. The purpose of this hashcode is to help the ASP.NET runtime verify the integrity of the view state contents. That is, it checks whether the contents may have been tampered with during posting. If ASP.NET detects a problem, then the view state contents are discarded, and the controls are restored to their initial values. The EnableViewStateMac attribute is really of little use; you should only use it if you decide to implement 3DES encryption. Even then, we recommend you consider using HTTPS over 3DES encryption. HTTPS is a proven, secure encryption technology that is widely known and trusted by users of Internet-based applications.

Implementing View State in Server Farms

You can implement view state in a server farm using a simple modification to the <machineKey> element. By default, view state works with a random validation key that indicates the integrity of the view state data. For example, this is a <machineKey> element with default attribute values:

```
<machineKey validationKey="AutoGenerate" decryptionKey="AutoGenerate"
        validation="SHA1"/>
```

In a server farm, you must manually set the validationKey attribute to a cryptographic key that is consistent for all servers in the farm. Otherwise, one server (in the farm) will assume that the view state for another server is corrupted, and the view state data will not be restored. The validation key must be between 20 and 64 bytes and is represented as a hexadecimal string, from 40 to 128 characters in length. The recommended key length is 128 hexadecimal characters (or 64 bytes). You can create the key value using a specialized .NET Framework class called RNGCryptoServiceProvider, which resides in the System.Security.Cryptography namespace. The sample project contains a page called ap_crypto.aspx, which demonstrates how to generate a 128-character cryptographic key. Listing 2-3 shows the simple code.

Listing 2-3. Generating a 128-Character Cryptographic Key

```
Imports System.Text
Imports System.Security.Cryptography

Private Sub Page_Load(ByVal sender As System.Object, _
    ByVal e As System.EventArgs) Handles MyBase.Load
    Response.Write("The 128-character cryptographic key is: " & _
        GenerateCryptoKey())
End Sub

Private Function GenerateCryptoKey() As String

    ' Step 1: Initialize a byte array
    Dim buff(63) As Byte

    ' Step 2: Declare the class
    Dim rngKey As RNGCryptoServiceProvider = _
        New RNGCryptoServiceProvider()

    ' Step 3: Populate the buffer with key bytes
    rngKey.GetBytes(buff)

    ' Step 4: Transfer the key to a string
    Dim i As Integer
    Dim sb As StringBuilder = New StringBuilder(128)
    For i = 0 To buff.Length - 1
        sb.Append(String.Format("{0:X2}", buff(i)))
    Next

    Return (sb.ToString)

End Function
```

This listing initializes a byte array and then populates it with a cryptographic key using the RNGCryptoServiceProvider class. Notice the use of the Format() function to map the generated bytes to a hexadecimal character representation. This is one example of a generated key:

```
0CB9F8A3F24CBB5C724AD939CE7AC075D6266224CBF92D88A46BD09E7397735ADFF161
D9309B7353E82DB7FFCEE74D73412A68830543BD6FCACDE303C98F4500
```

Simply copy this key value to the Web.config file of every server in the Web farm to share view state across the farm.

View State vs. Session State

Observant readers will notice the similarity between view state and session state when it comes to storing session-specific, custom values. Both approaches use a straightforward, key-based system for getting and setting values:

```
Dim MyObject As System.Object ' Generic object
Session("MyData") = MyObject ' Add an object to session state
ViewState("MyData") = MyObject ' Add an object to view state
Dim MyObject As Object = Session("MyData")   ' Get an object from session state
Dim MyObject As Object = ViewState("MyData")   ' Get an object from view state
```

Classic ASP users are trained to be wary of using Session variables because they incur a high performance and scalability cost. Session variables have been overhauled in ASP.NET and are now a viable choice for persisting session-specific information. Some of the same limitations that affected Session variables in classic ASP still apply in ASP.NET, but the technology is better. Chapter 4, "Optimizing Application and Session State Management," discusses this topic in greater detail. For now, the discussion focuses on whether view state or session state is a better choice for storing session-specific custom objects.

Perhaps surprisingly, Session variables are often the better choice, especially on stand-alone Web servers, for the following reasons:

Session variables can hold a wide range of object types, as long as they are thread-safe. View state can only hold simple object types, or objects that support binary serialization. Session variables have no such limitation, as long as the session state mode is set to InProc (in-memory) or SQLServer. The StateServer mode employs binary serialization, so it is not suitable for all object types.

Session variables are more efficient at storing large and complex objects, especially when the Session State mode is set to "InProc." View state must serialize all objects to bytes, and large objects require storing a large number of bytes.

Session variables are persistent for the entire duration of the client's session. View state is only persistent for the current page, except for server controls that are exactly duplicated across multiple pages.

Session variables are more efficient to serialize. An object serializes more efficiently to an InProc Session variable than it does to a view state byte stream.

Session variables provide more privacy for sensitive information compared to view state because Session data is stored on the server, whereas view state data is marshaled between the client and server.

Still, there are times when you will want to use view state over Session variables. The reasons are as follows:

View state is efficient at storing simple object types.

View state does not consume server memory resources for storing objects in the same way that InProc (in-memory) session variables do.

View state does not time out, whereas Session variables will time out by default. Sessions will also be destroyed if changes are made to the Web.config file or if IIS gets reset.

View state only requires a minor special configuration for a server farm environment (implementing a consistent validation key). However, session state management in this environment requires special considerations. For example, it must exclude InProc session state, which is only valid if the request returns to the same server. Instead, the SQLServer or StateServer modes must be used, which will likely not perform as fast as view state.

In summary, Session variables may be a better choice than view state for storing complex or large, session-specific custom objects. This is especially true on stand-alone Web servers that support low to moderate traffic volumes. In a server farm environment, view state is usually a better choice compared to session state management. In addition, view state is most suitable for storing simple object types.

Keep in mind, however, that view state offers one significant convenience over Session variables. Namely, view state automatically rehydrates Web page controls, restoring both their properties and their data. Session variables will store data, but it is up to the developer to manually rehydrate the Web page controls using this data. Convenience often comes with a price, and you should always consider alternatives to view state if your Web application is focused on persisting data rather than control states.

Further Alternatives to View State

You can use caching in place of view state or session state, depending on what a specific Web page needs to do. Page-level output caching is a convenient way to store rendered content and is suitable for non-interactive, read-only pages. Alternatively, fragment caching allows you to mix cached and non-cached content. Finally, the Cache API allows you to cache objects and access them with a high level of control. Chapter 5, "Caching ASP.NET Applications," covers caching, along with session state management, and it discusses the similarities and contrasts between each technology.

Cookies are another technology you can use in conjunction with caching to replace view state, albeit with some limitations. Cookies are useful for storing limited amounts of information on the client, and they are suitable for persisting simple information, such as combo box selections. Cookies may be a good alternative for Web pages that do not cache content but that need to persist user input, selections, and preferences. You could use caching to persist control contents, and you could use cookies persist user selections and preferences. In combination, these two technologies may be a suitable and better-performing alternative to view state. Keep in mind, however, that the developer is then responsible for manually hydrating the Web page controls with cached data.

Understanding the ASP.NET Configuration System

ASP.NET provides an extensible, XML-based configuration system that is easy to use and easy to customize. The root configuration file, `Machine.config`, provides ASP.NET configuration settings for every application in the Web server. In addition, every ASP.NET application contains its own configuration file, called `Web.config`, which resides in the root of the application. This file provides configuration settings for all files in the root directory and for every child directory below the root.

`Machine.config` and `Web.config` are structured the same way, and they define many of the same settings. The `Web.config` file overrides many of the settings in `Machine.config`, within the scope of the specific ASP.NET application where

the Web.config file resides. ASP.NET also allows you to set up a hierarchy of
Web.config files so that every child directory can have its own. The settings in the
child directory's Web.config file override the settings in the root directory's
Web.config file. The root directory's file, in turn, overrides many settings in
the server-level Machine.config file. Certain settings in the Machine.config file have
server-level scope and cannot be overridden by individual Web.config files. This
includes, for example, the <processModel> configuration element, which controls
the behavior of the ASP.NET worker process. You can still access the configuration
values and modify them as needed, but you can only do this in Machine.config.

Benefits of ASP.NET Configuration

The ASP.NET configuration system provides several benefits over classic ASP:

XML-based file format: The configuration files are XML based, so they are
readable and can be edited in any XML editor or in Visual Studio .NET
directly. As of this writing, no editor exists specifically for ASP.NET configuration files. The one drawback to this is that you can easily introduce
syntax errors into the file during editing. These errors can break the build
during compilation, and you may only receive an ambiguously worded
error. Make sure you edit configuration files one key at a time and rebuild
the application often between edits. This will allow you to catch syntax
errors immediately after they occur.

Optimized access to settings: The ASP.NET runtime engine caches configuration settings, so they are readily accessible throughout the application.
The configuration file provides an excellent alternative to using Application variables for caching global configuration settings.

Automatic refresh when settings change: The ASP.NET runtime engine
automatically picks up changes to configuration files and applies them to
the local application for all subsequent requests. Configuration changes do
not require an IIS reset because the application will restart automatically
once all current requests have completed. (This feature is convenient, but
be aware that if your application uses in-memory session variables, then
this information will be lost during an application restart).

Extensible for adding custom settings: The ASP.NET configuration system
is extensible. The system uses handler classes for processing configuration
settings, and these existing classes may be used for processing your own
custom configuration settings. Alternatively, you can create custom handler classes to handle the processing.

Protected settings: ASP.NET configuration files are protected from direct browser access, so your settings are protected from prying eyes. You may still want to rethink storing passwords in the configuration files because any written password is automatically a security liability. For example, SQL connection strings are commonly stored in configuration files. (You can avoid storing connection strings directly by setting up a trusted connection between the Web server and the SQL Server. Chapter 3, "Writing Optimized Data Access Code," discusses trusted connections.)

Some of these advantages will be obvious to you, but others are probably unfamiliar and require further explanation. The issues will become clearer once you take a closer look at the ASP.NET configuration system. Before proceeding, we need to point out that there is some ambiguity to the term *configuration setting* because most ASP.NET configuration settings are multidimensional. For example, the <sessionState> configuration element provides several attributes, including mode and timeout. It becomes unclear whether the term *setting* refers to the element (which has no direct value) or to the attributes—or to both. To avoid confusion, we will refer to configuration elements and attributes, where the element holds the name and the attributes hold the values. We will use the term *configuration setting* for the sum total of a configuration element and its attributes.

The Machine.config File

The Machine.config file is located in the folder %windir%\Microsoft.NET\Framework\%version%\config, where %version% is a folder that is named for the current installed version of the .NET Framework. The Machine.config file serves two purposes. First, it defines what the configuration elements are. Second, it specifies initial values for every element's attributes. The Machine.config file is divided into two sections:

- **The configuration section handler (CSH) section**: This section provides definitions for the configuration elements, using section handlers. A section handler simply specifies the name of the configuration element and the name of the handler class that will process the configuration attribute values.

- **The configuration implementation section**: This section specifies initial attribute values for every configuration element. Essentially, this section implements the configuration elements defined in the previous section.

The terminology sounds confusing, but it is actually straightforward. Listing 2-4 shows a stripped-down version of the `Machine.config` file.

Listing 2-4. A Simple `Machine.config` File

```xml
<?xml version="1.0" encoding="UTF-8"?>
<configuration>

    <configSections>
        <sectionGroup name="system.web">
            <section name="httpHandlers"
                type="System.Web.Configuration.HttpHandlersSectionHandler,
                    System.Web"/>
            <section name="sessionState"
                type="System.Web.SessionState.SessionStateSectionHandler,
                    System.Web " allowDefinition="MachineToApplication"/>
            <section name="trace"
                type="System.Web.Configuration.TraceConfigurationHandler,
                    System.Web "/>
        </sectionGroup>
    </configSections>

    <system.web>
        <sessionState mode="InProc" stateConnectionString="
            tcpip=127.0.0.1:42424"
            stateNetworkTimeout="10" sqlConnectionString="data source=127.0.0.1;
            user id=sa;password=" cookieless="false" timeout="20"/>
        <trace enabled="false" localOnly="true" pageOutput="false"
                requestLimit="10"
                traceMode="SortByTime"/>
        <httpHandlers>
            <add verb="*" path="*.aspx"
                    type="System.Web.UI.PageHandlerFactory"/>
            <add verb="*" path="trace.axd"
                    type="System.Web.Handlers.TraceHandler"/>
        </httpHandlers>
    </system.web>

</configuration>
```

The `<configuration>` node is the root node for the overall file. The section handlers are contained within the `<configSections>` tags. A section handler is simply an XML tag that defines the name of the configuration element and the type (or *class*) that processes the configuration attribute values. Listing 2-4 shows section handlers for the <httpHandlers>, <sessionState>, and <trace> configuration elements. Notice the convention of using Pascal-case, or *camel-case*, for element and attribute names. The Web.config file is case sensitive and will generate compilation errors if it includes a section handler that does not use camel-case. For example, you must type the attribute value for <sessionState> mode as "InProc"—not as "Inproc" or a similar variation. Notice also the use of section groups, which organize section handlers into related groups. The listing shows a section group called system.web.

The lower half of the file, between the <system.web> tags, is the implementation section. This section specifies initial values for the configuration elements defined in the top half of the file. You do not see the attributes defined directly in the file; instead, you can only see where they are implemented. The handler classes actually define what the element attributes are. The handler class is also responsible for returning an object that provides programmatic access to the configuration element. For example, the handler class for <sessionState> returns an object of type HttpSessionState. Again, you can't tell this from the configuration file. The lesson here is to document your classes well should you develop your own custom handler classes! The .NET Framework provides a number of generic handler classes in addition to the specialized classes. You should find the available handler classes to be adequate for defining most configuration elements.

The Web.config File

The Web.config file is easy to understand once you know how the Machine.config file is structured. Everything you can do in Machine.config, you can also do in Web.config. This means you can create new section handlers and implement existing ones. When you create a new ASP.NET application project using Visual Studio .NET, it will automatically create a Web.config file in the root. If you open this file, you will notice that all of its contents are devoted to implementing existing configuration elements. In fact, <configSections> elements are not initially added to the file. You can override almost any configuration setting (with the exception of <processModel>) by adding it to the Web.config file and then changing one or more attribute values. Table 2-4 summarizes the ASP.NET configuration elements that are initially included in the Web.config file.

•

Table 2-4. The ASP.NET Configuration Elements

ELEMENT	DESCRIPTION
Authentication	This element sets the authentication policy for the application. Possible modes are "Windows," "Forms," "Passport," and "None."
Authorization	This element sets the authorization policy for the application. You can allow or deny access to application resources by user or by role. Also, you can use wildcards: * for everyone and ? for anonymous (unauthenticated) users.
Compilation	This element sets several compilation settings for the application, including whether the debug mode is "True." This mode inserts debugging symbols into the compiled page. Debug pages are larger and execute more slowly, so you should use them only for testing purposes.
Custom Errors	This element allows you to set custom error pages for specific errors if the mode is set to "On." If the mode is set to "RemoteOnly," then remote users will see custom errors, and local users will see standard ASP.NET error screens that contain full details of the error, including a stack trace. If the mode is set to "Off," then all users will see the standard ASP.NET error screens.
Globalization	This element sets the character encoding for requests and responses. The default value is "UTF-8."
SessionState	This element sets the Session State mode for the application. Possible modes are "InProc," "SQLServer," "StateServer," and "None." Chapter 4, "Optimizing Application and Session State Management," discusses session state.
Trace	This element sets attributes for application-level tracing. Trace logs may post directly to a page, or they may be stored in a trace.axd file. Chapter 8, "Debugging and Tracing ASP.NET Applications," discusses tracing.

The Machine.config file contains several other configuration elements that are not initially included in the Web.config file. The most important of these elements are <processModel> and <httpRuntime>, which directly affect the performance, availability, and stability of your ASP.NET applications. These elements are discussed in some detail in the "Optimal ASP.NET Configuration" section.

Custom Configuration Elements

The power of ASP.NET configuration lies in its extensibility. You can easily define custom configuration elements using generic handler classes. Alternatively, you can add custom elements as key-value pairs without having to define a handler class. The configuration files allow you to add custom elements in two ways:

- **Application settings**: Add key-value pairs to a specialized section handler called <appSettings>. The setting is defined and implemented in the same line using the key-value attribute values.

- **Custom configuration settings**: Add custom section handlers directly into <configSections>. You can either create a custom handler class or use a generic handler class. You must implement the setting in a separate area of the file.

The details of each approach will become immediately clear when you see some examples. But first we need to mention the System.Configuration namespace, without which it would not be possible to define and to read custom configuration settings. Table 2-5 summarizes the more important class members in the System.Configuration namespace.

Table 2-5. The System.Configuration *Namespace*

CLASS MEMBER	DESCRIPTION
IConfigurationSectionHandler	Defines the interface that must be implemented in all configuration handler classes for them to resolve configuration settings.
NameValueSectionHandler	Provides name-value pair configuration information for a configuration section handler. You can implement this class handler in your own custom sections.
DictionarySectionHandler	Provides key-value pair configuration information for a configuration section handler. You can implement this class handler in your own custom sections.
ConfigurationSettings	Provides access to configuration settings in a specific configuration section.

(continued)

Table 2-5. The `System.Configuration` *Namespace (continued)*

CLASS MEMBER	DESCRIPTION
AppSettings	Provides access to custom sections in the `<appSettings>` section group.
GetConfig()	Provides access to custom sections in the `<configSections>` section group.

The `System.Configuration` namespace includes generic handler classes you can use in custom configuration settings. These include NameValueSectionHandler and DictionarySectionHandler. The namespace includes a class called ConfigurationSettings, which gives you read-only, programmatic access to configuration settings once they have been defined and implemented.

Now let's take a look at examples of the two approaches for defining custom configuration elements.

Application Settings

Application settings are simply key-value pairs that you define to store custom values. They are stored as child `<add>` elements below the `<appSettings>` element, which in turn resides below the root `<configuration>` element. Each `<add>` element contains key and value attributes. Application settings are appropriate for simple information that is widely accessed throughout the ASP.NET application. Database connection strings are one good example:

```
<configuration>
    <appSettings>
        <add key="ConnectionString"
            value="server=machineName\sqlServer;uid=sa;pwd=;database=dev;" />
    </appSettings>
</configuration>
```

You have programmatic access to this key value using the `AppSettings` property of the ConfigurationSettings class:

```
' Retrieve the connection string from Web.config
Dim strConn As String = _
            ConfigurationSettings.AppSettings("ConnectionString")
Response.Write("The 'Connection String' is: " & strConn)
```

Application settings are quick and easy to use but are limited in what they can store.

Custom Configuration Settings

You must define custom configuration settings by adding a section handler to the `<configSections>` element. You can also add section groups to organize the custom section handlers. Consider the following example: Define a menu system that associates screen names with Web page names. The menu elements should be enclosed in a section group. The XML definition could look something like this:

```
<!-- configuration settings -->
<configSections>
        <!-- Declares a section group called myMenuGroup -->
        <sectionGroup name="myMenuGroup">
                <!-- Declares a section name called myMenuItem -->
                <section name="myMenuItem"
                   type="System.Configuration.DictionarySectionHandler, System,
                      Version=1.0.3300.0, Culture=neutral,
                      PublicKeyToken=b77a5c561934e089"/>
        </sectionGroup>
</configSections>
```

Notice that we have written a full type definition of the handler class for the `<myMenuItem>` element. The .NET runtime was unable to load the DictionarySectionHandler class unless the full type definition was provided. Now you can implement some menu items:

```
<!-- Menu details: key=[Screen Name]; value=[Web Page Name] -->
<myMenuGroup>
        <myMenuItem>
                <add key="Login" value="login.aspx"/>
                <add key="Browse" value="browse.aspx"/>
                <add key="Purchase" value="purchase.aspx"/>
                <add key="Tracking" value="tracking.aspx"/>
                <add key="Logout" value="logout.aspx"/>
        </myMenuItem>
</myMenuGroup>
```

You have programmatic access to the menu items using the `GetConfig()` static method of the ConfigurationSettings class:

```
' Retrieve myMenu items from Web.config
Dim dctMenuItems As IDictionary
Dim enmMenuItems As IDictionaryEnumerator

dctMenuItems = ConfigurationSettings.GetConfig("myMenuGroup/myMenuItem")
enmMenuItems = dctMenuItems.GetEnumerator()

While enmMenuItems.MoveNext()
    Response.Write(enmMenuItems.Key & ": " & enmMenuItems.Value & "<BR>")
End While
```

Optimal ASP.NET Configuration

Much of the discussion in this book focuses on how to improve the performance of your ASP.NET applications. The ASP.NET configuration system is as much about efficiency as it is about performance. It is efficient to store application-level configuration settings in XML-based files that are cached at runtime. In classic ASP, application-level information is typically stored in Application variables, which have more drawbacks than benefits. For example, Application variables must be compiled into the application, and their values can be changed in only two ways. One way is to reset the value in code, then recompile the Web application. This change requires an application restart to take effect. The other way is to provide programmatic access to the variable so that users can change the value at runtime. This approach creates concurrency problems and can lead to unstable Web applications. Classic ASP essentially provides no intrinsic support for a system administrator to update a configuration setting in an outside source location and then have the changes smoothly propagated through the Web application. Developers can, and do, implement workaround systems, but it shouldn't have to be that hard!

On the issue of performance, the ASP.NET configuration system provides several settings that directly control the performance and availability of ASP.NET applications. Two of the best examples include the <processModel> and the <httpRuntime> elements.

The ASP.NET Worker Process

ASP.NET provides new safeguards against performance crashes by isolating ASP.NET execution in a separate process from IIS. This process is called the *ASP.NET worker process*, or aspnet_wp.exe. Classic ASP applications typically run in the same process as IIS, which means that memory leaks and resource crunches can cause the IIS process to become unstable and lock up or crash. Classic ASP applications may also be configured to run in a separate process, but this approach may reduce application performance by up to a factor of 10. ASP.NET anticipates that issues and errors can occur in applications, so the worker process is designed to shut down and recycle automatically in the event that errors occur.

The Common Language Runtime (CLR) adds an additional level of stability because it provides type safety, optimized memory management, and automatic garbage collection. Stray pointers and unused references should never linger on the .NET managed heap as long as the application is written entirely using managed code. However, the .NET Framework supports unmanaged COM+ components, using its COM InterOp Services support. Unmanaged code operates outside of the control of the CLR and may generate memory leaks. ASP.NET applications that use unmanaged code are susceptible to the very application instability problems that the CLR is designed to prevent.

The ASP.NET worker process is designed with fault tolerance in mind to ensure the maximum availability for your ASP.NET application. ASP.NET is designed, under certain conditions, to shut down the existing worker process and to create a new process thread. This action may disrupt the requests for a certain number of users, but it may also prevent the application from experiencing a crash, which would ultimately affect all users for a certain period of time. The ASP.NET worker process is configured in the `Machine.config` file only, using the `<processModel>` element. Several of the element's attributes set the conditions under which the worker process must be recycled. This happens, for example, if the number of queued requests grows too large or if the process has been idle for a certain amount of time. Table 2-6 describes several of the `<processModel>` element's important attributes.

Table 2-6. The `<processModel>` *Configuration Element*

ATTRIBUTE	DESCRIPTION
Enable	Enables the processModel settings. The default value is "True."
Timeout	The total life of the process before it must be shut down and recycled. This is equivalent to an absolute expiration timestamp and will occur regardless of how well or poorly the process is running. However, the Timeout is specified in duration, rather than a specific date. The default value is "Infinite."
IdleTimeout	The amount of time that the process can be idle before it is shut down. The default value is "Infinite," meaning that an idle process will never shut down.

(continued)

Table 2-6. The `<processModel>` *Configuration Element (continued)*

ATTRIBUTE	DESCRIPTION
ShutdownTimeout	The amount of time that the process is given to shut down gracefully before it is killed. ASP.NET initially sets this value to 5 seconds, [0:00:05].
RequestLimit	The total number of requests to serve before the process is shut down. The default value is "Infinite."
RequestQueueLimit	The number of queued requests allowed before the process is shut down. ASP.NET initially sets this value to 5,000 requests. We recommend setting this number closer in line to 20 percent higher than your maximum expected loads.
RestartQueueLimit	The number of requests kept in queue while the process is restarting. For example, if the value is set to 10, then the 11th user would receive an HTTP 403 error, or equivalent, indicating that the server has understood the request but is refusing (too busy) to fulfill it. The default value is "10," but you may want to increase this value for high-volume Web sites.
MemoryLimit	The percentage of physical memory that the process is allowed to use before it must be recycled. ASP.NET initially sets this value to 60 percent, but you should choose a percentage with which you feel comfortable. Some administrators may feel more comfortable setting the percentage to 50 percent or lower, in order to stay well clear of the "red zone," in which all server processes begin to get affected by sharply reduced available memory. Of course, this percentage depends on what other processes and applications are running on the server.
ClientConnectedCheck	The amount of time that a request is left in the queue before ASP.NET checks to verify that the client is still connected. ASP.NET initially sets this value to 5 seconds, [0:00:05]. This feature is extremely useful for handling the scenario where a user gets impatient waiting for a server response and clicks the submit button (in other words, resubmitting the form) multiple times. Doing so effectively disconnects earlier requests. The clientConnectedCheck attribute saves ASP.NET from having to waste time servicing requests that are currently disconnected.

(continued)

Table 2-6. The `<processModel>` *Configuration Element (continued)*

ATTRIBUTE	DESCRIPTION
ResponseDeadlockInterval	Provides deadlock detection. The amount of time allowed for a response while a request is still executing. ASP.NET initially sets this value to 3 minutes, [0:03:00].
responseRestartDeadlockInterval	The amount of time to wait before restarting the worker process following a deadlock. ASP.NET initially sets this value to 9 minutes, [0:09:00].
MaxWorkerThreads	The maximum number of worker threads per CPU. ASP.NET initially sets this value to 25. We do not recommend changing this value, although the allowed range is from 5 to 100.
MaxIOThreads	The maximum number of IO threads per CPU. ASP.NET initially sets this value to 25. We do not recommend changing this value, although the allowed range is from 5 to 100.

The HTTP Runtime Engine

The HTTP runtime engine is responsible for managing the processing of HTTP requests. This includes delegating requests to the appropriate handler classes. The `<httpRuntime>` configuration element provides attributes for optimizing how the HTTP runtime engine works. The element can be included in the Web.config file and modified on a per-application basis. Initially, the element is defined in the Machine.config only, so it applies across all ASP.NET applications. The `<httpRuntime>` element settings provide an additional line of defense against application crashes. Table 2-7 summarizes several of the `<httpRuntime>` element's important attributes.

Table 2-7. The `<httpRuntime>` *Configuration Element*

ATTRIBUTE	DESCRIPTION
ExecutionTimeout	The amount of time before a request is timed out. ASP.NET initially sets this value to 90 seconds.
maxRequestLength	The maximum request length that ASP.NET will accept, in kilobytes (Kb). ASP.NET initially sets this value to 4096 Kb. This attribute is designed to prevent denial-of-service attacks that occur through repeated large file uploads that overwhelm a Web server. You should set this value close to the largest size file you expect to have uploaded.
MinFreeThreads	The minimum number of free threads that will be kept available for processing new requests. ASP.NET initially sets this value to 8.
MinLocalRequestFreeThreads	The minimum number of free threads that will be kept available for processing new local requests. New local threads may be spawned for multithreaded processing on the Web server. This attribute reduces the chances for deadlocks by ensuring that a minimum pool of threads is reserved for local, multithreaded processes.
AppRequestQueueLimit	The maximum number of requests that will be queued when no threads are available for additional processing. Additional requests will receive an HTTP 403 error, or equivalent, indicating that the server has understood the request but is refusing (too busy) to fulfill it. The default value is 100.

Summary

ASP.NET applications introduce a new architecture for building Web applications and a new set of programmable, extensible server controls. In this chapter we reviewed the architecture of ASP.NET applications and the role of HTTP handlers in servicing ASP.NET requests. The Page object is the programmatic cornerstone of Web forms, and it provides a number of directives that control the execution of the Web form. ASP.NET introduces the new view state, which conveniently preserves the contents of server controls between postbacks. However, this convenience may come at a performance price, so we also discussed the implications of disabling view state. ASP.NET provides an advanced configuration system using XML-based configuration files. We reviewed the `Web.config` file in detail and discussed how to create and use custom configuration settings. Finally, we reviewed ways to optimize your ASP.NET application.

CHAPTER 3

Writing Optimized Data Access Code

ADO.NET PROVIDES MANAGED data access and provides an impressive level of both functionality and flexibility. It also provides an unprecedented level of support for disconnected data access, which creates many new possibilities, such as the ability of disconnected Extensible Markup Language (XML) Web services to exchange DataSet objects across the wire. The ADO.NET programming model represents a new paradigm—one that requires innovative thinking to get the most out of it.

The goal of this chapter is to highlight ways for you to maximize the efficiency and performance of your ADO.NET code. There is no substitute for good design decisions in software development, and this is especially true for ADO.NET code. Well-designed ADO.NET code is efficient and performs optimally. Most applications are data-driven, so the application's performance and quality is often directly related to how well it handles data access and updates.

This chapter focuses on the following points:

- A review of the ADO.NET programming model, including the advantages and disadvantages of specific data objects

- A review of the role of XML in ADO.NET with a special focus on the DataSet object

- A review of data access best practices and design decisions, using common data access and update scenarios

Generally speaking, this chapter is equally divided between a review of the ADO.NET programming model and a review of how to make good data access design decisions. This chapter is not intended to be a complete tutorial on using ADO.NET, although the first half of the chapter may appear that way. Instead, this chapter aims to give the advanced developer a new perspective on optimal data access.

Overview of ADO.NET

The ADO.NET programming model is built around two groups of objects:

Managed provider objects: These objects provide direct, connected access to a data source and the ability to directly interact with a data source. This group includes the Connection, Command, DataAdapter, and DataReader objects. The DataReader object provides streaming, forward-only, read-only access to a data source and is the fastest way to access a data source.

The DataSet object: This object provides disconnected access to a data source, that is, without a persistent connection to the parent data source. In fact, the DataSet object has no ability to directly connect to a data source. Instead, the DataAdapter object acts as the intermediary between the DataSet object and the data source. The DataSet object provides the ability to navigate through hierarchical data and to manipulate data and the underlying schema, all without a persistent connection to the parent data source. The DataSet object tracks all changes made to the data set so that they may be later merged with the parent data source. Finally, the DataSet object has the ability to serialize to Extensible Markup Language (XML) as an *XML data document*, which is simply an XML document that preserves relational information.

The .NET Framework provides a number of namespaces that relate both directly and indirectly to data access (see Table 3-1).

Table 3-1. .NET Framework Namespaces Involved in Data Access

NAMESPACE	DESCRIPTION
System.Data	Provides base classes for ADO.NET, focused on the DataSet class and its child classes, such as DataRow, DataColumn, and DataRelation.
System.Data.SqlClient	The SQL Server .NET data provider.
System.Data.OleDb	The OLE DB .NET data provider.
System.Data.Common	Provides classes that are shared by all .NET data providers. Many of these classes are abstract and may be used to create custom data providers.
System.Data.SqlTypes	Provides classes for native data types in SQL Server.
System.Xml	Provides classes for processing XML.

(continued)

Table 3-1. .NET Framework Namespaces Involved in Data Access (continued)

NAMESPACE	DESCRIPTION
System.Xml.Schema	Provides classes for processing XML Schema Definition (XSD) schema files.
System.Xml.Xsl	Provides classes for processing Extensible Stylesheet Transformation (XSLT) transforms.

Figure 3-1 depicts the ADO.NET architecture and highlights the two distinct groups of objects in the model, namely, the .NET data provider, and the DataSet.

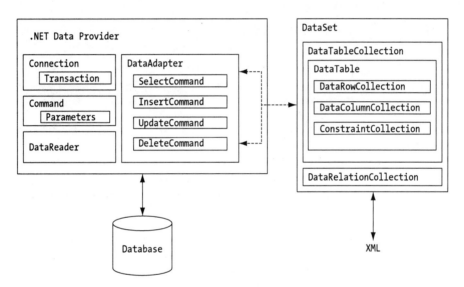

Figure 3-1. ADO.NET architecture

The DataSet side of the architecture is contained within the System.Data namespace. The .NET data provider side of the architecture depends on the nature of the backend data source and is contained either within the System.Data.SqlClient namespace or within the System.Data.OleDb namespace. The DataSet is strongly integrated with XML, as depicted by a double-headed arrow in the figure. The DataSet has no direct link to the data source but instead communicates via the .NET data provider. Table 3-2 summarizes the ADO.NET objects covered in this chapter.

Table 3-2. Important ADO.NET Objects

OBJECT	DESCRIPTION
Connection	Provides connectivity to the data source.
Command	Enables access to database commands for returning data, modifying data, running stored procedures, and sending or retrieving parameter information. Includes explicit functionality such as the ExecuteScalar() method for queries that return one summarized value and the ExecuteNonQuery() method for commands that do not return a resultset.
DataReader	Provides highly optimized, non-cached, forward-only, read-only streaming data access.
XmlReader	Provides highly optimized, non-cached, forward-only, read-only access to an XML data stream. This object contains the resultset for SQL Server stored procedures that contain the FOR XML clause. This object cannot be used for stored procedures that return standard resultsets.
DataAdapter	Provides the bridge between the DataSet object and the data source. The DataAdapter object uses a set of Command objects for selecting, inserting, updating, and deleting data in the data source. The DataSet communicates directly with the DataAdapter object, which in turn communicates the request to the data source.
DataSet	An in-memory representation of one or more tables with records, constraints on columns, and relations among tables. You can use it for storing and manipulating disconnected relational data, flat data, or XML data.
Typed DataSet	A specialized class that inherits from the DataSet class and that provides access to data using strongly typed methods, properties, and events. You can access data tables and columns by name, rather than by using collection-based syntax. A typed DataSet is generated using XSD schema information. The .NET Framework SDK provides a command-line tool called XSD.exe for generating typed DataSets. Visual Studio.NET provides alternate access to this tool within the XML Designer."
DataView	Provides an optimized, customized view of a DataTable. One DataSet object can have several associated DataView objects, each of which contains a different, filtered view of the same data set. DataView objects are also disconnected from the parent data source.

NOTE   *We often refer to a data provider object by its common name, such as* DataReader *instead of* SqlDataReader. *This implies that the discussion applies equally to all data providers. If we discuss a feature that is unique to a specific data provider, then we will refer to the specific version of the data provider object.*

Benefits of ADO.NET

ADO.NET provides three important benefits:

- A simple object model that provides strong support for disconnected data access

- Strong integration with XML, especially the DataSet object

- Performance advantages, including dedicated data providers, and objects dedicated to fast, efficient, streaming data access

- Automatic connection management, including pooling

The ADO.NET object model was designed with a focus on the developer, and the typical data access scenarios for which they code. Broadly speaking, data access falls into two areas: retrievals and updates.

Many Web applications are built solely around data retrievals, and provide few (if any) update screens. For this data access scenario, ADO.NET provides objects that support streaming data access, which is the fastest, most efficient way to retrieve data.

For Web applications that provide update capabilities, data access and synchronization has always been problematic. ADO.NET provides strong support for disconnected data access, including a specialized format called the *DiffGram*, which preserves a record of original and modified values in the same DataSet. Now, a Web application can deliver a disconnected DataSet to a client, which can in turn perform updates on the data. When the client is done, they can send the DataSet back to the Web server to have it synchronize the data changes. The DiffGram records error information for each row of data, which it can communicate back to the client in the event that the Web server encounters synchronization errors with the data updates.

Finally, ADO.NET provides strong integration with XML, particularly the DataSet object, which supports a range of methods for reading and writing XML and Extensible Schema Definition (XSD) schema information. The .NET Framework provides a number of classes for processing XML and XSD files, including reading documents, validating documents against schemas, and transforming XML using XSLT. Taken together, the System.Data namespace and the System.Xml namespace pack a powerful one-two punch that allows you to process XML data with a high level of sophistication. Some XML-related operations, such as generating XSD schemas and uploading XML documents to a DataSet, are a breeze to perform using the .NET Framework classes. Other operations, such as validating an XML document against multiple schema files, remain a difficult experience. But the functionality is there, and with perseverance your applications will be able to process XML in very sophisticated ways. This chapter pays particular attention to the strong integration of ADO.NET with XML.

Understanding the .NET Managed Data Provider

A .NET *managed data provider* is a set of objects for connecting to a data source, executing commands, and retrieving data. The .NET data provider is designed to be lightweight, creating a minimal layer between the data source and your code, thereby increasing performance without sacrificing functionality. ADO.NET currently offers four widely used managed providers:

SQL Server .NET data provider: This is the optimal choice for SQL Server 7.0 or greater. This provider uses the Tabular Data Stream (TDS) protocol, which is SQL Server's native data format. The TDS protocol operates by sending data packets over Remote Procedure Calls (RPC), and it is the fastest performing provider. To use this provider, you need to import the System.Data.SqlClient namespace into the .NET application.

OLE DB .NET data provider: This is the optimal choice for SQL Server 6.5 or earlier or any data source that supports native OLE DB providers, including Microsoft Access. The OLE DB .NET data provider must communicate to an OLE DB data source through two intermediate layers: the OLE DB provider and the OLE DB Service component, which provides connection pooling and transaction services. For this reason, the OLE DB .NET data provider is not as fast as compared to the SQL Server .NET data provider, especially for SQL Server 7.0 or greater. To use this provider, you need to import the System.Data.OleDbClient namespace into the .NET application.

Oracle .NET data provider: The optimal choice for Oracle. You can also use the OLE DB .NET data provider for accessing Oracle databases. However, the Oracle data provider will provide improved performance, especially for data retrieval operations. To use this provider, you need to import the System.Data.OracleClient namespace into the .NET application.

ODBC .NET data provider: This provider is designed to work with any non-OLE DB data source that supports native ODBC drivers. However, the Microsoft Web site states that this provider has only been tested with the ODBC drivers for SQL Server, Access, and Oracle. You can read more about the Oracle .NET data provider at `http://msdn.microsoft.com/library/default.asp?url=/library/en-us/dndotnet/html/ManProOracPerf.asp`.

ADO.NET ships with the SQL Server and OLE DB .NET data providers, but as of press time you must download the Oracle and ODBC data providers from Microsoft's Web site.

NOTE   *The Oracle and ODBC .NET data providers are available for download at* `http://msdn.microsoft.com/downloads`. *For Oracle, navigate to the .NET Framework ➤ Microsoft .NET Data Provider for Oracle node. For ODBC, navigate to the .NET Framework ➤ ODBC .NET Data Provider node.*

Microsoft is encouraging the development of additional OLE DB .NET data providers, so you can expect managed provider support for additional data sources to be forthcoming. The advantage of the data provider architecture is that it supports a consistent set of objects that shield the implementation details from the end user. All .NET data providers are required to implement a default set of objects: the Connection, Command, DataAdapter, and DataReader objects. This allows developers to focus on writing data access code that is independent of the specific backend data source.

Using the Connection Class

The .NET data provider includes a Connection class for establishing the connection to a data source. The following code shows how to open a connection to a SQL Server 7.0 (or later) database using the SqlConnection class:

```
Imports System.Data.SqlClient
Dim sqlConn As SqlConnection = New_
    SqlConnection(<SqlConnection.ConnectionString>)
sqlConn.Open()
```

The syntax to create and open a connection using the OleDbConnection class is almost identical to that for the SqlConnection class:

```
Imports System.Data.OleDbClient
Dim oleConn As OleDbConnection =
    New OleDbConnection(<OleDbConnection.ConnectionString>)
oleConn.Open()
```

These code samples illustrate the similarities between different data providers.

Using the Connection String Property

The ConnectionString property includes the source database name and other parameters needed to establish the initial connection. Developers frequently debate the best location for storing connection strings in an ASP.NET application, but one good choice is in the Web.config file as a custom configuration setting. The Web.config file has global scope for all files in the application. The file cannot be browsed directly from the outside, so an outside party cannot discover the connection string or any other information in the file. In addition, the Web.config file is easy to update and does not require any recompilation when the file contents change. When the Web.config file changes, ASP.NET automatically loads the new file as soon as all current application requests have been completed.

Custom application settings are stored as simple key-value pairs below the <appSettings> element, which in turn resides below the root <configuration> element. This is how you would store a database connection string:

```
<configuration>
    <appSettings>
        <add key="ConnectionString"
        value="server=machineName\sqlServer;uid=myId;pwd=myPwd;database=dev;" />
    </appSettings>
</configuration>
```

You can easily access the custom application setting from the code-behind file using the AppSettings property of the ConfigurationSettings class:

```
' Retrieve the connection string from Web.config
Dim strConn As String = ConfigurationSettings.AppSettings("ConnectionString")
Response.Write("The 'Connection String' is: " & strConn)
```

The ConfigurationSettings class is a member of the System.Configuration namespace. You will not need to import this namespace in the code-behind file for an *.aspx page, but you will have to import it for a Web service in the code-behind file for the *.asmx page. Chapter 2, "Introducing ASP.NET Applications," discusses how to store custom application settings in the Web.config file in great detail.

Table 3-3 provides an overview of important ConnectionString parameters, including some lesser-known parameters that may improve the performance of your data access code. Note that several parameters have alternative names, and you can pick whichever one you want to use.

Table 3-3. Important ConnectionString *Parameters*

NAME	DEFAULT	DESCRIPTION
Data Source/Server		The name or network address of the instance of SQL Server to which to connect. Use an Internet Protocol (IP) address instead of a Domain Name System (DNS) name. By using an IP address, the DNS name does not have to resolve, which may reduce the amount of time it takes to connect. In addition, problems with DNS name resolution will not interfere with data access.
Initial Catalog/Database		The name of the database with which to connect.
User ID		The SQL Server login account.
Password/Pwd		The password for the SQL Server login account.
Connect Timeout/Connection Timeout	15	The length of time (in seconds) to wait for a connection to the server before terminating the attempt and generating an error. You should never use a value of zero (0) because this may cause an indefinite wait if the database server is unresponsive.
Integrated Security/Trusted_Connection	"False"	Indicates whether the connection is trusted, which uses Windows Authentication credentials. To specify a trusted connection, set this parameter value to SSPI and omit the security credentials (name and password). Integrated security requires additional administrative work, as described in the "Using SQL Server 2000 Trusted Connections" section.

(continued)

Table 3-3. Important ConnectionString *Parameters (continued)*

NAME	DEFAULT	DESCRIPTION
Enlist	"True"	Transaction context setting. When "True," the connection pooler automatically enlists the connection in the creation thread's current transaction context. For better performance, set to "False" if the application is not using transactions.
Packet Size	8192	The size in bytes of the network packets used to communicate with an instance of SQL Server. You can adjust this parameter value based on the size of the data packets being transferred between the client and the server. This parameter can help optimize the communication performance. The range is 512–32, 767 bytes.

You can specify every connection parameter you might need in the connection string parameter. In addition, the Connection object exposes dedicated properties for a select group of parameters, including the DataSource, Database, ConnectionTimeout, and Packet Size parameters. To avoid confusion, we prefer to set all connection parameters in the connection string only.

The following example of a ConnectionString property for a SQL Server data source does not require transactional support:

```
Imports System.Data.SqlClient
Dim strConn As String
strConn = "server=192.168.64.84;uid=apress_dev;pwd=apress_pwd;database=apress;" & _
        connect timeout=300;enlist=false;"
Dim sqlConn As SqlConnection = New SqlConnection(strConn)
```

Much attention has been given to the fact that the .NET managed runtime environment automatically handles garbage collection. This leads some developers to erroneously assume that they do not need to close their database connections. This is not true, although developers are allowed to omit code that explicitly clears object references. However, just because this is allowed does not mean it is the best way. For optimum performance you should always explicitly clear unused object references so that they do not needlessly take up space on the stack for the finite amount of time that it takes the garbage collector to recognize that an object reference is going unused.

Closing the Connection

Connections are not implicitly released when the Connection object falls out of scope or is reclaimed by garbage collection. You must always close the connection when you are finished using it, by invoking the Connection object's Close() method. The Close() method releases the connection and returns it back to the pool if connection pooling is enabled. Otherwise, this method simply destroys the connection.

Keep in mind that different ADO.NET objects require the connection to remain open for different lengths of time. When a DataAdapter object opens a connection to fill a DataSet, the connection can be closed as soon as the DataSet has been filled. However, when the DataReader opens the connection, it must remain open throughout the lifetime of the DataReader. If two DataReader objects attempt to use the same open connection, then the second DataReader object will raise a SqlException indicating that the connection is already in use.

Now let's look at how you can optimize a database connection even further by taking advantage of connection pooling.

Connection Pooling

The .NET managed provider automatically provides connection pooling for your data access code. Connection pooling involves creating and maintaining a group (pool) of connections that can be handed out to applications that request a database connection. The time it takes to grab a connection from the pool is almost instantaneous compared to the seconds worth of delay it may take to establish a new connection over the network. The ConnectionString property includes several parameter settings that control and optimize the behavior of the connection pool. Table 3-4 provides a summary of the parameters that control connection pooling behavior.

Table 3-4. `ConnectionString` *Parameters for Connection Pooling*

NAME	DEFAULT	DESCRIPTION
Pooling	"True"	When "True," the connection is drawn from the appropriate pool or, if necessary, created and added to the appropriate pool. If "False," then connection pooling is disabled.
Connection Lifetime	0	When a connection is returned to the pool, its creation time is compared with the current time, and the connection is destroyed if that time span (in seconds) exceeds the value specified by `Connection Lifetime`. A value of zero (0) will cause pooled connections to never timeout as long as users are actively connecting to the system.
Connection Reset	"True"	Determines whether the database connection is reset when being removed from the pool. For Microsoft SQL Server version 7.0, setting to "False" avoids making an additional server round trip when obtaining a connection, but you must be aware that the connection state, such as database context, is not being reset.
Max Pool Size	100	The maximum number of connections allowed in the pool.
Min Pool Size	0	The minimum number of connections maintained in the pool.

To get the most out of connection pooling, keep the following important facts in mind as you develop your data access code:

- Open a connection right before you need it, not earlier.

- Close a connection as soon as you are done using it. Do not leave a connection open if it is not being used.

- Clear references to unused connection objects.

- Complete any pending transactions before closing a connection.

- You can disable connection pooling (using the Pooling parameter).

- Connections are only given from the pool if they match a prior connection string exactly. Even whitespace variations between connection strings will cause the pool to treat these as different connections.

- Pooled connections will continue to be returned from the pool for as long as the Connection Lifetime parameter will allow. Set this parameter to a higher value if you do not expect connection details to change in the short term.

- Active connections are not shared. A connection will only be given to a new requestor when the previous connection owner has called its Close() method.

Using SQL Server 2000 Trusted Connections

Earlier in this chapter, we showed how you can store connection string information in the Web.config file and then retrieve it dynamically at runtime. The Web.config file is protected from outside browsing, but it still stores its information as plain text, including passwords. Some users may feel uncomfortable with this potential security liability and may prefer an alternative approach for connecting to a database.

If your Web application supports Windows authentication and uses SQL Server 2000, then you can connect to the database without a connection string. The alternative is to request a *trusted connection* from SQL Server using authenticated Windows credentials. You implement trusted connections as follows:

1. The database administrator specifies Windows accounts or groups that are permitted to access the SQL Server database. Each Windows account must be mapped to an appropriate SQL Server account or database role. For example, read-only users are given a specific Windows account that maps to a SQL login account with read-only access.

2. The user signs on to the application using Windows credentials and then makes a request to the database.

3. Windows will not open a trusted connection unless the user is currently authenticated.

4. SQL Server matches the authenticated Windows account against the list of accounts to which it permits access. Once a match is made, SQL Server will process the database request.

A trusted connection (also known as *integrated security*) allows a client to connect to a SQL Server 2000 database without having to specify security credentials, such as the name and password. You still need to specify a connection string, but it omits the security credentials. The following is one example of a connection string, as it appears in the Web.config file:

```
<configuration>
        <appSettings>
                <add key="ConnectionString" value="server=192.168.1.1;
                        Integrated Security="SSPI";database=dev;" />
        </appSettings>
</configuration>
```

Internet Information Server (IIS) automatically uses a machine-level Windows account to impersonate anonymous Web users. For secure operations you can extend this system to require that all users authenticate themselves using a domain-level Windows account. The simplest approach is to set up a limited number of Windows accounts that map to specific types of database operations. For example, you could specify one account for read-only operations and one account for read/write operations. A certain amount of application logic may be required if you support multiple Windows accounts for different operations and then need to dynamically switch users between read-only access vs. read/write access.

Having a limited number of accounts not only simplifies the administrative work, but it also helps overcome an important limitation of trusted connections with respect to connection pooling. Namely, connection pools only work for individual accounts and will not work across multiple, separate accounts. If you want your trusted users to pull connections from the same pool, then they will need to be authenticated under the same domain-level Windows account. In addition, this domain account must include both IIS and SQL Server in the same domain or in a trusted domain.

Windows authentication is actually the default authentication mode for SQL Server 2000. Mixed-mode authentication is a hybrid approach that uses either SQL login credentials or Windows authentication credentials. In mixed-mode authentication, the SQL login credentials will be used if they are supplied and if Windows authentication has not been specifically requested via the connection string.

Using the Command Class

The Command class executes stored procedures and Transact-SQL statements. It provides several dedicated methods for executing different types of queries:

ExecuteReader(): This is optimized for retrieval queries that will return one or more records. This method returns the resultset as a DataReader object, which provides a forward-only data stream.

ExecuteScalar(): This is optimized for queries that return scalar values. It returns the resultset as a singleton value. This method will return only the first field value in the first row in the event that multiple fields and/or records are returned. Because .NET enforces strict data typing rules, you must cast the scalar value to the appropriate data type before working with it.

ExecuteNonQuery(): This is optimized for Transact-SQL statements. It returns the number of rows affected for UPDATE, INSERT, and DELETE operations; otherwise, it returns –1.

ExecuteXmlReader(): This is optimized for SQL Server stored procedures that return the resultset as XML, using the FOR XML clause. This method returns a forward-only XML data stream that may be accessed using an XmlReader object.

The Command class provides an overloaded New() constructor for initializing the object. It may include a Connection object reference directly as follows:

```
Dim sqlConn As SqlConnection = New SqlConnection(<Connection String>)
Dim sqlCmd As SqlCommand = New SqlCommand(cmdText, sqlConn)
```

The cmdText parameter is the query to be executed: either the name of the stored procedure or the Transact-SQL string. The Command class requires more initialization information than you can add in the New() constructor. Optimally, you should always specify the CommandType property, which indicates what kind of query you will be executing. For example, Listing 3-1 shows how to use the SqlCommand object's SqlCommand.ExecuteReader() method to execute a query and return a SqlDataReader object.

Listing 3-1. Using the Command Object's `ExecuteReader()` *Method*

```
Dim sqlDR As SqlDataReader
Dim sqlConn As SqlConnection = New SqlConnection(<Connection String>)
Dim sqlCmd As SqlCommand = New SqlCommand("CustOrderHist", sqlConn)
Try
    'Specify the stored procedure and connection
    With sqlCmd
        .CommandType = CommandType.StoredProcedure
        .CommandBehavior = CommandBehavior.CloseConnection
        .CommandTimeout = 60
    End With
    sqlDR = sqlCmd.ExecuteReader()
Finally
End Try
```

This code includes the `CommandBehavior` enumeration, which indicates how the Command object should return a resultset and how the Command object should behave once the query has been executed and the return resultset is no longer needed. For example, a value of `CloseConnection` indicates that the connection should be automatically closed once the associated data object has been closed (in this case, the DataReader object). You should always set this property, especially when you are retrieving an object such as the DataReader, which should never leave a connection open. Table 3-5 summarizes the members in the `CommandBehavior` enumeration.

Table 3-5. `CommandBehavior` *Enumeration Members*

MEMBER	DESCRIPTION
CloseConnection	When the command is executed, the associated Connection object is closed when the associated DataReader object is closed.
SchemaOnly	The query returns schema (column) information only.
SequentialAccess	Provides a way for the DataReader to handle rows that contain columns with large binary values. SequentialAccess enables the DataReader to load each row of data as a binary stream. You can then use the `GetBytes()` or `GetChars()` method to specify a byte location to start the read operation and a limited buffer size for the data being returned. SequentialAccess allows you to choose any starting read position in the row. However, once you have read past a location in the returned stream of data, data at or before that location can no longer be read from the DataReader.

(continued)

Table 3-5. CommandBehavior *Enumeration Members (continued)*

MEMBER	DESCRIPTION
SingleResult	The query returns a single result set.
SingleRow	The query is expected to return a single row. You can still return multiple resultsets, but each one will only contain a single row.
Default	Use this setting when you expect the query to affect the state of the database, such that you cannot determine in advance what to do with the Command and Connection objects following completion of the query. Default sets no CommandBehavior flags, so ExecuteReader(CommandBehavior.Default) is functionally equivalent to calling ExecuteReader().

Listing 3-1 also includes the CommandTimeout property, which it sets to a value of 60 seconds. This property sets the query timeout—that is, the amount of time that the Command object will wait before aborting a query. It is important to set this property, especially when you anticipate variable delays in query processing time. If you do not set this property, then the command object will wait indefinitely until the database returns a result, and this can be confusing for the user, who may assume that the application has become unresponsive. Conversely, do not set the CommandTimeout property to an unreasonably low value; otherwise, the user may frequently encounter timeout exceptions, when in reality, you are not allowing enough time for the query to reasonably finish processing. Finally, do not get confused between the Connection object's ConnectionTimeout property and the Command object's CommandTimeout property. The former specifies the amount of time to allow a database connection to be established. The latter specifies the query timeout only.

Some stored procedures return output parameters in place of a resultset. If the Command object's CommandType property is set to CommandType.StoredProcedure, then the Parameters property allows you to access the input and output parameters and return values from the stored procedure. These parameters are accessible independent of the Execute() method called. However, in the case of ExecuteReader(), the output parameters and return values are not accessible until the DataReader is closed.

Output parameters are tricky to work with because you are required to specify the name and type of each output parameter in advance in order to capture their values. This makes code harder to create and harder to maintain, especially if the underlying stored procedure ever changes. If possible, avoid using output parameters in favor of using the ExecuteScalar() and ExecuteNonQuery() methods.

Using the ExecuteXmlReader() Method

To take advantage of SQL Server 2000's XML functionality, the SqlCommand object exposes the ExecuteXmlReader() method for retrieving an XML data stream. The ExecuteXmlReader() method returns a System.Xml.XmlReader object populated with the results of the SQL statement specified for a SqlCommand.

```
Dim myXR As System.Xml.XmlReader
myXR = sqlCmd.ExecuteXmlReader() ' The SqlCommand object is already initialized
```

You can only use the ExecuteXmlReader() method for SQL Server stored procedures that return XML data using the FOR XML clause. The XmlReader provides forward-only, read-only access to the returned stream of XML data.

The XmlReader has the following advantages:

- The XmlReader is a streaming reader that provides fast access to an XML data stream. The XmlReader does not have to retrieve and cache all of the data before exposing it to the caller. This design is especially optimal for large returned XML documents.

- The XmlReader has methods and properties that can read and navigate the elements, attributes, and contents of the XML stream.

The XmlReader has the following disadvantages:

- The XmlReader maintains an open connection to the database until it is closed and the connection can be closed and released. The XmlReader's active connection is not available to the connection pool as long as the XmlReader remains open.

- The XmlReader requires additional processing on the database server to process the FOR XML clause and return data as XML.

 NOTE *The sample project that accompanies this chapter contains complete code samples for each of the Command object's* Execute*() *methods. Please refer to the ExecSP* functions in the DataAccess component of the AspNetChap3 sample project.*

Using the DataReader Class

All .NET data providers support the DataReader object, which is created by the Command object's ExecuteReader() method. The DataReader provides an unbuffered sequential stream of data for fast, efficient access to a resultset. The DataReader is a good choice for retrieving large amounts of data because the data is not cached in memory.

The DataReader object has the following advantages:

A DataReader requires the lowest amount of memory and resource overhead, especially compared with the DataSet object. Lower overhead translates to increased application performance. By reading directly from the database, you can bypass storing data in a cached DataSet object, which requires memory overhead. Always use the DataReader object when you intend to use a resultset only once.

The DataReader is optimized for read-only access, which is a common operation on data-driven Web sites.

The DataReader provides schema information in addition to data. You can use the GetSchemaTable() method of the DataReader to obtain the column metadata.

You can bind the DataReader to a wide range of ASP.NET Web controls.

The DataReader has the following disadvantages:

The DataReader retains an active database connection for as long as it remains open. Minimize the amount of time you use an expensive Connection object. Open the connection right before the ExecuteReader() method, read the data off the DataReader, close the DataReader, and then immediately close the database connection.

The DataReader requires an active database connection for access. It cannot be disconnected, cached, or serialized.

The DataReader may cause contention in the connection pool if active connections are not used efficiently and closed in a timely manner. Contention is the state where the maximum number of requested connections exceeds the number of connections in the pool. Contention minimizes the overall responsiveness and scalability of the calling application.

The DataReader is limited to forward-only, read-only data access. The DataReader cannot update records in the database, nor can it support complex operations such as sorting or directly accessing specific records in a resultset. (The latter example has one exception: DataReader objects may be opened using SequentialAccess, where they retrieve each record as a binary stream. Even so, data access is still forward only).

The DataReader does not return data from multiple, non-joined database tables or from different data sources.

Accessing Data Within a DataReader

The DataReader object provides a Read() method for accessing each record of data in the resultset. Within each record (or row) you can access the fields either by column name or by ordinal reference, as shown here:

```
Dim strResult As String
While (sqlDR.Read())
        strResult = sqlDR.GetString(0) & " : " & sqlDR("CustomerName")
End While
```

The DataReader object provides a set of typed accessor methods for accessing fields with known data types. If you know the underlying data type for a column value, then the typed accessor method lets you access this value in its native data type. For example, the GetDateTime(), GetFloat(), GetInt32(), and GetString() methods offer the best performance because they eliminate data type conversions when retrieving a column value.

The following code shows how you can retrieve a native integer field, then immediately cast the value to a string. Explicit casting is more efficient than assigning the integer field value to a string variable directly:

```
Dim intResult As Int32
Dim strResult As String
While (sqlDR.Read())
    intResult = sqlDR.GetSqlInt32(0)
    strResult = CType(intResult, String) ' Cast the integer to a string
End While
```

The SqlDataReader object (in contrast to the OleDbDataReader object) actually exposes two sets of type accessor methods. The first is a set of generic data access methods provided directly by the .NET Framework. These methods include GetString() and GetBoolean(), and they do not account for specific SQL Server data types. The second set of data access methods is provided by the Data.SqlClient namespace directly. These methods include GetSqlDouble() and GetSqlMoney(), and they account for specific SQL Server data types. These specialized data access methods allow you to work with these data types safely in the .NET managed environment.

NOTE *SQL Server and the .NET Framework use different typing systems. You may lose data if you attempt to map a SQL Server data type to a .NET data type. For this reason, the .NET Framework exposes a* SqlDbType *enumeration that allows managed code to reference SQL Server data types directly.*

The .NET Framework's System.Data.SqlTypes namespace provides constructs for handling type conversions between SQL Server and the .NET Framework. It provides structures for mapping SQL Server data types to .NET. It also provides an enumeration for setting the SQL Server data type of input and output parameters that will be used when calling SQL Server stored procedures from .NET managed code.

Consider the Orders table in the Northwind database, which contains an integer field for the Order ID. The SQL Server data type for this field is int. You can declare a variable to reference this field's values using the SqlInt32 structure from the Data.SqlTypes namespace:

```
Imports System.Data.SqlTypes
Dim intOrderID As SqlInt32
```

Now let's say you want to call a stored procedure that includes the Order ID as an input parameter. This is where you use the enumeration to assign the int SQL Server data types to the input parameter. For example:

```
Dim myParameter As New SqlParameter("@OrderID", SqlDbType.Int)
```

As if this was not enough, the SqlDataReader class also provides dedicated typed accessor methods that automatically convert the SQL Server data type to the appropriate .NET Framework data type. For example, you can capture a SQL

Server int field from the DataReader using the GetSqlInt32() accessor method. This method in turn returns a data type represented in .NET by the SqlInt32 structure. For example:

```
Imports System.Data.SqlTypes
Dim intOrderID As SqlInt32
intOrderID = sqlDataReader.GetSqlInt32(0)
```

Typed accessor methods promote type safety and prevent type conversion errors. You should always take advantage of the typed accessor methods when using the SqlDataReader object.

> **NOTE** *For a complete list of typed accessor methods, refer to the .NET Framework Developer's Guide at* http://msdn.microsoft.com/library/ default.asp?url=/library/en-us/cpguide/html/ cpconmappingnetdataproviderdatatypestonet frameworkdatatypes.asp.

> **NOTE** *For information on the* System.Data.SqlTypes *namespace, refer to* http://msdn.microsoft.com/library/ default.asp?url=/library/ en-us/cpref/html/frlrfSystemDataSqlTypes.asp.

Data Binding Using a DataReader

The DataReader also supports binding to a data-oriented Web control in ASP.NET. Data controls can be single-value (Label), multi-value (ListBox), or multi-record (DataGrid). For multivalue and multirecord cases, the control will automatically loop through the data source during binding, reading each row in turn to retrieve the required data. The following code demonstrates how to bind a DataReader to a DataGrid Web control. Note that this code uses the wrapper functions that are included in the sample project:

```
Dim sqlDR As SqlClient.SqlDataReader
Dim DataGrid As System.Web.UI.WebControls.DataGrid
Try
      objDB = New Apress.Database(strConn)
      arrParams = New String() {"@CustomerID", SqlDbType.Char, "ALFKI"}
      sqlDR = objDB.ExecSPReturnDR("CustOrderHist", arrParams)
      ' Bind the DataReader to the DataGrid
      DataGrid1.DataSource = sqlDR
      DataGrid1.DataBind()
Finally
End Try
```

We will not discuss data binding in any detail because there is little to say in terms of optimizing this process. Data binding in ASP.NET is a faster, more efficient process than it has been in the past, but keep in mind that bound controls can generate a lot of output bytes during rendering. Be judicious about how much data you bind and, where possible, always disable the view state for a bound control. This is especially true for DataGrid controls, which can generate lengthy view state records. Always disable view state for controls that do not need to post their contents back to the server. This is almost always true for DataGrids that only display data and that do not support direct updates in the grid.

Using the DataAdapter Class

The DataAdapter class is the bridge between a disconnected DataSet object and a data source. Specifically, it has two main purposes:

- To retrieve data from a data source and populate the tables within a DataSet

- To resolve data modifications made in the DataSet with the data source

The DataAdapter uses the Connection object to connect to the data source. It uses the Command object to retrieve data from, and resolve data to, the data source. The DataAdapter actually provides four properties to assign Command objects: one property each for SELECT, UPDATE, INSERT, and DELETE commands. Table 3-6 defines these properties.

Table 3-6. DataAdapter Properties

PROPERTY	DESCRIPTION
SelectCommand	An auto-generated or user-defined Command object that retrieves data from a data source
InsertCommand	An auto-generated or user-defined Command object that inserts data from a data source
UpdateCommand	An auto-generated or user-defined Command object that updates data from a data source
DeleteCommand	An auto-generated or user-defined Command object that deletes data from a data source

The DataAdapter provides two main methods for selecting and updating data, as summarized in Table 3-7.

Table 3-7. DataAdapter Methods

METHOD	DESCRIPTION
Fill()	Populates a DataSet with the results from the SelectCommand
Update()	Resolves the changes made in the DataSet and executes the appropriate command (InsertCommand, UpdateCommand, DeleteCommand) on the data source

The DataAdapter Fill() method implicitly uses the SelectCommand property to retrieve the column names, data types, and data values to create and populate the tables in the DataSet. The following code shows how to populate a DataSet with a DataAdapter:

```
' Create and initialize a new DataAdapter object
Dim sqlAdapt As SqlDataAdapter = New SqlDataAdapter()
sqlAdapt.SelectCommand = sqlCmd
' Open the Connection object
m_sqlConn.Open()
sqlAdapt.Fill(sqlDS)
m_sqlConn.Close()
sqlAdapt = Nothing ' sqlAdapter is no longer needed
```

(This code assumes that the Connection and Command objects have already been created and initialized, as shown in earlier sections). An alternative approach to this listing is to create the DataAdapter by passing the Command object into the New() method of the DataAdapter without explicitly setting the SelectCommand property:

```
Dim sqlAdapt As SqlDataAdapter = New SqlDataAdapter(sqlCmd)
```

The Command properties are auto-generated using the CommandBuilder class. Listing 3-2, which was taken from the UpdateCustomerProfile() function in the sample project's DataAccess class, shows how to do this. In this example, the DataAdapter Update() method call would have failed had the UpdateCommand property not been auto-generated using the SqlCommandBuilder class.

Listing 3-2. Updating the Database Using the SqlCommandBuilder Class

```
Try
    Dim sqlAdapt As SqlDataAdapter = New SqlDataAdapter(sqlCmd)
    Dim custCB As SqlCommandBuilder = New SqlCommandBuilder(sqlAdapt)
    ' Open the Connection object and populate the DataSet
    m_sqlConn.Open()
    sqlAdapt.Fill(sqlDS, "Customers")
    m_sqlConn.Close()
    ' Code to modify data in DataSet here
    Call UpdateData(sqlDS, arrParams)
    'Update method would have failed without the SqlCommandBuilder
    sqlAdapt.Update(sqlDS, "Customers")
    m_sqlConn.Close() Finally
End Try
```

You can also specifically define the Command properties associated with the Update() method at design-time as well as associate them with a set of stored procedures. This will provide some level of performance advantage compared to setting these properties at runtime.

Understanding the DataSet Class

The DataSet provides a virtual snapshot of a database and stores it as a disconnected, in-memory representation of a collection of data tables, relations, and constraints. The DataSet class allows data to be updated while being physically disconnected from the data source. By design, the DataSet has no direct knowledge of the underlying data source, but instead relies on the DataAdapter class to open this connection as needed. The DataSet represents the disconnected portion of the ADO.NET architecture, and the .NET managed provider represents the connected portion.

The DataSet class is strongly integrated with XML and can serialize to both XML and XSD files. The XML file provides a representation of the data that preserves the relational information. The XSD file represents the schema for the DataSet. The DataSet natively serializes with XML and XSD in both directions, meaning that it can both read and write XML and XSD files.

For writing purposes, the DataSet can infer its own schema and incorporate this information into the XML file that it generates, on a per-query basis. For performance reasons, it is not optimal to have the DataSet infer its own schema. In addition, this approach may lead to inaccuracies. A better approach is to have the DataSet reference and incorporate a specific XSD schema, which allows it to generate a more exact XML representation of the data.

For reading purposes, you can populate a DataSet with relational data using well-formed XML, with or without a specific XSD schema file. Typed DataSets are a special form of the DataSet that incorporate XSD schema information into strongly typed members that can be referenced from code just like a standard class attribute. As we discuss, XSD schemas are a powerful tool for validating data structures, and they improve the efficiency of working with the DataSet class.

The DataSet class is important for XML Web services, which can exchange relational data by leveraging the DataSet's ability to serialize to XML. The DataSet allows XML Web services to produce and exchange relational data as XML files that can be marshaled across the wire. Once these files reach their destination, they may be processed using standard XML-based technologies such as XSLT (for transformations) and XPATH (for queries). Alternatively, the XML data can be reassembled into a new DataSet object.

Many books highlight examples of how the DataSet class interacts with XML, but they do not provide a context as to why this is beneficial. From a pure performance standpoint, XML serialization is a processor-intensive operation that introduces an additional layer for working with data. In other words, for some operations it will be sufficient to manipulate the in-memory data tables directly, without ever needing to represent the data as XML. In short, XML serialization is a processor-intensive operation that should be used only when needed. In our opinion, there are four important scenarios where you need to use XML serialization:

- For exchanging relational data with XML Web services over Hypertext Transfer Protocol (HTTP)

- For validating data against a specific XSD schema

- For generating typed DataSets

- For persisting relational data in an XML repository

It is especially advantageous to persist complex, hierarchical data as XML, if possible, because this can eliminate the need for multiple subqueries to retrieve all of the child information (assuming that the data is complex enough to require multiple database calls to assemble the complete data set).

Clearly, XML integration is the most important feature of the DataSet class and is the focus of our discussion. But before we go too far down this road, let's briefly review the other important features, benefits, and uses of the DataSet class.

Features of the DataSet Class

The DataSet is a disconnected, in-memory representation of a data source that preserves the schema information. The DataSet contains a collection of DataTable objects that each represent a table of data and that can originate from multiple underlying data sources. A DataTable may represent a physical database table or the contents of a query that derives information from multiple, related database tables. Each DataTable object is comprised of a collection of DataRow and DataColumn objects. The DataColumn objects represent the schema information for the table, and the DataRow objects contain the actual record data for the table.

You can create a DataSet in the following three ways:

- Manually, by programmatically instancing the DataTable, DataRelation, and Constraint objects within the DataSet and then populating the DataTables with data

- Automatically, by populating the DataSet from an existing relational data source using the DataAdapter object

- Automatically, by loading the contents and schema information directly into the DataSet from XML and XSD files

Because the DataSet is disconnected, any operation will take effect against the in-memory data, not against the actual data source. The DataAdapter object provides the connection between the DataSet and the underlying data source, and it can be created and destroyed as needed without any effect on the contents of the DataSet. Once the DataSet is created and filled, it can be accessed programmatically as long as it is retained in memory. This is in contrast to the DataReader object, which requires a persistent connection to the data source.

The command methods exposed by the DataAdapter synchronize and guarantee data concurrency between the data source and the DataSet's DataTable objects. The DataAdapter object provides commands for all four types of database operations: SELECT, INSERT, UPDATE, and DELETE. For example, when the DataSet calls the Update() method on the DataAdapter, the DataAdapter analyzes the changes that have been made before they are committed. The Update() method provides this information back to the DataSet on a per-record basis. This information is encapsulated by the DataRowState enumeration value for each DataTable.DataRow object. The enumeration provides before and after values for the update and allows for more programmatic checks before the updates are actually committed.

The DataSet has the following advantages:

The DataSet is versatile and can perform complex operations such as sorting, filtering, and tracking updates.

The DataSet provides the GetChanges() method, which generates a second DataSet that contains the subset of records (from the original DataSet) that have been modified. This is especially useful when you need to send record updates across the wire and want to minimize the amount of sent data.

The DataSet is disconnected from the underlying data source. The DataSet allows you to work with the same records repeatedly without having to requery the data source.

The DataSet can be cached in memory and retrieved at any time. The DataSet is a good solution for paging through data in a DataGrid. The DataSet can be cached and rebound to the DataGrid as the page index changes. The underlying data source does not need to be requeried.

The DataSet can contain multiple tables of results, which it maintains as discrete objects. A DataSet can simultaneously represent data from multiple sources, for example, from different databases, from XML files, from spreadsheets, and so on. Each data source is contained in a separate DataTable object within the DataSet. Once the data resides in the DataSet, you can treat it as a homogeneous set of data—that is, as if it had come from a single source. You can work with the tables individually or navigate between them as parent-child tables.

The DataSet can be bound to a wide range of ASP.NET Web controls and .NET Windows Form controls.

The DataSet provides excellent support for XML and will natively serialize to XML and XSD files that represent relational data.

The DataSet provides excellent support for XML Web services. The DataSet provides a powerful way to exchange data with other components and applications using XML representations of the DataSet contents.

The DataSet does have some disadvantages. The DataSet has higher memory and processor demands than other data objects, which can potentially lead to lower application performance. The DataSet object is not the optimal solution for straightforward, one-time data retrieval operations. The DataReader object is a faster, more efficient solution for quick data retrievals that do not need to be cached or serialized. Similarly, the XmlReader object is a faster solution for processing the resultsets from stored procedures that natively return XML. (However, the XmlReader lacks the DataSet object's ability to natively serialize relational data to XML).

Using the DataSet Object

There are two common purposes for using the DataSet object. The first involves updating data in an underlying data source. The second involves serializing relational data to and from XML and XSD files. In the following section we discuss the first application: accessing and updating data using the DataSet object.

Updating Data Using the DataSet

The DataSet object allows you to modify a disconnected set of records and then synchronize the updates with the parent data source. This is especially useful in a Web application because updates on the client are always disconnected from the parent data source on the server. The DataSet object may hold one or more DataTable objects, each of which represents a specific database table or the results of query. The DataSet object allows you to make updates to one or more of the available DataTable objects with no special coding other than making sure you reference the correct DataTable object that you are modifying.

The DataSet object reduces the burden on the developer by managing concurrency during disconnected updates to data. The DataSet object tracks modifications to the data and also preserves the original values for reference purposes. In addition, the DataSet object tracks errors that occur during updates—for example, errors that are caused by modifying a data field with an incorrect data type. In short, the DataSet object provides a record of updates that can be examined prior to synchronizing the updates with the parent data source.

The following is the workflow for updating a DataSet on a Web client and synchronizing the updates back to the parent data source:

1. On the server, populate a DataSet with records from the parent data source.

2. On the server, disconnect the DataSet from the parent data source and then bind it to a DataGrid. (Alternatively, you can render the data in another format that allows updates to the DataSet. For our purposes, we assume a DataGrid.)

3. On the server, assign the DataSet into the cache, using a unique cache key name. For example, use the client's session ID as the key name. The cached copy of the DataSet will be used later for reference and to avoid another round trip to the database.

4. Deliver the Web form (with the bound data) from the server to the client for display and updates.

5. On the client, modify one or more DataTables in the DataSet by adding, updating, or deleting DataRows.

6. Submit the Web form from the client back to the server.

7. On the server, retrieve the original cached DataSet.

8. On the server, copy Web client changes to the original DataSet. (This step may seem confusing, but it is required because you cannot retrieve the DataSet directly from the DataGrid Web control.)

9. On the server, examine the modified records for errors using the DataSet's HasErrors property. (The DataTable object also provides the HasErrors property.)

10. If you do not find any errors, proceed with the update by initializing a DataAdapter object and passing it the modified DataSet.

11. If you find errors, then examine the specific error messages using the DataRow object's RowError property. If the errors cannot be handled on the server, then raise the error messages back to the Web client.

These steps are specific to Web applications and are more complicated than what you would need for a Windows (desktop) application. In a desktop application, you can retrieve the DataSet directly from the DataGrid object's DataSource property:

```
Private dsCustomers As DataSet
dsCustomers = CType(DataGrid1.DataSource, DataSet)
```

Unfortunately, in a Web application you must manually store the original DataSet object and then manually update the changes from the DataGrid. If the client has updated a DataGrid, then the easiest approach is to retrieve the values directly from the edited DataGrid item. Then, simply retrieve a cached copy of the original DataSet and update it directly using the edited values. We show an example of how to do this in the next section.

Once you have a reference to the modified DataSet, you can examine the DataSet for changes and errors and then update the data source. This check is useful if you have a multirow DataSet and do not know in advance which, if any, rows have been modified. The following code outlines this process:

```
' Look for modifications and errors
' Note: The DataSet object's HasChanges() method can return Added, Deleted,
' Detached, Modified, and Unchanged records
If dsCustomers.HasChanges(DataRowState.Modified) Then
    If dsCustomers.HasErrors Then
        Dim sqlDR As DataRow
        For Each sqlDR In dsCustomers.Tables(0).Rows
            If sqlDR.HasErrors Then
                Err.Raise(vbObjectError + 512, , sqlDR.RowError) ' Raise error
            End If
        Next
    Else
        ' Commit the update
    End If
End If
```

The DataSet class also supports the GetChanges() method, which returns a second DataSet that contains just the modified records from the original DataSet. This method is convenient for filtering modified records, but you must also check for errors in any of the DataSet's DataTable objects. After calling the GetChanges() method, you should check for DataTable errors using the DataTable object's HasErrors property. If this property returns "True," then you can use the GetErrors() method to extract an array of DataRow objects for the individual rows that have errors. If possible, you should resolve the errors within each DataRow and then call the DataTable object's AcceptChanges() method. Once all errors have been resolved, you can pass the DataSet of modified records to a DataAdapter object in order to synchronize the updates with the parent data source.

Note that the DataTable object's AcceptChanges() method only needs to be called if you will be performing successive updates on the DataTable. This method will reset the DataSet object's tracking parameters. For example, let's say you modify a DataSet and then call AcceptChanges(). If you continue to modify the DataSet, then its HasChanges property will reflect only those changes made since AcceptChanges() was last called. Similarly, the GetChanges() method will only contain records that were modified since AcceptChanges() was last called.

Sample Code for Updates Using a DataGrid Control and a DataSet Object

The sample project for this chapter provides two Web pages that illustrate how to update changes in a disconnected DataSet back to the parent data source. The pages are as follows:

- **UpdateDSWithDataGrid1.aspx**: This page demonstrates how to use the DataSet and DataAdapter objects to update a data source. It uses the SQLCommandBuilder to auto-generate the update Command object.

- **UpdateDSWithDataGrid2.aspx**: This page demonstrates how to use the DataSet and DataAdapter objects to update a data source. It uses a parameterized stored procedure for the update Command object.

The update process is confusing the first time you attempt it, but with practice you should quickly grow to appreciate how well it works. Let's review the update process here, using the code from UpdateDSWithDataGrid1.aspx.

Figure 3-2 shows a DataGrid that is bound to a DataSet of customers from the Northwind database. This DataSet is also stored in the server cache so that you can access the original data without another round trip to the database. Notice that the DataGrid is in Edit mode for Customer ID AROUT.

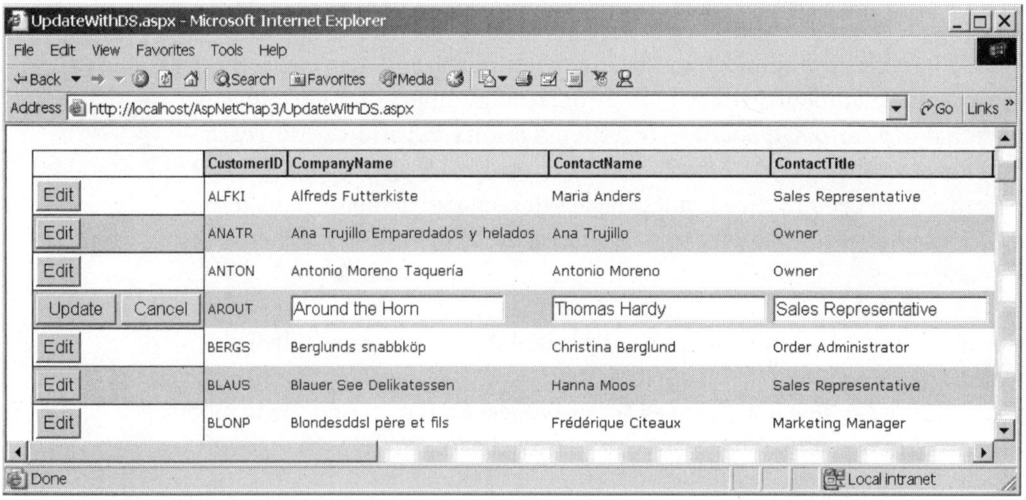

Figure 3-2. The UpdateWithDS.aspx *screen*

The Update button triggers the DataGrid's Update() event in the code-behind file. It is here that you implement the code for updating the parent data source:

```
Sub DataGrid1_Update(ByVal sender As Object, _
        ByVal e As DataGridCommandEventArgs)
    ' Step 1: Retrieve the modified DataGridItem (row)
    Dim dgItem As DataGridItem
    dgItem = e.Item
End Sub
```

The DataGrid1_Update() event handler tells you which data row has changed. You can then extract the user's changes directly from the DataGridItem object (dgItem) and assign them to the original DataSet. First, you must retrieve a reference to the affected DataRow (in the original DataSet). The index of the affected DataRow matches the index of the DataGridItem because, in this example, the binding sequence was not affected by subsequent sorting. You can then set a reference to the affected DataRow as follows:

```
Dim sqlDR As DataRow
sqlDR = dsCustomers.Tables(0).Rows(e.Item.ItemIndex)
```

The following is how you copy the CompanyName field value from the DataGrid to the affected DataRow:

```
' Update the DataRow using the DataGridItem
Dim txtControl As System.Web.UI.WebControls.TextBox
txtControl = dgItem.Controls(2).Controls(0)
sqlDR("CompanyName") = txtControl.Text
```

You may want to use another method of referencing the DataGrid item values if you are not comfortable with the syntax shown here.

Next, you use a SqlDataAdapter object to update the data source with the changes. Using the SqlCommandBuilder object, you are able to auto-generate the update Command object that the DataAdapter uses. The SqlCommandBuilder object must be initialized with the stored procedure that is used to originally select the data, which in this example is called GetAllCustomerDetails:

```
sqlConn = New _
    SqlConnection(ConfigurationSettings.AppSettings("ConnectionString"))
sqlAdapt = New SqlDataAdapter(New SqlCommand("GetAllCustomerDetails", sqlConn))
sqlCB = New SqlCommandBuilder(sqlAdapt)
```

The final step is to execute the update using the DataAdapter's Update()
method. You simply need to pass in the modified DataSet, and the update will
execute. It is not efficient to pass in the entire original DataSet when you know
that only one row has changed. For efficiency, you extract the subset of modified
records from the original DataSet into a second DataSet using the GetChanges()
method. It is the second DataSet that actually gets updated to the data source:

```
If dsCustomers.HasChanges(DataRowState.Modified) Then
    If Not dsCustomers.HasErrors Then
    ' Extract the modified records
    Dim dsChanges As DataSet
    dsChanges = dsCustomers.GetChanges()
    ' Commit the update
    sqlAdapt.Update(dsChanges)
    End If
End If
```

Note that the GetChanges() method will accept a DataRowState modifier to
return a specific kind of updated record, such as a deleted record. Without a modifier, this method returns all added, deleted, detached, and modified records.

For the full code listing, please see UpdateDSWithDataGrid1.aspx in the sample project.

Integrating the DataSet Object with XML

The DataSet object is strongly integrated with XML and can serialize its relational
data to XML and XSD files. The benefit of this is that different applications can
share relational data using self-describing XML files, even if they are written in different languages and are potentially running on different platforms. The XML and
XSD files combine to document the relational structures in the data and to document the data types of each field. Web service components that deliver XML data
files benefit greatly from using the DataSet object because there is little coding
involved for serializing data to XML. Table 3-8 summarizes the XML-related methods that the DataSet class supports for reading and writing XML and XSD content.

Table 3-8. XML-Related Methods in the DataSet Class

METHOD	DESCRIPTION
GetXml()	This method returns the XML representation of the data stored in the DataSet as a string, without an XML schema. This method is equivalent to calling the WriteXml() method while setting XmlWriteMode to IgnoreSchema.
GetXmlSchema()	This method returns the XML schema that represents the data stored in the DataSet as a string.
ReadXml()	(Overloaded.) This method reads XML data and schema information into the DataSet. This method reads from a filestream, from a file, or from objects derived from the TextWriter and XmlWriter classes. It optionally includes an enumeration called XmlReadMode that provides the following options:
	IgnoreSchema: This ignores inline schema information and uses the DataSet's current schema. This will cause exceptions if the incoming data does not match the DataSet's current schema.
	InferSchema: This ignores inline schema information and infers the schema as it reads the data into the DataSet.
	ReadSchema: This reads inline schema information and loads data into the DataSet.
	DiffGram: This reads the DiffGram into the DataSet and applies the changes contained in the DiffGram.
	Fragment: This reads XML documents into the DataSet, including those generated from SQL Server using the FOR XML clause. This mode reads schema information from the inline namespaces that are in the document.
	Auto: This applies the most appropriate mode: InferSchema, ReadSchema, or DiffGram
ReadXmlSchema()	This method reads an XML schema into the DataSet.

(continued)

Table 3-8. XML-Related Methods in the DataSet Class (continued)

METHOD	DESCRIPTION
WriteXml()	(Overloaded.) This method writes out the XML representation of the data stored in the DataSet. This method writes out to a filestream, to a file, or to objects derived from the TextWriter and XmlWriter classes. It optionally includes an enumeration called XmlWriteMode that provides the following options:
	IgnoreSchema: This writes the current contents of the DataSet as XML without schema information.
	WriteSchema: This writes the current contents of the DataSet as XML with inline schema information.
	DiffGram: This writes the current DataSet in DiffGram format, which includes original and current values.
WriteXmlSchema()	This method writes the DataSet structure as an XML schema. This method writes out to a filestream, to a file, or to objects derived from the TextWriter and XmlWriter classes.
InferXmlSchema()	This method infers the schema for a file or TextReader that has been loaded into the DataSet.

Generating XML from a DataSet

Let's jump right into an example. Listing 3-3 shows how to generate an XML document from a populated DataSet and then query the XML directly using an XPATH statement. This example simulates a scenario where a Web service generates an XML file of relational data and delivers it to a consumer. The consumer resides on a non-Microsoft platform and cannot work with the ADO.NET DataSet object. Instead, the consumer uses XPATH queries on the XML document to drill down into the data. You can find the code for this example in ExecSPReturnXSD.aspx within the sample project that accompanies this chapter.

Listing 3-3. Using the QueryProducts() Method

```
Imports System.Data
Imports System.Xml

Sub QueryProductList()
Dim objDB As Apress.Database
Dim strConn, strJSScript As String
Dim arrParams() As String
Dim sqlDS As DataSet
```

```vb
    Try
        ' Retrieve the connection string
          strConn = ConfigurationSettings.AppSettings("ConnectionString")

        ' Step 1: Instance a new Database object
        strConn = ConfigurationSettings.AppSettings("ConnectionString")
        objDB = New Apress.Database(strConn)

        ' Step 2: Load Products into DataSet [ProductList]
        arrParams = New String() {}
        sqlDS = objDB.ExecSPReturnDS("ProductList", arrParams)

        ' Step 3: Load the DataSet XML into an XmlDataDocument
        sqlDS.EnforceConstraints = False
        Dim xmlDataDoc As XmlDataDocument = New XmlDataDocument(sqlDS)
        xmlDataDoc.Normalize()

        ' Step 4: Use XPATH to query all nodes where UnitsOnOrder > 70
        Dim objXmlNode As XmlNode
        Dim objXmlParentNode As XmlNode
        Dim strProductID As String
        Dim objXmlNodes As XmlNodeList = _
            xmlDataDoc.SelectNodes("//UnitsOnOrder[.>70]")

        ' Step 5: Iterate through the XmlNodeList returned from the XPATH query
        Dim enmNodes As IEnumerator = objXmlNodes.GetEnumerator
        While enmNodes.MoveNext
            objXmlNode = CType(enmNodes.Current, XmlNode)
            objXmlParentNode = objXmlNode.ParentNode
            strProductID = objXmlParentNode.Item("ProductID").InnerText
            Response.Write("Product ID: " & strProductID & " has " & _
                objXmlNode.InnerText & " units on order." & "<BR>")
        End While
        Response.Write("(" & objXmlNodes.Count & " Products matched)")
    Catch err As Exception
        ' Error handling code goes here
    Finally
        objDB = Nothing
    End Try

End Sub
```

In Steps 1 and 2, Listing 3-3 populates a DataSet object with the available products in the Northwind database. (We have created a new stored procedure for this purpose called `ProductList`, which simply returns all of the records in the Products table.) In Step 3, the DataSet object gets loaded into an XmlDataDocument object, which maps the relational data into an XML document. There is a lot of complexity in this transformation that is completely taken care of for you. Listing 3-4 shows the schema file that represents the resultset. It was generated using the DataSet object's `GetXmlSchema()` method.

Listing 3-4. The Schema File

```
<?xml version="1.0" encoding="utf-16"?>
<xs:schema id="NewDataSet"
    targetNamespace="urn:products-schema" xmlns:mstns="urn:products-schema"
    xmlns="urn:products-schema" xmlns:xs=http://www.w3.org/2001/XMLSchema
    xmlns:msdata="urn:schemas-microsoft-com:xml-msdata"
    attributeFormDefault="qualified" elementFormDefault="qualified">
  <xs:element name="NewDataSet" msdata:IsDataSet="true">
    <xs:complexType>
      <xs:choice maxOccurs="unbounded">
        <xs:element name="Table">
          <xs:complexType>
            <xs:sequence>
              <xs:element name="ProductID" type="xs:int" minOccurs="0" />
              <xs:element name="ProductName" type="xs:string" minOccurs="0" />
              <xs:element name="SupplierID" type="xs:int" minOccurs="0" />
              <xs:element name="CategoryID" type="xs:int" minOccurs="0" />
              <xs:element name="QuantityPerUnit" type="xs:string" minOccurs="0" />
              <xs:element name="UnitPrice" type="xs:decimal" minOccurs="0" />
              <xs:element name="UnitsInStock" type="xs:short" minOccurs="0" />
              <xs:element name="UnitsOnOrder" type="xs:short" minOccurs="0" />
              <xs:element name="ReorderLevel" type="xs:short" minOccurs="0" />
              <xs:element name="Discontinued" type="xs:boolean" minOccurs="0" />
            </xs:sequence>
          </xs:complexType>
        </xs:element>
      </xs:choice>
    </xs:complexType>
  </xs:element>
</xs:schema>
```

The schema file provides you with two important types of information. First, the resultset contains a sequence of fixed elements (or fields) that represent a product record. This set of elements starts with the `ProductID` field and ends with the `Discontinued` field. The sequence of elements is contained within a Table element. Second, you know the data type for each element, which allows you to validate the record fields should you need to add additional records.

To retrieve the actual XML, you can call the XmlDataDocument object's `InnerXML()` method. This is a portion of the first record in the XML file:

```
<NewDataSet>
        <Table>
                <ProductID>1</ProductID>
                <ProductName>Chai</ProductName>
                <UnitsOnOrder>0</UnitsOnOrder>
                <Discontinued>false</Discontinued>
        </Table>
</NewDataSet>
```

In Step 4, we execute an XPATH query directly against the XmlDataDocument to retrieve all nodes where the UnitsOnOrder field value is greater than 70. You accomplish this using the XmlDataDocument object's `SelectNodes()` method. Finally, in Step 5 you iterate through the returned list of nodes using the standard enumerator interface. The output is as follows:

```
Product ID: 64 has 80 units on order.
Product ID: 66 has 100 units on order.
(2 Products matched)
```

Listing 3-3 is short, but it clearly demonstrates the powerful functionality that the DataSet and XmlDataDocument objects have with very little code.

DataSet Validation Using XSD Schemas

An XSD schema file describes the structure of a relational data set and the data types that it contains. XSD schema files serve two important purposes. First, they fully describe a data set, which is essential when you deliver an XML file to an outside consumer. Second, they serve as an excellent validation tool, especially when you are adding additional records to a data set and need to verify that you are using the correct data types.

Let's consider an example. Listing 3-5 shows how to use an XSD schema to validate new DataRow records in a DataSet object.

Listing 3-5. Using an XSD Schema

```
Imports System.Data
Imports System.Data.SqlClient
Imports System.Xml
Imports System.IO


Sub ValidateSchema()
        ' Purpose: Demonstrate how to validate a DataSet using an XSD Schema
        Dim objDB As Apress.Database
        Dim strConn, strJSScript As String
        Dim arrParams() As String
        Dim sqlDS As DataSet

    Try
            ' Step 1: Instance a new Database object
            strConn = ConfigurationSettings.AppSettings("ConnectionString")
            objDB = New Apress.Database(strConn)

            ' Step 2: Load Products into DataSet [ProductList]
            arrParams = New String() {}
            sqlDS = objDB.ExecSPReturnDS("ProductList", arrParams)

            ' Step 3: Write out the DataSet Schema to an XSD file
            Dim xsdFile As File
            If xsdFile.Exists("c:\temp\products.xsd") Then _
                xsdFile.Delete("c:\temp\products.xsd")
            Dim sw As StreamWriter
            sw = New StreamWriter("c:\temp\products.xsd")
            sqlDS.Namespace = "urn:products-schema" ' Assign a namespace
            sw.Write(sqlDS.GetXmlSchema)
            sw.Close()

            ' Step 4: Read the XSD file into a StreamReader object
            Dim myStreamReader As StreamReader = New _
                    StreamReader("c:\temp\products.xsd")

            ' Step 5: Create a blank DataSet and load the XSD schema file
            Dim sqlDS2 As DataSet = New DataSet()
            sqlDS2.ReadXmlSchema(myStreamReader)

            ' Step 6A: Manually add a product correctly (required fields only)
            Dim dr As DataRow = sqlDS2.Tables(0).NewRow
```

```
            dr("ProductID") = 200
            dr("ProductName") = "Red Hot Salsa"
            dr("Discontinued") = False
            sqlDS2.Tables(0).Rows.Add(dr)


            ' Step 6B: Manually add a product incorrectly (Set ProductID to a string)
            dr = sqlDS2.Tables(0).NewRow
            dr("ProductID") = "XJ8" ' expected type is Int32: this assignment will fail
            dr("ProductName") = "Red Hot Salsa"
            dr("Discontinued") = False
            sqlDS2.Tables(0).Rows.Add(dr)

    Catch sqlError As SqlException
            ' Error handling code goes here
            Response.Write(sqlError.Message)
    Finally
            objDB = Nothing
    End Try
End Sub
```

In Steps 1 and 2, a DataSet object gets populated with the available products in the Northwind database, using the ProductList stored procedure created for the previous example. In Steps 3 and 4, the XSD schema information is written out to a file called products.xsd. The schema is generated using the DataSet object's GetXmlSchema() method. Notice that the code provides a target namespace called urn:products-schema to uniquely identify this schema. In Step 5, an empty DataSet object is created and is loaded with the XSD schema file that was just generated. Step 6A demonstrates how to add a valid new product record. Step 6B attempts to add a new record that is invalid. The ProductID field has an Int32 data type, but in Step 6B, the field gets assigned a string value. The following SqlException error gets raised when Step 6B attempts to execute:

```
Couldn't store <XJ8> in ProductID Column.  Expected type is Int32.
```

Extended Validation Using the XmlValidatingReader Class

There are different variations on how you can perform validation using an XSD schema file. The System.Xml.Schema namespace provides a class called XmlValidatingReader that validates an XML file against one or more XSD namespaces. In this example, there are actually three schema namespaces that are used in the construction of the XML file:

- urn:products-schema

- http://www.w3.org/2001/XMLSchema

- urn:schemas-microsoft-com:xml-msdata

The first namespace, urn:products-schema, is the custom namespace created to represent the Products table. The second namespace (ending in XMLSchema) is a standard namespace that must be included in all XSD schema files. Finally, the third namespace is Microsoft specific and describes the NewDataSet element, among other things.

The XmlValidatingReader class is not straightforward to use because it provides a large number of properties that can be set in many different combinations. We will not discuss the class in any detail here because we would require an entire chapter to do the subject justice. Suffice it to say that the .NET Framework provides a large number of classes for working with XML and XSD, including classes that will validate well-formed XML documents against multiple XSD schemas.

 NOTE   *You can read more about the XmlValidatingReader class, and XSD validation in general, using .NET, at* http://msdn.microsoft.com/library/ en-us/cpguide/html/ cpconvalidationofxmlwithxmlvalidatingreader.asp.

Now let's turn our attention to typed DataSets, which represent another interesting example of XML integration with the DataSet object.

Typed DataSets

A *typed DataSet* is a class that inherits from the DataSet object and incorporates a specific XSD schema. A typed DataSet is essentially a special compilation of the DataSet object that is bound to a specific structure, represented by the XSD schema. As such, all the DataSet methods, events, and properties are available in the typed DataSet object. Additionally, a typed DataSet provides strongly typed methods, events, and properties for the schema information.

You have already seen how to generate an XSD file programmatically. Visual Studio .NET provides another option for generating these files. You can use the Visual Studio Component Designer tool to generate an XSD schema from a database table or stored procedure with the following steps:

1. In the ASP.NET application, add a DataSet item to the `Components` direc-
    tory. You will see a new `.xsd` file in the `Components` directory.

2. Open the Server Explorer and add a data connection to your database.

3. Drag and drop the table or stored procedure from the Server Explorer to
    the DataSet form. The Component Designer will populate the XSD
    schema into the `.xsd` file.

Once you save the .xsd file, the XSD schema becomes automatically recognized as a valid data type that you can reference programmatically. The
AspNetChap3 sample project provide an example, which includes
the dsCustOrderHist typed DataSet. This has been generated and stored in the
`dsCustOrderHist.xsd` file.

Keep in mind that a typed DataSet is not automatically a populated DataSet
object. By creating a typed DataSet you have actually generated a new class that
forms the shell of a schema-specific, populated DataSet. For example, you can
use the DataAdapter `Fill()` method to write data to the typed DataSet in the
same way as you would to an untyped DataSet. This is an example showing how
you can fill the custom `dsCustOrderHist` typed DataSet created earlier:

```
' Create a new Typed DataSet object
Dim sqlDS As New dsCustOrderHist ()
Try
    Dim sqlAdapt As SqlDataAdapter = New SqlDataAdapter(sqlCmd)
    m_sqlConn.Open()
    sqlAdapt.Fill(sqlDS, "CustOrderHist")
    m_sqlConn.Close()
Finally
End Try
```

A typed DataSet object allows access to tables and columns by name, instead
of using collection-based methods, as shown in this code:

```
sqlDS = objDB.ExecSPReturnDS("CustOrderHist", arrParams)
'Read the row values by name
For Each myRow In sqlDS1.CustOrderHist.Rows
    strResults = strResults & (myRow.ProductName.ToString) & "  " & _
        (myRow.Total.ToString) & vbCrLf
Next myRow
```

For a regular DataSet, the line inside the For...Next loop would have read as
follows:

```
strResults = strResults & (myRow("ProductName")) & "  " &_
    (myRow("Total")) & vbCrLf
```

This may not seem like a huge difference until you consider that typed DataSet properties, such as `ProductName`, show up in Visual Studio's IntelliSense viewer. For untyped DataSets the developer must manually type the name of the field index. In this case, simple spelling errors in the field name can cause run-time errors. So, not only does a typed DataSet improve the readability of code, but it makes it easier to write and allows the Visual Studio .NET code editor to catch exceptions related to invalid casting at compilation time rather than at runtime.

NOTE   *Although you do not have to include the table name when calling the* `Fill()` *method for an untyped DataSet, you must include the table name defined in the XSD schema when filling a typed DataSet. If the table name is not included, then the filled DataSet will contain two tables, one with the generic name of "Table" that contains all the data and the second empty table defined with the name in the XSD schema ("CustOrderHist" in our sample).*

The DiffGram Format

A *DiffGram* is simply a specialized XML format that tracks original and current data values in a DataSet. Microsoft outlines the DiffGram format in this schema:

`urn:schemas-microsoft-com:xml-diffgram-v1`

DataSets can both generate DiffGrams and load them. For example, if you modify data in a DataSet, you can then generate a DiffGram that records the original and current (modified) values. The DiffGram can be loaded into another DataSet, which can then re-create the original and current values, as well as the row order and any row-level errors due to updates. One thing a DiffGram does not do is preserve schema information. You will need to transport this information in a separate file. Note that Web service methods that return DataSets will automatically use the DiffGram format.

The sole purpose of the DiffGram format is to provide an XML format for transporting DataSet update information. DiffGrams carry a large footprint because they include multiple XML records for each actual data record. You may never need to use DiffGrams directly, and in fact, you should use them sparingly. Because Web service methods automatically use the DiffGram format, you should never return DataSets directly from Web services unless you specifically need to do so.

NOTE *You can read more about the DataSet and XML, including DiffGrams, at* http://msdn.microsoft.com/library/ default.asp?url=/library/en-us/cpguide/html/ cpconxmldataset.asp.

Using the DataView Class

The DataView class deserves special mention because it is useful for optimizing data access code. The DataView class holds a customized and optimized view of a DataSet. The DataView does not carry the high overhead of the DataSet object because it does not preserve the same level of information. Yet you can still use it for complex operations such as sorting, filtering, searching, editing, and navigating. For example, if you need to bind a subset of a DataSet to a grid, then the DataView object can capture the exact subset. You can then bind the DataView object, as opposed to the entire DataSet object.

You can create a DataView either by referencing the DefaultView property of a DataTable or by using the DataView constructor. This is how you establish a reference to the DefaultView:

```
Dim sqlDV As DataView
Dim sqlDS As DataSet
' Assume that the DataSet object is populated
sqlDV = sqlDS.Tables(0).DefaultView
```

The constructor for the DataView can be empty, or it can accept a DataTable along with filter criteria, sort criteria, and a row state filter:

```
myView = New DataView(Table As System.Data.DataTable, RowFilter As String, _
        Sort As String, RowState As System.Data.DataViewRowState)
```

You can create multiple, distinct DataViews for the same DataTable. This is helpful if you need to represent data from the same DataTable source in different ways.

As an example, let's look at the code from ExecSPReturnDS.aspx in the sample project (specifically, the GetDVBindDG() method). Listing 3-6 retrieves the CustOrderHist dataset, which contains the total number of products ordered by each customer. Let's say you are only interested in seeing customers who ordered more than 15 products. You can use a DataView to create a filtered view of the CustOrderHist dataset.

Listing 3-6. Creating a Filtered View of a DataSet

```
Dim myView As DataView
Try
    objDB = New Apress.Database(strConn)
    arrParams = New String() {"@CustomerID", SqlDbType.Char, "ALFKI"}
    sqlDS = objDB.ExecSPReturnDS("CustOrderHist", arrParams)
    myView = New DataView(sqlDS.Tables(0), "Total>15", "Total", _
            DataViewRowState.CurrentRows)
    ' Bind the DataView to the DataGrid
    DataGrid1.DataSource = myView
    DataGrid1.DataBind()
Finally
End Try
```

You can make changes to the DataView using the `AddNew()` and `Delete()` methods. The `RowState` filter property tracks changes to the DataView and lets you create yet another filtered view of the data. For example, this is how you filter the DataView to show new or deleted rows only:

```
' Set the RowStateFilter to display only Added and Deleted rows.
myView.RowStateFilter = DataViewRowState.Added Or DataViewRowState.Deleted
```

You can also cache the DataView in memory, which makes it an excellent alternative to the DataSet for situations where you need to hold the data in memory but want to use as little memory as possible.

Using the SqlException Class

Data access programming is vulnerable to exceptions because there are many factors that can cause issues, including database errors, improperly formatted queries, and timeouts. The .NET Framework provides specialized exception classes for handling and interpreting data access errors. The SQL Server .NET Managed Provider provides the SqlException class, which specifically handles SQL errors. This class is derived from the standard Exception class and provides a similar interface.

The SqlException object actually exposes a collection of one or more SQL errors, each of which is encapsulated by a SqlError object. You can reference the collection directly, as a SqlErrorCollection object, or indirectly, via the SqlException object's Errors property.

Listing 3-7 comes from `ShowSQLExceptions.aspx` and shows how you can trap for, and iterate through, a collection of SQL errors.

Listing 3-7. Trapping and Iterating Through Exceptions

```
Sub CreateSqlException()
    Try
        ' Execute data access code
    Catch err As SqlException
        ' SQL Error handling code goes here
        Dim i As Integer
        Dim sqlErr As SqlError
        For i = 0 To err.Errors.Count - 1
            sqlErr = err.Errors(i)
            Response.Write("Error #" & sqlErr.Number & ": " & _
                err.Message & "<BR>")
        Next i
        If m_sqlconn.State = ConnectionState.Open Then m_sqlconn.Close()
    Catch err2 As Exception
        ' Standard exception handler here
    Finally
        m_sqlconn = Nothing
        objDB = Nothing
    End Try
End Sub
```

For example, if you call a nonexistent stored procedure, you will get the following exception:

```
Error #2812: Could not find stored procedure 'ProductList2'.
```

It is interesting to note the effect of a SQL error on the state of the connection to the database. Every error is associated with a severity level, and the SqlConnection object will automatically close if an error is raised with a severity level of 20 or greater. Be sure to always check the connection state in your error handler and to close it if it is still open. We prefer this approach to evaluating the severity level because open SQL connections may cause downstream exceptions that are difficult or impossible to handle. Finally, notice Listing 3-7 includes a second, standard exception handler. The SqlException handler will trap only SQL errors, so to be safe you should always include a handler for the standard Exception class. This will trap all exceptions that the SqlException handler does not.

The SqlException class provides other properties not covered here, including a Source property. This will provide the detailed call stack that led to the error. This information is useful for developers but bewildering for end users, so our approach is to write the source information to a private application event log and suppress it from the end user's view. In closing, make sure you always implement the provider-specific exception class in your data access code. The OleDbException class holds errors for OLE DB data sources just as the SqlException class holds errors for SQL Server data sources.

Making Data Access Design Decisions

ADO.NET introduces new possibilities for data access programming, which complicates the design process for developers. At the risk of oversimplifying the issue, three main factors influence design decisions:

- The application architecture

- The format in which the consumer expects to receive data

- The format in which the consumer expects to communicate data updates

For the purposes of this discussion, ASP.NET enables two main kinds of applications:

- **N-tier Web applications**: Each logical process is separated in discreet classes, such as business components, data components, and frontend components.

- **Web services**: These are distributed components that send and receive data using XML.

We will ignore the obvious variations that each application type can provide and distill the issue down to one simple difference: Data is exchanged as XML, or it is not. Furthermore, some applications and components simply retrieve data, and others also allow updates to data.

Data Access Design for N-Tier Web Applications

N-tier applications separate application logic into distinct components, which includes separating data access logic into separate classes. N-tier application architecture has become a standard design because it applies equally well to small, medium, or large applications. Partitioned logic is not only easier to build and maintain, but it enables components to be flexibly distributed across physical servers as the application load increases.

N-tier Web applications follow a typical design:

1. Write the frontend user interface using Web forms.

2. Write the business rule components as separate classes that can be called from the code-behind file in the Web forms.

3. Create a dedicated data access component in a separate class module. This component ideally provides a set of generic functions that encapsulate the ADO.NET object calls. In addition, you may choose to write dedicated functions that are tied to specific database entities in your backend database.

4. Use typed DataSets where possible because they provide the functionality of the DataSet class along with the convenience of strong-typing for the DataTable fields. There is a performance penalty with typed DataSets compared to standard DataSets; however, you may find this a small price to pay compared with the benefits of coding with strongly typed accessors. The performance penalty will likely increase in relation to the complexity of the underlying XSD schema. However, the exact performance price can only be determined by testing your specific Web application.

The advantages of n-tier application design for data access are as follows:

Data access routines are centralized. Changes to any data access routine only need to be made in one component. Code becomes much easier to maintain.

There is less repeated code in the application, which makes it easier to maintain and reduces the size of the compiled executable. This indirectly improves the responsiveness of the application because the ASP.NET worker process has a smaller binary file with which to work.

Separate components can be located on different physical machines if required. This can improve the responsiveness of the overall application.

The disadvantages of n-tier application design for data access are as follows:

Development time is increased in the short term because you need to create several components. (You can minimize this development time by designing your data access components for flexible reuse so that they may be used in another Web application with little or no recoding.)

Centralized data access classes can be difficult to write in such a way that they handle all data access scenarios for your application. For example, let's say you do not incorporate output parameters into your wrapper classes. Then, once the application is deployed, a data access requirement arises that can only be handled by a stored procedure that returns an output parameter. You may need to modify the data access wrapper functions to accommodate output parameters, which could impact existing calls. The moral of the story is to think ahead and anticipate as many of your data access needs as possible.

The sample application that accompanies this chapter provides an example of a data access class. It is a huge convenience to be able to call single methods that will assemble the parameter string and instance the required ADO.NET objects for you. In addition, it is more convenient to be able to update global changes to your data access code in one location as opposed to several. We faced this situation recently when we moved a Web application into a production environment and immediately encountered query timeout errors across the application. It turned out that the CommandTimeout parameter was not set high enough for the production environment, even though it had been set perfectly for the development environment. The application's data access component was already using a single private global value for this parameter, so it was a quick operation to update the value and recompile the class. (Of course, you could also store the CommandTimeout parameter in the Web.config file so that you can modify its value without recompiling the data access component.)

Data Access Design for Web Services

Web services exchange data as XML, and as you have seen, the .NET Framework provides a huge amount of functionality for working with XML. The DataSet class will handle most data access scenarios—from simple data retrievals to complex data updates. The DataSet class will serialize to XML and XSD files in a way that preserves the relational structures in the data. For updates, the DataSet works with the DiffGram schema format, which tracks before and after values as well as errors that arise due to updates. Whatever data access operation you need to perform, there is a good chance you can accomplish it using ADO.NET and XML.

Web services follow a typical set of design principles when it comes to data access:

Data requests and responses are exchanged as XML inside a Simple Object Access Protocol (SOAP) envelope. The consumer application must have the ability to format SOAP requests. Optionally, the consumer should be able to work with XML documents, especially if it calls Web service methods that generate schema-specific XML documents.

Web service methods return targeted information. They should return all of the information for a specific kind of request. You should never have to invoke two or more Web service methods for the same related request.

Web services use targeted methods for updating data. Unless you need to support complex XML structures such as the DiffGram, the best approach for updating data with a Web method is to use a targeted method that calls a specific update stored procedure. Web services can easily throw back exceptions, so the consumer can always stay informed about errors during updates.

Web service methods use the most efficient return data type. For example, scalar values should be returned as integers, strings, or another appropriate data type, rather than as a serialized DataSet. In addition, arrays of data may be more efficient than returning a serialized DataSet. For example, we typically use DataReader objects within the Web service method and map the resultset to an array of strings that holds the name-value pairs. This approach enables the Web method to use an efficient object for data access and to return data with an efficient footprint.

The advantages of Web services for data access are as follows:

Web service methods will work with a wide range of common data types, as well as custom data types, as long as they are tied to an XML schema file.

Web service methods for accessing data provide the same level of functionality as standard data access methods, but with the added benefit that they are not tied to a particular consumer. A Web service component meets all the needs for servicing a local consumer and can also service outside consumers should the need arise. Local and remote consumers alike can use data access code that is written into Web service components.

Web service methods can return XML documents, which gives the consumer application flexibility in processing the resultset.

The disadvantages of Web services for data access are as follows:

Complex data structures and complex updates typically must involve the DataSet object, which has the highest resource footprint of the available data access objects. Web service methods that exchange and work with DataSets will not perform as well as methods that work with simple data types. They require more resources to work with, and to serialize, and they generate larger XML documents. Recall also that Web services automatically generate DataSets in the DiffGram format, which creates multiple XML records per record of actual data.

Web services carry additional overhead compared to local components because they require SOAP and typically require a proxy class. If you are certain you will never to need to invoke data remotely, then you should avoid Web services in favor of using components that can be installed locally to your ASP.NET application.

Web services only support stateless, single method calls.

In our recent applications we have moved a fair amount of data access code to Web services. This is mainly because the applications make liberal use of real-time validation, which uses Web services that are hooked into client-side scripts. So, for example, as the user fills in a form field, the application will perform a real-time check against the database for duplicates and other potential validation problems. At the same time, we often need to call these same methods from the server-side code-behind file. We can do this easily by setting Web references between the client ASP.NET application and the Web services. This allows us to invoke the Web services in the same way as we would invoke a regular component. In theory we are taking a performance hit by calling a Web service method from code-behind file instead of calling a standard component. In reality, we have found the performance to be fast enough and certainly acceptable for our particular ASP.NET applications. Ultimately, you need to decide the approach that works best for you.

Decision Flow Diagram

Data access design decisions are complicated and are largely dictated by the application architecture and by the format in which data must be exchanged (that is, XML vs. non-XML). Figure 3-3 presents a decision flow diagram that attempts to capture a broad range of data access scenarios. The diagram suggests primary and alternate data access methods based on a particular data access scenario. The diagram does not encompass all factors, but at the least it will help you start thinking about the best approach for your particular data access scenario.

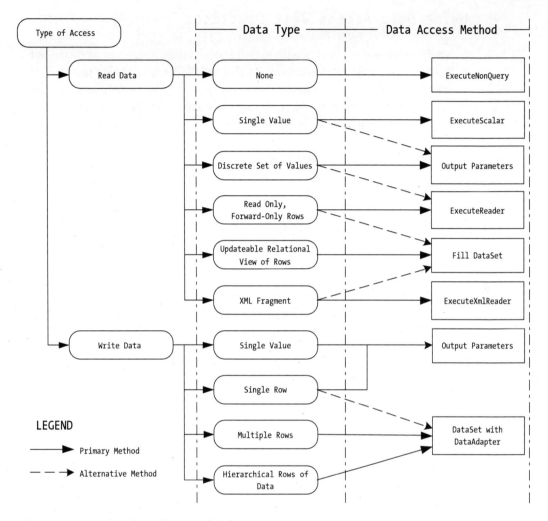

Figure 3-3. Decision flow diagram for data access

NOTE *For more information on data access design using ADO.NET, refer to the MSDN article ".NET Data Access Architecture Guide" at* `http://msdn.microsoft.com/library/` `default.asp?url=/library/en-us/dnbda/html/daag.asp`.

Using Data Access Best Practices

Good data access code begins with making good design decisions, as discussed in the previous sections. In addition, it helps to follow a list of best practices, which you can think of as a checklist that keeps your code efficient and may also buy you extra performance. The following are some generally recognized best practices for writing data access code:

- Use the appropriate data access object.

- Use stored procedures, not embedded Transact-SQL.

- Use complex stored procedures, not multiple retrievals.

- Use SQL data types with SQL Server.

- Use connection pooling.

- Use centralized data access functions.

- Use good programming sense.

- Use exception handling appropriately.

- Use helper technologies.

Now, let's discuss each of these in turn.

Use the Appropriate Data Access Object

You have seen the distinctiveness of each of the ADO.NET objects. The easiest and smartest step you can take is to always use the most appropriate data object for the given scenario. Always use streaming data access for read-only, data retrieval operations. Use the DataSet object for data update operations only if you need to perform the updates in disconnected mode. (Alternatively, write dedicated update stored procedures that resolve updates for you.) Use the DataView object when you want to work with filtered views of a larger DataSet object. The DataView object provides many of the benefits of the DataSet object, but without as much overhead.

Use Stored Procedures, Not Embedded Transact-SQL

An accepted Transact-SQL design approach is to compile your Data Manipulation Language (DML) statements into stored procedures. Stored procedures execute much faster than Transact-SQL statements because they are precompiled on the database server and are reusable. The ADO.NET Command object will allow you to execute embedded Transact-SQL statements directly by assigning the statement to the CommandText property and by setting the CommandType enumeration to Text. You may have seen code that dynamically assembles a Transact-SQL string. However, you should *always* avoid this approach. Not only does Transact-SQL execute more slowly than a stored procedure, but you can also introduce parsing errors into the Transact-SQL statement, which will in turn generate runtime errors. Worse yet, if your application executes any dynamic Transact-SQL statement, then you may inadvertently allow the application to execute commands that modify the database structure (such as dropping tables). Always execute stored procedures, and use input parameters, preferably with strong typing.

TIP *Keep the size of the returned resultset to a minimum by filling it with just the records that you need. This is especially important for database query results that will be marshaled over the wire to Web clients. Also, avoid using the wildcard (*) in SQL queries. Always specify the exact fields you want to extract.*

Use Complex Stored Procedures, Not Multiple Retrievals

Use complex stored procedures that return multiple resultsets, rather than making multiple calls to multiple stored procedures. ADO.NET makes it easy to work with multiple resultsets, for example, by using the SqlDataReader object's NextResult() method. This is code that demonstrates how to iterate through every record in every returned resultset:

```
sqlDR = objDB.RunQueryReturnDR("MyStoredProcedure")
Dim arrResult(0) As String
Do
    While sqlDR.Read() ' Position the pointer on the first record
        i += 1
        ReDim Preserve arrResult(i)
```

```
            arrResult(i) = sqlDR("ProductNumber")
        End While
    Loop While (sqlDR.NextResult()) ' Move to the next resultset
```

If possible, write your stored procedures to batch-related resultsets. This helps to reduce network traffic and overhead on the database server.

Use SQL Data Types with SQL Server

The .NET Framework and SQL Server use different data types that do not always convert with each other. The System.Data.SqlTypes namespace provides a set of .NET Framework structures that represent SQL Server data types in the managed environment. In addition, the SqlDataReader class provides typed accessor methods that automatically map retrieved field values into the appropriate structure. Always use typed accessor methods when retrieving SQL Server data to avoid type conversion errors.

Use Connection Pooling

Always use connection pooling. The SQL Server managed provider supports connection pooling by default with little effort required on the part of the developer. The most work you have to do is to modify the connection string to override default settings for connection pooling parameters.

Use Centralized Data Access Functions

Always centralize your data access functions in a dedicated class file. This enables you to maintain your database code in one central location, which makes it easier to write and to maintain. The sample project that accompanies this chapter provides one example of a data access class (the source code file is DataAccess.vb). It implements wrapper functions for basic data access operations, including:

- Executing a stored procedure and returning a DataReader

- Executing a stored procedure and returning a DataSet

- Executing a stored procedure and returning an XmlReader

- Executing a stored procedure with no return value

These wrapper functions encapsulate the details of setting up the Connection and Command objects, as well as any additional objects. This code becomes repetitive, and the last thing you want to do is to have the same constructs included in dozens of locations throughout your code. Not only is this hard to maintain, but it also artificially inflates the size of the application executable.

NOTE *Microsoft provides a .NET component called the* Data Access Application Block, *which contains optimized data access wrapper functions. You can read more about this and download the code at:*
`http://msdn.microsoft.com/library/`
`default.asp?url=/library/en-us/dnbda/html/daab-rm.asp.`

Use Good Programming Sense

The .NET managed runtime environment provides advanced garbage collection designed to optimize resource usage and remove unnecessary references. However, you should always implement the fundamental housekeeping rules that keep your code readable and efficient. In particular, always clear object references when you are done with them. If you use data connections, make sure you keep the connection open for as short a time as possible. Open the connection just before it is needed, and close it as soon as it is no longer required. Never leave open connections in your code, especially if you are working with streaming data objects such as the DataReader. In summary, close connections and clear unused object references: This is good coding practice, and it makes good sense.

Use Exception Handling Appropriately

Exception handling is expensive, especially throwing errors. Always implement structured error handling in your applications, but design your code to avoid falling into exception handlers. This may seem obvious except to developers who are used to coding inline, such as when using classic ASP. Inline code often uses `On Error Resume Next` constructs that allow code to continue executing past errors in order to then check for an expected error result. This approach is unnecessary in the .NET managed environment. Design your code to use exception handlers as destinations of last resort. Use the multitude of error and type checking functions to detect errors before the compiler is forced to raise a runtime error.

Throw exceptions only if absolutely necessary because this is an expensive operation. The exception classes provide a large amount of information that may go unused by the calling code that receives the thrown error. In this case, it is better to raise a custom error, using Err.Raise, than to throw an exception. This operation will transmit basic error information, such as an error number, source, and message, but it will avoid expensive information such as the detailed call stack.

Finally, if you provide more than one Catch statement with differing filter criteria, remember to order them from most-specific type to least-specific type. For example:

```
Try
Catch SqlErr as SqlException
Catch err As Exception
Finally
End Try
```

Use Helper Technologies

ASP.NET provides technologies that complement ADO.NET in providing optimized data access. In particular, ASP.NET supports a sophisticated set of caching options ranging from page-level output caching to data caching using the Cache API. Caching is an important consideration in the design of ASP.NET applications. It is considerably faster to read data from a cache than it is to access it fresh from a data source. Caching reduces the number of queries executed against the database and delivers data more responsively. Caching does come with a price in terms of increased memory usage, particularly if you are caching large DataSets. However, caching is efficient in ASP.NET and will almost always prove to be worth the small price you pay in increased resource usage. The one caveat with caching is that it can only provide a stale view of data, so you need to factor in the appropriate refresh rate into a caching implementation.

NOTE *Please refer to Chapter 5, "Caching ASP.NET Applications," for a complete discussion on caching.*

ASP.NET and the .NET Framework provide additional features that can serve as helper technologies for data access. Above all, keep in mind that with ASP.NET you have access to the full .NET Class Framework, and this alone is a powerful advantage, both for data access code and beyond.

Summary

ADO.NET provides a powerful, extensible object model for data access, as well as an unprecedented level of integration with XML. In this chapter we reviewed the ADO.NET object model, which is divided into two groups: the managed data provider and the DataSet. We also covered optimal settings for the Connection and Command objects. We discussed the DataReader, XmlReader, and DataSet objects in detail, and we reviewed the optimal data access scenario for each object. The DataSet object provides disconnected access to data and works with the managed provider to synchronize changes back to the parent data source. We reviewed how the DataSet integrates with XML and how you can use an XSD schema to preserve relational information in XML. Finally, we reviewed data access design decisions and best practices.

CHAPTER 4

Optimizing Application and Session State Management

ASP.NET *STATE MANAGEMENT* is the ability of a Web application to persist information, both at the application and session levels. There are two main types of state in a Web application:

- **Application state**: This is information that applies to all clients of the Web application. This information is shared by, and managed for, multiple clients.

- **Session state**: This is information that applies to a specific client session. You manage this information for individual clients.

Application and session state management are important for personalizing Web applications and for persisting information that is widely used across a Web application. ASP.NET expands the range of options available for managing application and session state. In particular, it overcomes previous limitations of classic ASP for managing state across Web farms.

You continue to manage application state using the Application object (technically, the `HttpApplicationState` class). In addition, ASP.NET provides the `Cache` class, which offers more granular control over managing application data.

Session state management has been greatly expanded compared to classic ASP; you are no longer confined to just using in-process Session objects. In classic ASP, developers liked Session objects for their ease of use but disliked them for negatively impacting application scalability and performance. ASP.NET faces similar challenges; however, the actual performance implications may surprise you. As we discuss in this chapter, Session objects are not necessarily performance killers. On the contrary, when used correctly, they can greatly improve the performance of your application and minimally impact scalability. Most books simply make a cursory reference to the "performance impact" of using Session objects. We, on the other hand, take the discussion a step further by running performance tests for each session mode and examining the numbers.

Overview of Session Management

ASP.NET provides a wide range of session state management capabilities, which allows for the dedicated storage and retrieval of user-specific information. Web applications are built on Hypertext Transfer Protocol (HTTP), which is inherently a stateless protocol. Web servers cannot typically recognize when a set of requests originates from a single user. (The exception would be if the user has a unique Internet Protocol that the Web application can reference from the HTTP Headers collection). This limitation makes it challenging to tailor a Web application experience to a single user. Personalized application sessions can usually only occur if the Web server retains session-specific information between requests. This process typically requires infrastructure support from the Web server and participation from the client. The server and the client establish a unique reference number for the session, or *session ID*, which is typically stored in a cookie on the client machine. Cookies alone may also enable session management because they allow session-specific information to be retained in a text file on the client machine. Cookies pass between the client and server during requests, which enables the server to customize a response based on client-specific information.

But cookies will only get you so far because they are limited both in size and in the complexity of information they can store. Cookies are limited to 4KB in size and are only capable of storing strings. You must store complex information, such as an array or an ADO.NET DataSet, in more sophisticated ways on the server side.

NOTE   *Some developers prefer to create custom session management code rather than using the Session object. One approach is to persist session information in hidden fields or in the Uniform Resource Locator (URL) querystring. An alternate approach is to store session information in a back-end database and key the records using the session ID key that is automatically generated when you enable session state management. In these cases, neither the Web server nor the client requires direct session management support.*

There is actually a dual challenge to retaining and providing session-specific information. On the one hand, there is the challenge of how to retain and procure the information. And on the other hand, there is the challenge of how to do it *quickly*. Users will not appreciate their richly tailored individual experience if it requires them to wait for long periods of time between requests to the Web application.

Managing Session State in Classic ASP

Session state management was available in classic ASP, but it was much maligned for four important reasons:

Performance: Classic ASP provides in-process session management only. All session-specific information has to be stored in the Web server's memory heap, which becomes a drain on available resources as the number of sessions increases. This is especially true if the session-specific information is large or takes time to serialize. Session management in classic ASP is widely considered to have unacceptable impacts on application scalability.

Reliability: In-process session information will not persist if the Web server process ends unexpectedly or the connection between the client and the server is dropped.

Web farms: The in-process nature of classic ASP session management means that only one server at a time can retain session information. This limitation makes classic ASP session management incompatible with Web farms because this architecture routes a single user's requests to the most available server in the farm. Session information will get lost unless the user is consistently routed to the same machine. In recent years this has not been as much of an issue because modern load-balancing routers have the ability to consistently route a user to the same machine for every request. However, the user is still exposed to the risk of losing their session information if their specific server crashes between requests and they are forced to route to a different machine.

Cookie support: Classic ASP requires cookies for managing sessions, which is a problem for the minority of clients that do not enable cookies. Although this only affects a small number of clients, the greater problem is the lack of any alternative to using cookies.

Classic ASP developers use their skills to overcome these limitations as best they can. An especially popular approach is to retain all session information in a dedicated database, using the session ID as a primary key for referencing the information. This approach is not without its performance implications because database calls are slower than pulling data from memory. But the performance hit is worthwhile given that data is guaranteed to be available, especially from clustered SQL Servers, which are highly available. Of course, database server crashes will interrupt access to data. However, developers can greatly reduce the likelihood of crashes through a combination of reliable database software (SQL Server!) and fail-over measures, such as clustering database servers.

Managing ASP.NET Session State

ASP.NET addresses the limitations of classic ASP in the following ways:

Process independence: ASP.NET continues to support traditional in-process session state storage, which stores session values in the same process as the ASP.NET worker process. However, ASP.NET also provides two modes for storing session state out-of-process. The StateServer mode stores session state in a separate thread that is managed by a separate NT service. The SQLServer mode stores session state in a dedicated SQL Server database. Process independence improves the reliability and durability of session state information by decoupling it from the ASP.NET application's worker process. If this process crashes, then session state information does not need to be lost.

Cookieless support: ASP.NET does not require cookies for managing sessions. Cookie-based session state management continues to be the default, where the session ID is stored in a cookie on the client machine. In cookieless mode, ASP.NET automatically appends the session ID to all URLs. The drawback to this approach is that the Web application must contain relative links, with no absolute links. Otherwise, the session ID will fail to append to the URL, and the session association will be lost.

Web farms: ASP.NET provides the StateServer and SQLServer session state modes, which decouples session state management from an application's ASP.NET worker process. Multiple computers in a Web farm can manage session state using a centralized StateServer thread or a centralized SQL Server database. These session state modes are easy to configure and require no special coding.

In the "Understanding Session State Modes" section, we examine the various ASP.NET session state modes in detail. In addition, we discuss the performance implications of each mode. Clearly, there are performance implications when you require a server to manage session information. This task is an additional burden on the server and requires it to allocate valuable resources, both in terms of memory and processor utilization. The key is to pick a session state mode that provides the best session management for your application with the lowest overhead. That is, you must pick a mode that offers the optimal balance between performance and reliability for your particular state management requirements.

Configuring and Using ASP.NET Session State

Session state is enabled by default for a new ASP.NET project and is set to InProc (in-process) mode (described next). You configure session state in the Machine.config and Web.config files using the <sessionState> element:

```
<sessionState
        mode="Off|InProc|StateServer|SQLServer"
        stateConnectionString="tcpip=127.0.0.1:42424"
        sqlConnectionString="server= machineName\sqlServer;uid=sa;pwd=;"
        cookieless="true|false"
        timeout="20"
/>
```

In this example, the pipe symbol (|) indicates a mutually exclusive choice of options, and the connection string and timeout properties have default examples. Note that the Web.config file is case sensitive, so make sure you type all mode values using the correct case. "InProc" is a valid mode value, but "Inproc" is not. There is no special user interface (UI) for the Web.config file; otherwise this detail would be taken care of for you.

The minimum required <sessionState> attributes are mode, cookieless, and timeout (set in minutes). The stateConnectionString attribute is only required when the session mode is StateServer. Similarly, the sqlConnectionString attribute is only required when the session mode is SQLServer.

You can further configure session state at the individual page level using the EnableSessionState attribute of the @ Page directive:

```
<%@ Page EnableSessionState="True|False|ReadOnly" %>
```

If the attribute value is "True," then either a new session will be created or an existing session will be used. If the value is "False," then no new session will be created and no session values may be accessed on the page. If the value is "ReadOnly," then session values may be retrieved, but not modified.

Understanding Session State Modes

ASP.NET provides four modes for managing session state on the server:

- **Off**: Session state is disabled.

- **InProc**: Session state is stored and managed in-process, on the same thread as the ASP.NET application.

- **StateServer**: Session state is stored out-of-process and is managed by an NT Service called *ASP.NET State Service*.

- **SQLServer**: Session state is stored and managed by a SQL Server database called *ASPState*. A batch file that ships with .NET, called `InstallSqlState.sql`, creates this database.

Let's discuss each of the modes in turn, excluding the Off mode, which warrants no further explanation.

Using InProc Session State

The InProc mode is the default mode for session state and is equivalent to what classic ASP provides. This mode is the easiest to configure and only requires you to update the `Web.config` file:

```
<sessionState mode="InProc" cookieless="false" timeout="20"  />
```

The advantages of the InProc mode are as follows:

- It is easy to configure.

- It is the fastest mode available because session items are stored in the same thread as the ASP.NET application.

The disadvantages of the InProc mode are as follows:

- Session items are available on a single server only; you cannot share them across multiple Web servers.

- Session items are not durable. You will lose them if the server crashes or is restarted.

- Session items use up server memory and may negatively impact the scalability of the application.

The InProc mode is an excellent choice if the session items are modest in size and you are not concerned about potentially losing session items and having to re-create them. E-commerce applications, for example, cannot afford to lose session data. However, other applications can use Session objects to reduce redundant database calls that would return duplicate information. These applications can easily re-create session items if they are lost.

Using StateServer Session State

The StateServer mode provides out-of-process session storage and management. This mode stores session items in a dedicated process managed by an NT service called *ASP.NET State Service*. You configure the StateServer mode in a two-step process. First, you update the Web.config file:

```
<sessionState mode="StateServer" stateConnectionString="tcpip=127.0.0.1:42424"
        cookieless="false" timeout="20" />
```

Next, you have to start the ASP.NET State Service because its default startup type is manual. Open the MMC snap-in from the Windows Start menu button by selecting Start ➢ Programs ➢ Administrative Tools ➢ Services.

Highlight the ASP.NET State Service entry, as shown in Figure 4-1, and click the Start button. Alternatively, you can right-click the entry and select Start from the pop-up menu.

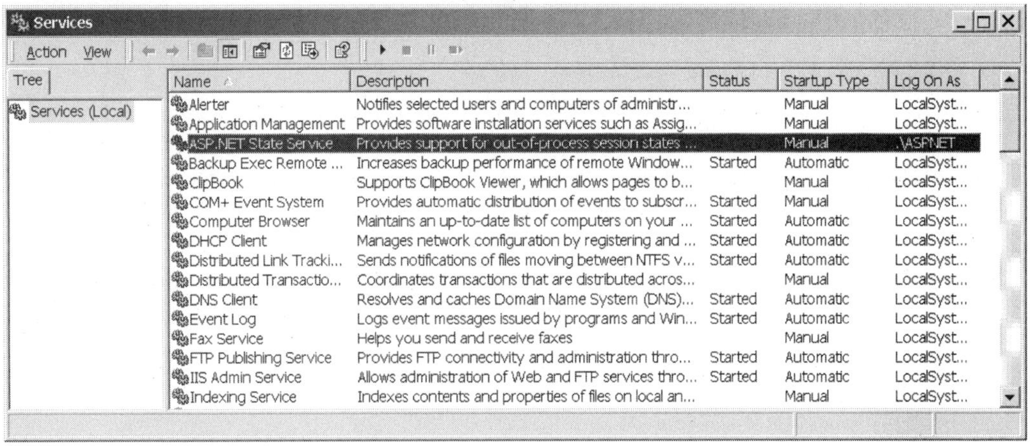

Figure 4-1. The ASP.NET State Service

If you forget to start the service but you update the Web.config file, then your application will throw the following error:

```
System.Web.HttpException: Unable to make the session state request to the
session state server. Make sure that the ASP.NET State service is started
and that the client and server ports are the same.
```

The advantages of the StateServer mode are as follows:

- Session storage is out-of-process, so it does not directly impact the scalability of the ASP.NET application.

- You can share session items across multiple Web servers.

The disadvantages of the StateServer mode are as follows:

- There is a high performance cost of marshaling session items across processes, even within the same server.

- There is a high performance cost of marshaling session items between servers if you have multiple servers accessing the same state service.

- Session items are not durable. You will lose them if the dedicated process crashes or is restarted.

- Session items must support binary serialization to work with the StateServer mode. Popular objects such as the DataSet object do support binary serialization. However, others such as the equally useful DataView object do not.

The StateServer mode is often the worst choice you can make for managing session state. The cost of marshaling data across process boundaries is high, even if the size of the data is small. If you must access Session data from multiple servers, then SQLServer mode is often a better choice.

In ASP.NET 1.1, by default, only the local machine can connect to its ASP.NET State Service. You can grant non-local machines access to the State Service via a registry setting. This is an improvement over ASP 1.0, which did not restrict access to the StateServer mode from any machine.

Using SQLServer Session State

The SQLServer mode provides out-of-process session storage and management using a SQL Server database. You configure the SQLServer mode in a two-step process. First, you update the `Web.config` file:

```
<sessionState mode="SQLServer"
    sqlConnectionString="server= machineName\sqlServer;uid=myid;pwd=123;"
    cookieless="false" timeout="20" />
```

You have some flexibility in the format of the SQL connection string. You could use the following alternate format:

```
<sessionState mode="SQLServer"
    sqlConnectionString="data source= machineName\sqlServer;
        user id=myid;password=123;" cookieless="false" timeout="20" />
```

Note that the connection string does not include a database name. In fact, the application will generate a runtime error if you include a specific database name in the connection string. For security purposes, you may prefer to use a trusted connection in place of specifying SQL credentials in the database connection string. (Chapter 3, "Writing Optimized Data Access Code," describes SQL Server trusted connections in detail.)

Next, you need to run the SQL batch script that creates the SQL Server session state database:

1. Open SQL Query Analyzer.

2. Open the `InstallSqlState.sql` script in a new window. The script is located at `%windir%\Microsoft.NET\Framework\%version%`, where `%version%` is a folder that is named equal to the current installed version of the .NET Framework.

3. Execute the SQL script in Query Analyzer.

The script creates a new database called `ASPState`, which contains a number of stored procedures for writing to, and reading from, the `tempdb` database. When a user assigns a session item, the information is inserted into a temporary table in the `tempdb` database. The new record includes an expiration timestamp that is equivalent to the `<sessionState>` element's timeout attribute value, in `Web.config`.

The advantages of the SQLServer mode are as follows:

*   Session storage is out-of-process, so it does not directly impact the scalability of the ASP.NET application.

*   You can share session items across multiple Web servers and potentially persist them until the service is stopped or the session item is explicitly removed.

*   It is highly efficient storage and retrieval for simple data types and small DataSets.

The disadvantages of the SQLServer mode are as follows:

- It offers less efficient storage and retrieval for large DataSets.

- It potentially impacts application scalability when session items are large and/or the number of session reads and writes is high.

- It only works for objects that can be serialized (in other words, objects based on classes that implement the ISerializable interface).

The SQLServer mode is typically your only choice for session state if you need to guarantee that the session information will be durable. The exception would be if your ASP.NET application stores small strings, and you are willing to persist this information in cookies on the individual client machines. The SQLServer mode is an excellent combination of performance and durability, and it will typically have limited impact on the scalability of an ASP.NET application. This is provided that the session items are modest in size and the number of session reads and writes remains reasonable. The SQLServer mode may not be a good choice if you are persisting large amounts of data, especially in combination with complex object types, such as the DataSet object. The process of serializing information to and from the database is extremely fast for a smaller number of users. But you are likely to notice a measurable delay if your application makes a high number of concurrent requests to the database, especially for larger amounts of information.

Analyzing Session State Performance

We have all heard about the supposed performance implications of using Session objects, but rarely do we see actual performance numbers in print. There is probably a good reason for this—namely, that no published set of numbers really applies to your application. But there is value in looking at the relative performance numbers for a simple ASP.NET Web page that retrieves data from a SQL Server database. ASP.NET introduces a new and unfamiliar set of session management options, and it is interesting to look at how each mode performs relative to the others.

Visual Studio .NET Enterprise Edition provides a tool called Microsoft Application Center Test (ACT), which is a stress test tool for Web applications. The tool allows you to record a Web session and then execute it for multiple simulated users. ACT provides summary statistics and performance counter numbers for the test runs. These metrics enable you to analyze performance and scalability issues with your application. Chapter 7, "Stress Testing and Monitoring ASP.NET Applications," discusses how ACT works in great detail. For now, show simulations for an increasing number of concurrent browsers and measure three important performance and scalability counters:

- **Time to Last Byte (TTLB)**: This counter measures (in milliseconds) how long it takes for the Web application to service a request. TTLB is a key indicator of how scalable an application is.

- **Requests/Sec**: This counter measures how many pages the Web application can serve per second. (This counter is a good measure of scalability.)

- **% Committed Bytes in Use**: This counter measures the amount of memory being utilized on the Web server. This measure includes all processes running on the machine, so you need to adjust the final numbers for the amount of memory usage that is unrelated to the Web application.

Processor utilization is another important metric because it indicates whether your hardware is a limiting factor to your application's scalability. This metric factors into Transaction Cost Analysis (TCA), which provides a quantitative measure of the processing cost of your application for a specific user load. Note that TCA is not a part of this chapter's load testing because our purpose is to study the relative performance of each session state mode. However, Chapter 7, "Stress Testing and Monitoring ASP.NET Applications," discusses it in detail.

ACT also provides a summary of the HTTP Errors count, which is important because performance metrics are only relevant when a significant percentage of the requests have been successfully processed. As the number of concurrent browsers increases, the chance for errors increases as well. A successful request will return an HTTP response code of 200. ACT will commonly return two additional response codes:

- Response code 403 indicates that the server understood the request but is refusing to fulfill it.

- Response code 500 indicates that the server encountered errors in attempting to fulfill the request.

Response code 403 is frequently returned for higher numbers of concurrent browsers. We do not consider performance numbers meaningful unless greater than 97.5 percent of the requests are fulfilled successfully. For this reason, in the following performance test, we ignored all test runs with greater than 10 concurrent browsers.

Sample Web Page with Session State

The sample Web "application" is a single Web page called
`ap_SalesQueryWithSession.aspx`, which executes a stored procedure in the

Northwind database and binds the resulting DataSet to a DataGrid on the page. Specifically, the page executes the [Employee Sales By Country] stored procedure, which accepts two input parameters: @BeginningDate and @EndingDate. Figure 4-2 shows the Web frontend screen for this stored procedure.

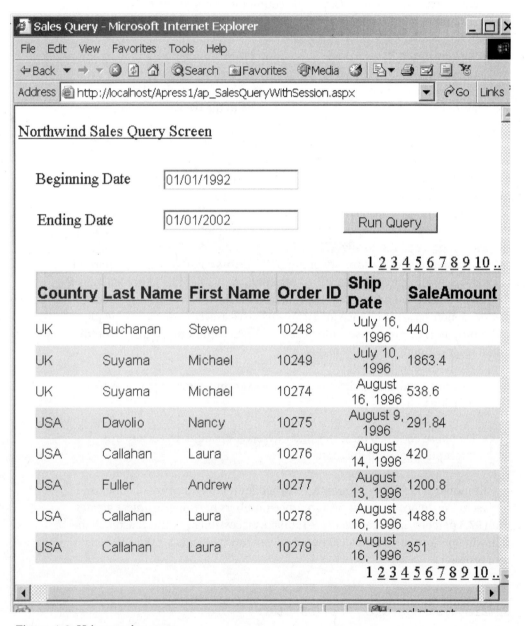

Figure 4-2. Using session state

The first time that the page executes, it retrieves a DataSet directly from the database. This DataSet gets bound to the DataGrid and then assigned to a Session object. In addition, the search parameters are persisted directly to view state so that they are available for comparison purposes. On subsequent requests, the code compares the current textbox values with the values in view state. If they are the same, then the code attempts to retrieve the DataSet from the Session object. If they are different, then the code executes a fresh database request.

This logic is handled inside of the BinDataGrid() function, as shown in Listing 4-1.

Listing 4-1. The BindDataGrid() *Function*

```
Private Sub BindDataGrid()
    Dim objDB As Apress.Database
    Dim arrParams() As String
    Dim sqlDS As DataSet
    Dim blnRefreshDS As Boolean = False
    Dim strJSScript As String = False

    ' Retrieve the connection string from Web.config
    Dim strConn As String
    strConn = ConfigurationSettings.AppSettings("ConnectionString")

    Try
        ' Did the search criteria change?
        If viewstate("BeginningDate") <> Me.ap_txt_beginning_date.Text Then _
            blnRefreshDS = True
        If viewstate("EndingDate") <> Me.ap_txt_ending_date.Text Then _
            blnRefreshDS = True
        ' Look for an existing DataSet object in a session variable
        sqlDS = CType(Session("sqlDataView"), DataSet)
        If sqlDS Is Nothing Then blnRefreshDS = True
        If blnRefreshDS Then
            ' Step 1: Instance a new Database object
            objDB = New Apress.Database(strConn)
            ' Step 2: Execute [Employee Sales By Country]
            arrParams = New String() { _
                "@Beginning_Date", Me.ap_txt_beginning_date.Text, _
                "@Ending_Date", Me.ap_txt_ending_date.Text}
            sqlDS = objDB.RunQueryReturnDS("[Employee Sales By Country]", _
                arrParams)
            Session("sqlDataView") = sqlDS ' Assign DataSet to Session object
```

```
            ' Persist the search parameters in ViewState, for future comparison
            viewstate("BeginningDate") = Me.ap_txt_beginning_date.Text
            viewstate("EndingDate") = Me.ap_txt_ending_date.Text
        End If


        ' Bind the DataView to the DataGrid
        DataGrid1.DataSource = sqlDS
        DataGrid1.DataBind()

    Catch err As Exception
        ' Report the error in a JavaScript alert
        strJSScript = "<SCRIPT LANGUAGE='JavaScript'>alert('" & _
            err.Message"');</SCRIPT>"
        RegisterStartupScript("JSScript1", strJSScript)
    Finally
        objDB = Nothing
    End Try


End Sub
```

Note that Listing 4-1 uses a wrapper function called `RunQueryReturnDS()`, which is a member of a custom data access component that encapsulates ADO.NET database calls. You can view the code listing for this component in the sample project that accompanies this chapter.

Stress Testing with Session State

We stress tested the sample page in four groups of tests: one group for each of the four session state modes. We performed the testing within each group as follows:

1. We configured the page for one of the session state modes: Off, InProc, StateServer, or SQLServer.

2. ACT recorded a Web browser session with three steps:

    a. Load `ap_SalesQueryWithSession.aspx` into the browser for InProc, StateServer, and SQLServer modes. For Off mode, load `ap_SalesQueryWithDataSet.aspx`.

    b. Enter a Beginning Date of 01/01/1992 and an Ending Date of 01/01/2002.

    c. Click the Submit Query button twice: first, to retrieve a DataSet from the database and, second, to retrieve the DataSet from the Session object.

3. The recorded script ran three times, one time each for one, five, and 10 concurrent browsers. The script ran for a 35-second interval with a five-second warm-up period.

The database returned 809 records per query for the time period from 01/01/1992 to 01/01/2002. ACT generated from roughly 600 to 900 connections per test during the 35-second testing interval, depending on the session mode. This means that the tests created anywhere from 200 to 450 Session objects during the testing interval.

We executed the tests in two groups of runs with different architectures:

Group A: We executed these tests against a dedicated Web server using recorded scripts in ACT. The database resided on a separate server on the network. The ACT scripts were executed from the database server against the Web server to avoid generating simulated requests on the same server that processes them. This design spreads the processing burden between multiple servers so that IIS and SQL Server do not have to compete for processor time on the same server. This design should prevent the test results from being skewed by an overburdened processor.

Group B: We executed these tests on a single server that runs the Web server, the SQL Server, and the test scripts. This architecture imposes a high processor burden on the server, but it does not unusually skew the memory usage numbers. We chose this architecture because authentication issues prevented the Group A test results from generating memory usage numbers. For the client machine to bind to these remote counters, the Web server must authenticate requests using a domain account with administrative access (to the Web server). We chose not to set up these permissions levels for this round of testing.

The Group A tests represent better testing practices because the architecture spreads the processing burden between multiple servers. We ran the Group B tests because we could not otherwise generate memory usage numbers for different session state modes.

Before proceeding, we should point out that, in reality, you would likely not design a Web application to have tens to hundreds of session-stored data sets. The ACT tests represent unusually stressful conditions that would not likely be duplicated in the field because you would make a different design decision to avoid this situation. But this is, after all, what stress testing is all about.

Analyzing the Stress Testing Results

By session mode, Table 4-1 shows the change for Group A in the all-important Time To Last Byte (TTLB) parameter as the number of concurrent browsers increases. The numbers are normalized per 100 requests. You will recall that this parameter is a key indicator of application scalability.

Table 4-1. Normalized TTLB by Session State Mode (in Milliseconds per 100 Requests)

CONCURRENT BROWSERS	MODE = OFF	MODE = INPROC	MODE = STATESERVER	MODE = SQLSERVER
1	7.81	4.54	8.27	8.47
5	28.28	20.25	27.25	29.29
10	89.38	46.08	77.29	85.11

The TTLB numbers are similar for Off, StateServer, and SQLServer modes. However, the numbers are lower for InProc mode by up to a factor of two. This number becomes important when the Web server is under heavy load. A lower TTLB number translates into less latency—that is, more requests serviced per second. The testing results indicate this, as shown in Table 4-2, which presents Group A average request rates for each of the session state modes.

Table 4-2. Average Requests per Second by Session State Mode

CONCURRENT BROWSERS	MODE = OFF	MODE = INPROC	MODE = STATESERVER	MODE = SQLSERVER
1	18.86	24.17	18.31	18.11
5	21.66	25.74	21.54	21.34
10	17.23	23.8	18.11	17.6

These numbers may not look very different, but they can translate into a dramatically different number of total serviced requests. For example, over the course of the 35-second testing interval with 10 concurrent users, the Off mode serviced 603 total requests, and the InProc mode serviced 833 total requests.

Based on these numbers, the total number of serviced requests, from highest to lowest, is as follows: InProc, StateServer, SQLServer, Off.

This sequence should sound entirely logical: InProc mode is fastest because it operates in memory and on the same worker process as the application. StateServer mode is the next fastest because it also operates in memory, although you take a responsiveness hit for the time it takes to marshal session data across processes. SQLServer is the next fastest because it takes time to exchange session information with the database. Finally, the Off mode is the least responsive because every response must be regenerated freshly.

One of the knocks against classic InProc session variables is that they are scalability killers. They exhaust server resources rapidly as the number of concurrent users increases. This is a double hit when you consider that the Web server could be using some of this memory for caching, which would help service requests even faster by avoiding a complete re-creation of the response. In fact, session variables continue to use server resources, even if the user is not actually storing any session-specific information. Even a lightly used session variable continues to consume server resources. The overall result is that the Web server services fewer requests as the number of concurrent users increases.

The numbers in Table 4-2 appear to verify this trend, although with an interesting twist. Each mode services the most requests for five concurrent users but a fewer number for one user and for 10 concurrent users. Figure 4-3 shows a graph of the Group A average requests per second by session state mode.

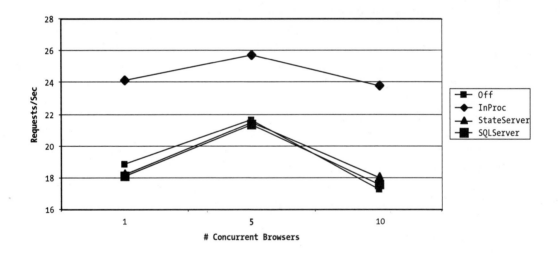

Figure 4-3. Group A: Average requests/sec by session state mode

This "triangular trend" indicates that five concurrent users receive better responsiveness than one concurrent user. This trend may reflect the influence of SQL Server, which caches data pages for successive requests, and SQL connection pooling, which makes a set of connections readily available for multiple users. The number drops again for 10 concurrent users because it exceeds the pool number and begins to be high enough to burden the server.

A better measure of scalability changes is to look at the change in TTLB as the number of concurrent users increases. Figure 4-4 graphs the change in TTLB for each session state mode as the number of concurrent users increases. The numbers are normalized based on 100 requests to adjust for the fact that differ-ent session modes service different numbers of requests. For example, in the Group A tests, InProc mode serviced 846 total requests, and SQLServer mode serviced 634 total requests.

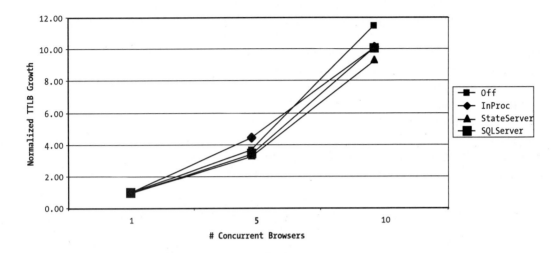

Figure 4-4. Group A: Normalized TTLB by session state mode

The TTLB numbers shown in Figure 4-4 exhibit subtle differences, except for InProc mode, which experienced the lowest TTLB numbers. This indicates that the InProc mode can service a superior number of requests and remain more responsive than other session modes. We attempted to test more than 10 concur-rent browsers, but the number of request errors exceeded 20 percent, which would not produce meaningful numbers for comparison.

Based on our limited data set, it is useful to look at relative growth rates in TTLB, as shown in Figure 4-5. The TTLB is normalized for each session mode, based on one concurrent user. For example, TTLB grows a factor of 10.05 for SQLServer mode as the number of concurrent browsers increases from 1 to 10.

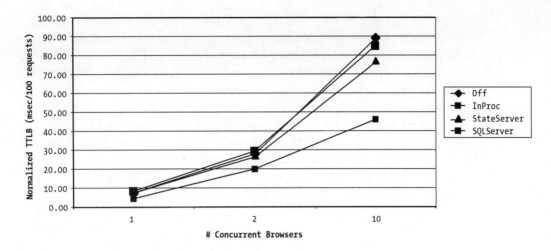

Figure 4-5. Group A: Normalized TTLB growth by session state mode

The differences in the TTLB growth rates are subtle, and it is perhaps a stretch to infer patterns from them. However, based on these numbers, the growth rate in TTLB for each session mode from highest to lowest is as follows: Off, InProc, SQLServer, StateServer.

This trend indicates that the Off mode experiences the greatest growth in TTLB as the number of concurrent users increases. The InProc mode and the SQLServer mode experience lesser growth in TTLB, and the StateServer mode experiences the lowest. The results simply indicate the trend in TTLB growth and are not a replacement for actual stress testing and observation at higher user loads. These limited results simply indicate that responsiveness goes down as the number of concurrent browsers increases and that the Off mode experiences the greatest decrease in responsiveness. As the stock market mantra goes, current results are not an indication of future performance. In a similar sense, TTLB growth changes at low user loads may not indicate their behavior at higher (and more critical) user loads.

A further note of wisdom is that every system will experience bottlenecks at some level, whether it is related to the processor speed, to available memory, to network latency, or to the number of active threads being processed. Your goal must be to stay ahead of the curve by designing your system to manage its expected loads as efficiently as possible. Ultimately, performance tuning is important because it allows your system to handle higher loads without a redesign or without having to purchase bigger, more expensive hardware.

The other piece of the scalability puzzle is memory usage. We were unable to generate memory usage numbers for Group A tests because ACT could not bind to the remote Memory counter on the Web server (recall that ACT is running on a separate server from the Web server). However, ACT has no problem binding to the Memory counter on the same server. As a workaround, we ran an alternative set of tests on a single server (Group B).

Figure 4-6 shows the Group B normalized TTLB values, based on 100 requests. The result pattern is different from the equivalent Group A test. The SQLServer and StateServer modes experience much higher TTLB values, compared to the InProc and Off modes, by up to two orders of magnitude. This difference may reflect the greater processor burden on the single server. Simply put, with more demands on the processor, the SQLServer and StateServer modes suffered because they are more dependent on processor availability. We are not attempting to explain the numbers away, but we are simply presenting the TTLB test results so that you can keep them in mind when evaluating the memory usage results.

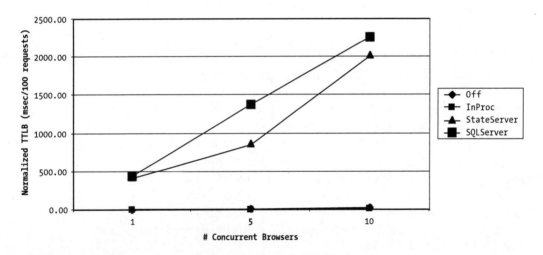

Figure 4-6. Group B: Normalized TTLB by session state mode

Figure 4-7 shows actual memory usage by session mode where memory usage is defined as the percentage of committed bytes in memory (as compared to the total amount of memory available). This is an actual measure of memory usage on the server, and it reflects the level of burden that each session mode places on available server memory.

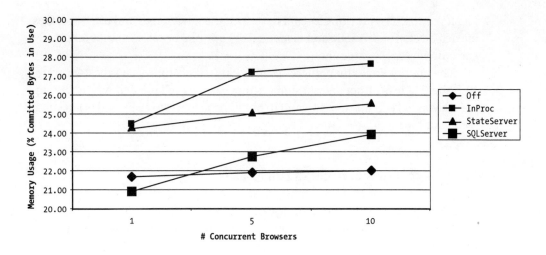

Figure 4-7. Group B: Actual memory usage by session state mode

The InProc mode clearly uses the highest amount of memory, followed by the StateServer mode. The Off mode uses the least amount of memory, which is to be expected. The SQLServer mode falls somewhere in between, although it is interesting to note that its growth curve in memory usage is steeper than for other modes. It is unfortunate that ACT could not generate meaningful numbers with more than 10 concurrent browsers because it would be interesting to see where the trends continued.

Memory usage numbers are an important indication of how a session mode impacts server resources. But as with every counter, it only tells a part of the story. For example, from Figure 4-7 alone, you might infer that the InProc mode is a potential scalability killer because it exerts the highest burden on server memory. But then, consider that it services a far greater number of requests than the other modes. Increased memory usage may be a small price to pay for the far greater number of requests that you can service, compared to other session modes. Add to this the fact that the InProc mode experiences lower TTLB growth rates than other session modes (based on both Group A and Group B test results). The InProc mode suddenly appears to be an attractive option for managing session state.

In closing out this section, we want to emphasize its overall message, which is that session state performance is not as clear-cut as many texts would lead you to believe. For example, many texts brand the InProc mode as a guaranteed scalability killer that should always be avoided on heavily trafficked Web sites. Our tests have demonstrated that the picture is more complex because the InProc mode offers far superior performance in exchange for higher memory usage.

Of course, there are other considerations that go into choosing a session state mode. For example, if you must persist session state to disk or manage it in a Web farm, then InProc mode will not meet your needs, no matter how good or bad it may be. The previous section described the advantages and disadvantages of each session state mode and discussed the optimal usage scenarios for each mode.

The bottom line is that only you can decide which approach is best for your Web site. There is no set of test numbers that can ever tell the definitive story, and we ask you to keep this in mind and to possibly be inspired to extend our testing with your own.

Programming with Session State

Session objects provide a straightforward application programming interface (API) that is easy to code against. Table 4-3 summarizes useful Session object members.

Table 4-3. Session Object Members

MEMBER	DESCRIPTION
SessionID	This read-only property gets the unique session ID used to identify the session.
Timeout	This read-write property gets or sets the timeout period (in minutes) between requests before the session is terminated.
Keys	This read-only property gets a collection of the keys of all values stored in the session.
IsReadOnly	This read-only property gets a value indicating whether a session is read-only. You set this property at the individual page level using <%@ Page EnableSessionState="ReadOnly" %>.
Add()	This method adds a new item to session state. Its syntax is Add(name As String, value As Object).
Clear()	This method clears all values and references from session state.
Abandon()	This method cancels the current session. If the session gets reinitialized, then the user gets a new session with a different session ID. Session objects store information by associating an object reference with a named index, or *key*, as follows: Session("[Name]") = [Object] Or, alternatively: Session.Add("[Name]", [Object])

NOTE *If you add a session variable that already exists, then the existing session variable will simply be updated with the new object or value. The previous object, or value, will be overwritten without a warning.*

Recall that in .NET, all data types inherit from the System.Object type. This enables Session objects to store virtually any .NET data type with two important exceptions:

If the session mode is StateServer, then you can only assign objects that support binary serialization. For example, the DataSet object supports serialization, and the DataView object does not. *Serialization* is the process that allows an object to be represented in an XML document or as a binary stream. The object may then be stored, or transported in this form, and then faithfully re-created from the XML document or stream. However, if the session mode is InProc, then the object need not support binary serialization.

You should not store objects, such as the DataReader, that maintain open connections to a database in Session objects. If you must assign a data object to a session, then use a disconnected object such as a DataSet or DataView.

You can iterate through a collection of session keys using the following:

```
Dim objKey As [Object]
For Each objKey in Session.Keys
    Console.WriteLn(objKey.Name) ' Write out the name of the key
Next
```

Retrieving session values is as simple as assigning the stored object back to a local variable:

```
sqlDV = Session("sqlDataView")
```

This method implicitly casts the session reference to the appropriate data type. You need to do this step because the Session object stores its references as Object data types for maximum flexibility. An alternative to implicit casting is to explicitly cast the data type when the reference is retrieved:

```
Dim sqlDV As DataView
sqlDV = CType(Session("sqlDataView"), DataView)
```

Explicit casting is always preferable to implicit casting. Once you have retrieved an object reference, you should always verify it was retrieved successfully before using it in code. The easiest way to do this is to execute the assignment and then check to see if the object exists:

```
sqlDV = CType(Session("sqlDataView"), DataView)
If sqlDV Is Nothing Then
    ' Recreate the object
End If
```

Finally, the Session object provides two event handlers for adding code when a session is first created and when it is abandoned. The "Understanding the Global.asax File" section discusses the `Session_Start()` and `Session_End()` event handlers in more detail.

Session State Management in Web Farms

ASP.NET makes it easy to manage session state in Web farms. The StateServer and SQLServer modes are equally good candidates for centralized session state management, so you need to decide which mode is right for your application. The StateServer mode may offer better performance than the SQLServer mode. However, the SQLServer mode guarantees that session state information will be durable. The StateServer mode cannot provide the same guarantee because it provides in-memory storage.

Keep in mind that you may not need a centralized State server in your Web farm. If you are using an IP redirector, such as Cisco's LocalDirector or F5 Network's BIGIP, then a client's requests get routed to the same server for the duration of their session. In this case, you can maintain session state on individual servers, using either the InProc or StateServer modes. You do run a risk that IP redirection may not always work. If a server crashes or becomes unavailable, then the client will be routed to another server, which will have no record of their session information. For this reason, you may want to consider using centralized session state management.

If you decide on using the StateServer mode, then you need to start the ASP.NET State Service on one of the servers in the Web farm. You must designate only one server in the Web farm for managing session state because you are proceeding on the assumption that there is no fixed redirection of requests in the Web farm. The advantage of this approach is its flexibility in being able to manage state for all servers in the Web farm. However, the disadvantage of this approach is that it creates a single potential point of failure. In exchange for flexibility, you run a higher risk that the State server may fail and be completely unavailable for all servers in the Web farm.

Next, you need to modify the Web.config file for each server in the Web farm to point to the centralized State server. For example:

```
<sessionState mode="StateServer" stateConnectionString="tcpip=127.0.0.1:42424"
        cookieless="false" timeout="20" />
```

Obviously, for this connection string to work, the State server must provide a fixed IP and must not use Dynamic Host Control Protocol (DHCP). If you decide on using the SQLServer mode, then you need to set up a central database server and run the SQL script that creates the ASPState database. Next, you need to modify the Web.config file for each server in the Web farm to point to the same SQL Server database. For example:

```
<sessionState mode="SQLServer"
    sqlConnectionString="server= machineName\sqlServer;uid=myId;pwd=myPwd;"
    cookieless="false" timeout="20" />
```

If the reliability of your session is of utmost importance, then you can implement state management on a cluster of multiple database servers so that no single point of failure exists.

This concludes the discussion of session state management. Next, turn your attention to the topic of application state management.

Overview of Application Management

Application state management enables information to be shared between multiple users of the same Web application. In classic ASP, you manage application state using an HttpApplicationState handler, which is encapsulated by the ASP Application object. This object is still available in ASP.NET, although it has additional members and gives you new ways to enumerate through a collection of HttpApplicationState variables. The Application object is easy to work with, in terms of configuration and coding, and this makes it a tempting option. Unfortunately, the Application object is also problematic because it does a poor job of synchronizing changes from multiple users. Only one user at a time (technically, one thread at a time) should be allowed to modify an Application object variable. This is a big issue in the .NET environment, which supports free-threaded objects. To ensure single-thread updates, the Application object provides Lock() and UnLock() methods that prevent other users from simultaneously updating the object. The Lock() method actually locks the *entire* Application object, even though the user may be updating just one of several available object variables. This feature can cause concurrency problems if several users attempt to lock the object at the same time. Ultimately, concurrency problems lead to scalability problems as users are forced to wait to commit their changes. Worse yet, concurrency lockups could cause one or more users to deadlock and experience instability with their sessions. As a result, Application state is only appropriate for values that are read often but are updated infrequently.

ASP.NET provides a new and superior alternative to the Application object in the form of a Cache engine, which provides better control over data storage and retrieval. The Cache engine provides a more sophisticated API than the Application object as well as better concurrency handling. The following sections demonstrate the different options that ASP.NET provides for managing application state.

Permanent vs. Transient Application State

You need to store two kinds of information at the application level:

- **Permanent information**: This applies globally across an application and changes rarely. Examples include connection string information or configuration setting values referenced throughout the application.

- **Transient information**: This information is still global in scope, but it changes with some frequency; examples include counters, such as a Web site visitor counter. Users must all modify the same copy of this value to keep a running count.

Although you could store both kinds of information in an Application object, ASP.NET provides better alternatives.

Understanding Permanent Application State

You can store permanent information in the Web.config file and reference it programmatically at runtime. At the simplest level, you can assign custom information to a new key within the <appSettings> node:

```
<appSettings>
    <add key="ConnectionString" value="server=;uid=sa;pwd=ap1;database=dev;" />
    <add key="SysAdminEmailAddress" value="sysadmin@yourcompany.com" />
</appSettings>
```

You can then reference these keys from any code-behind file using the ConfigurationSettings object, which is a member of the `System.Configuration` namespace:

```
Dim strConn As String
strConn = ConfigurationSettings.AppSettings("ConnectionString")
```

The `<appSettings>` element is useful, but it is restricted to storing name-value pairs. The `Web.config` file also allows you to define a custom configuration section, which can have a more complex structure. For example, you could define a section that tracks parent (myMenuGroup) and child (myMenuItem) menu options:

```
<configSections>
        <!-- Declares a section group called myMenuGroup -->
        <sectionGroup name="myMenuGroup">
                <!-- Declares a section name called myMenuItem -->
                <section name="myMenuItem"
                    type="System.Configuration.DictionarySectionHandler, System"/>
        </sectionGroup>
</configSections>
```

You could then implement the sections as follows:

```
<myMenuGroup>
        <myMenuItem>
                <add key="Login" value="login.aspx"/>
                <add key="Logout" value="logout.aspx"/>
        </myMenuItem>
</myMenuGroup>
```

You must define and implement custom configuration settings inside `Web.config`. Once you do this, you can reference the settings from any code-behind file in the project using the `GetConfig()` method of the ConfigurationSettings object:

```
Dim dctMenuItems As IDictionary
Dim enmKeys As IDictionaryEnumerator
```

```
dctMenuItems = ConfigurationSettings.GetConfig("myMenuGroup/myMenuItem")
enmKeys = dctMenuItems.GetEnumerator()
While enmKeys.MoveNext
    If enmKeys.Value.GetType.ToString = "System.String" Then
        Response.Write(enmKeys.Key & " = " & enmKeys.Value & "<BR>")
    End If
End While
```

The `Web.config` file is an excellent choice for persisting permanent application information that must be referenced by, but never altered by, the application. Clearly, the `Web.config` file is only capable of storing a limited range of data types, so it is most suitable for storing configuration values. An added advantage is that the application automatically picks up changes to this file without requiring a restart. (ASP.NET automatically restarts when it detects a change event.) This makes it easy to change application settings on the fly or to deploy multiple versions of the same `Web.config` file to different environments, such as staging and production.

CAUTION   *The* `Web.config` *file is a text file and should therefore not be used for storing sensitive information. IIS will not allow the* `Web.config` *file to be accessed by an outside browser, but you should still be cautious with the type of information you store in this file.*

Some developers refuse to store SQL connection string information in the `Web.config` file. We, on the other hand, store SQL login credentials as long as they reference an account that has highly restricted access to the database.

Chapter 2, "Introducing ASP.NET Applications," discusses the `Web.config` file in great detail.

Understanding Transient Application State

ASP.NET provides two main classes for managing transient application state:

- HttpApplicationState

- Cache

Let's discuss each of these in turn.

Configuring and Using the HttpApplicationState Class

The HttpApplicationState class is instanced once for every ASP.NET application, and it provides shared application state for all requests. This class is conveniently exposed by the Page object's `Application` property. From here on, we refer to the HttpApplicationState class as the *Application object*, which represents a single instance of the class. Think of the Application object as a collection container that enables you to manage a collection of globally scoped variables. Like the Session object, the Application object provides a straightforward API that is easy to code against. Table 4-4 summarizes useful Application object members.

Table 4-4. HttpApplicationState Class Members

MEMBER	DESCRIPTION
Add()	This method adds a new item to application state. Its syntax is `Add(name As String, value As Object)`.
Lock()	This method locks access to a specific application state variable.
Unlock()	This method unlocks access to a specific application state variable.
Set()	This method sets the value of a specific application variable. Its syntax is `Set(name As String, value As Object)`.
Contents	This read-only property gets a reference to the collection of Application variables that were added through code using the Application object's API.
StaticObjects	This read-only property gets a reference to the collection of Application objects that were added in `Global.asax` using the `<object>` tag.
RemoveAll()	This method removes the entire collection of Application variables.
Remove()	This method removes a specific Application variable from the collection. Its syntax is `Remove(name As String)`.
RemoveAll()	This method removes the entire collection of Application variables.

The Application object is programmatically accessible via the `Application` property of the Page object. Unlike the Session object, the Application object does not require any settings in the `Web.config` file. You can add application-level variables to the collection in two ways:

- Programmatically using the Application object's API

- Using the `<object>` tag in `Global.asax`

For example, you can assign a String object programmatically:

```
Dim objStr As System.String
Page.Application.Add("myStr", objStr)
```

Alternatively, you can instance the String object at the application level in `Global.asax`:

```
<%@ Application Codebehind="Global.asax.vb" Inherits="Apress1.Global" %>
<object runat="server" id="myStr" class="System.String" scope="application" />
```

Now that you have instanced the String object, you can set and retrieve its value from any page within the application. For example, on `Page1.aspx`, you can set the value:

```
' Set the string
Dim MyString1 As String = "My global string value."
Page.Application.Set("myStr", MyString1)
```

Then on `Page2.aspx`, you can retrieve the value:

```
' Retrieve the string
Dim MyString2 As String = Page.Application.Item("myStr")
Response.Write("MyString2 = " & MyString2.ToString())
```

Observant readers will notice that we assigned MyString1 to the Application object without locking the object first. Had we been more careful, we would have used the available locking methods:

```
' Alternative set
Dim MyString2 As String = "My global string value2."
Page.Application.Lock()
Page.Application.Set("myStr", MyString2)
Page.Application.UnLock()
```

The moral of the story is that the Application object allows you to set values without requiring the safety check of the `Lock()` and `UnLock()` methods. Without this check, you risk a collision with another user who is updating the Application object at the same time. On the other hand, if you keep the Application locked for too long, you risk a deadlock with another user.

In summary, the advantages of the Application object are that Application objects are easy to code with and easy to configure.

The disadvantages of the Application object are as follows:

- You cannot share Application objects across multiple Web servers. Stored values are only available to the application thread that instanced them.

- Application objects are not durable. They reside in memory and will be lost if the dedicated process crashes or is restarted.

- Application objects greatly impact scalability because they are multi-threaded and run a high risk of causing deadlocks and concurrency issues when multiple users attempt updates at the same time.

- Application objects use memory resources, which can potentially have a significant impact on the Web application's performance and scalability—particularly if the Application object stores significantly sized objects, such as a populated DataSet.

- Application objects do not optimize resource usage, for example, by expiring underused items. Application items remain in memory all the time, whether they are heavily used or not.

Let's now take a look at another alternative for managing transient application state: the Cache class.

Configuring and Using the Cache Class

ASP.NET supports application data caching, which allows expensive resources to be stored in memory for fast retrieval. Chapter 5, "Caching ASP.NET Applications," discusses caching in full detail, so this section serves as a quick introduction to the feature. We present just enough detail to demonstrate how caching is a good alternative to the Application object for managing transient application state.

The Cache class provides optimized storage for persisting objects in memory. Unlike the Application object, cached items remain available only for as long as they are needed. You can assign cached items with expiration policies. The Cache class provides much more control over cached items compared to the Application object. These advantages include the following:

- **Customized expiration**: You can assign cache items individual expiration policies that indicate when they should expire and be removed from the cache. The Cache class supports three expiration modes, including absolute, sliding, and dependency expiration:

  - Absolute mode specifies an exact date and time for expiring the item.

  - Sliding mode specifies a time interval for expiring the item, based on the last time that the item was accessed.

  - Dependency mode links an item's expiration to a fixed resource, such as a file. The item automatically expires and refreshes whenever the dependency changes.

- **Memory management**: The Cache class automatically removes underused items from the cache. In addition, items will be systematically evicted from the cache when server resources become low.

- **Concurrency management**: The Cache class automatically manages concurrent updates to the same item, without requiring that the user place a lock on the item.

Durability is the key difference between items stored in the cache vs. those stored in an Application object. Cache items are not guaranteed to persist in memory, although you can ensure they will by setting specific expiration policies. As server resources become low, the Cache class will evict items based on their relative priority. Heavily used items have high priority and will typically be evicted last. You can set items with specific priorities to influence their eviction order. But, ultimately, all items are subject to eviction if server resources become tight enough. The Application object, on the other hand, will continue to hold its references, regardless of the impact on server resources.

Like the Application object, the Cache class allows you to add items implicitly, using basic key-value pairs:

```
Dim sqlDS As DataSet
Page.Cache("MyDS") = sqlDS
```

The Cache class also provides explicit Add() and Insert() methods for adding cache items with advanced settings, such as expiration policies and priorities. The Insert() method is overloaded, so it provides the most flexibility for adding items. For example, this is how you add an item using a 30-minute sliding expiration:

```
Dim sqlDV As DataView
Page.Cache.Insert("MyDV", sqlDV, Nothing, Cache.NoAbsoluteExpiration, _
    New TimeSpan(0, 0, 30))
```

You can retrieve items from the cache implicitly:

```
Dim sqlDV As DataView
sqlDV = Page.Cache("MyDV")   ' Returns Nothing reference if item has been evicted
```

Or, explicitly using the Get() method:

```
Dim sqlDV As DataView
sqlDV = Page.Cache.Get("MyDV") ' Returns Nothing reference if item has been evicted
```

Finally, you can explicitly remove items from the cache using the Remove() method:

```
Dim MyDS As DataSet
MyDS  = Page.Cache.Remove("MyDS") ' Evaluates to True
```

Because cache items may expire, or be evicted, any code that uses them must have the ability to re-create the object in the event that it cannot be pulled from the cache. Consider the following code, which uses the GenerateDataSet() method to create a populated DataSet object:

```
If Not IsNothing(Page.Cache.Item("MyDS")) Then
    sqlDS = Page.Cache.Get("MyDS")
Else
    sqlDS = GenerateDataSet() ' Regenerate the DataSet
    Page.Cache.Insert("MyDS", sqlDS, Nothing, "12/31/2020", _
        Cache.NoSlidingExpiration)
End If
```

In this example, the code attempts to retrieve the DataSet from the cache. If it cannot be found, then it must be regenerated and added to the cache again. This example illustrates an important point: The Cache class is best suited for storing objects that have page-level scope and that can be re-created if needed. The Cache is global to an application, so it may technically be used for storing "application-level" objects. But in practice, you would not want every page to have to check for, and re-create, the Application object item. However, this is not an issue for page-level objects.

The Cache class is a superior alternative to the Application object for all purposes except when you need to store a truly global object reference—that is, a reference that may be accessed from any page within an application and that must be counted on to be there. The Application object is not as efficient as the Cache class, but it does offer more convenience when you want to guarantee that an item will always be available. The Application object does not persist items in the event that the application crashes, but then, neither does the Cache class.

In summary, the advantages of the Cache class are as follows:

- The Cache class optimizes memory management by using expiration policies and by automatically removing underused items.

- The Cache provides automatic concurrency management.

- The Cache class is easy to code with and easy to configure.

The disadvantages of the Cache class are as follows:

- Cache items are not guaranteed to be persistent in the cache. This requires contingency coding in code blocks that use cached object references.

- You cannot share cached objects across multiple Web servers. Object references are only available to the application thread that instanced them.

This concludes our discussion on application state management. Next, we discuss the Global.asax file and show how it helps you design optimal ASP.NET applications.

Understanding the Global.asax File

The Global.asax file provides access to events handlers for the HttpApplicationState class, for the HttpSessionState class, and for any HTTP module registered for the application. The file is optional, and you are not required to implement any of the event handlers. The Global.asax file essentially provides a gateway to all HTTP requests received by the application. It provides a centralized location where you can intercept client requests and use that information to modify custom application state information. The Global.asax file generally serves two purposes:

- Handling events for the Application and Session objects

- Centralizing application-wide tasks

This section focuses on the role of Global.asax both for state management and for centralizing application-wide tasks.

Table 4-5 summarizes the important Application and Session object event handlers that you can access in the Global.asax file.

Table 4-5. Global.asax *Event Handlers*

EVENT HANDLER	DESCRIPTION
Application_Start()	Called the first time an HttpApplication class is instanced. The Global.asax file has access to a pool of HttpApplication instances, but this event handler is called only once.
Application_BeginRequest()	Handles the HttpApplication BeginRequest() event. This is called when a new HTTP request is received by the application.
Application_EndRequest()	Handles the HttpApplication EndRequest() event. This is called when an HTTP request has finished processing but before the response has been delivered to the client.
Application_End()	Called when all HttpApplication instances unload. This occurs when the application is restarted, which may occur manually or when the Web.config file changes.
Application_Error()	Called when an unhandled exception is raised anywhere in the application. You can add generic code for managing unhandled exceptions, such as logging the issue and emailing a system administrator.
Session_Start()	Called when a new session is started.
Session_End()	Called when a session is abandoned. This event handler will not be called if the client simply closes their browser. It will be called when the current session is explicitly abandoned.

For example, consider a simple set of counters that track the following information:

- AllRequests: This tracks the total number of requests received by the application.

- AllUniqueSessions: This tracks the number of unique sessions created in the application.

- SalesQueryCounter: This tracks the number of requests for a specific page in the application, namely, ap_SalesQuery.aspx.

Listing 4-2 shows one example of how the Global.asax file manages these counters.

Listing 4-2. Seeing Global.asax in Action

```
Public Class Global
    Inherits System.Web.HttpApplication
    Sub Application_Start(ByVal sender As Object, ByVal e As EventArgs)
        ' Fires when the application is started
        Application("AllRequests") = 0
        Application("AllUniqueSessions") = 0
        Application("SalesQueryCounter") = 0
    End Sub

    Sub Session_Start(ByVal sender As Object, ByVal e As EventArgs)
        ' Fires when the session is started
        Application("AllUniqueSessions") += 1
    End Sub

    Sub Application_BeginRequest(ByVal sender As Object, ByVal e As EventArgs)
        ' Fires at the beginning of each request
        Application("AllRequests") += 1
        If InStr(Me.Request.Url.ToString, "ap_SalesQuery.aspx") > 0 Then
            Application("SalesQueryCounter") += 1
        End If
    End Sub
End Class
```

These counters are all initialized in the Application_Start() event, which fires the first time the application is instanced. The AllUniqueSessions counter gets incremented in the Session_Start event (assuming that session state is enabled for the application). Finally, the SalesQueryCounter counter gets incremented in the Application_BeginRequest event, which fires every time the application receives a new request. The code uses the Request object's Url property to determine which page the user has requested.

Managing Unhandled Exceptions with the Application_Error() Event Handler

The Application_Error() event handler is another useful method that is called whenever an unhandled exception occurs anywhere within the application. You can design an application for all foreseeable exceptions, but it is likely that unhandled exceptions will occur, particularly when the application is moved from a development to a production environment. Listing 4-3 shows how you can have unhandled exceptions logged to the application event log, then emailed to the system administrator.

Listing 4-3. Managing Unhandled Exceptions with the Application_Error()
Event Handler

```
Imports System.Diagnostics
Imports System.Web.Mail


Sub Application_Error(ByVal sender As Object, ByVal e As EventArgs)

    ' Step 1: Write an error to the event log
    Dim strMessage As String
    strMessage = "Url " & Me.Request.UserHostAddress & Me.Request.Path & _
        " Error: " & Server.GetLastError.ToString()

    Dim Log As New EventLog()
    Log.Source = "ASP.NET 1.0.3705.0"
    Log.WriteEntry(strMessage, EventLogEntryType.Error)

    ' Step 2: Send a mail message to the System Administrator
    Dim objMail As Mail.MailMessage = New Mail.MailMessage()
    With objMail
        .BodyFormat = Mail.MailFormat.Html
        .To = "sysadmin@yourcompany.com"
        .From = "sysadmin@yourcompany.com"
        .Subject = "Exception Report for " & Me.Request.UserHostAddress
        .Body = "<html><body><h2>" & Me.Request.UserHostAddress & _
            Me.Request.Path & "</h2>" & Me.Server.GetLastError.ToString() & _
            "</body></html>"
    End With

    ' Step 4: Send the Mail message (SMTP must be configured on the Web server)
    Dim objSmtpMail As Mail.SmtpMail
    objSmtpMail.SmtpServer = "MySMTPServer"
```

```
        objSmtpMail.Send(objMail)
        objSmtpMail = Nothing
        objMail = Nothing
End Sub
```

As an added convenience, you can set the `<customErrors>` element in the `Web.config` file to automatically redirect remote users to a friendly custom error page. This redirection will occur after the `Application_Error()` event handler has been called. Local users (in other words, developers who are working on local-host) will continue to see a standard error screen that displays full exception details, including the call stack:

```
<customErrors mode="RemoteOnly" defaultRedirect="ap_CustomErrorPage.aspx"/>
```

In summary, the `Global.asax` file serves as a central location for efficiently managing application and session state and as central location for managing application-wide tasks. The `Global.asax` file plays a key role in developing optimal ASP.NET applications.

Using a Custom Base Class for Global.asax

The Application object is not the only way to store application-wide values. In fact, it may be inefficient to store certain kinds of information this way. For example, consider the counter example from Listing 4-2. The three counters are initialized and incremented within the `Global.asax` file only, and they are never modified outside of this file. There is no need to use an Application object for storing this information, particularly if you want to keep the counter values private and inaccessible from the rest of the application.

An alternative approach to using the Application object is to create a custom base class for the `Global.asax` file. This base class inherits from the HttpApplication class, just like the default Global class that sits behind the `Global.asax` file. The custom base class provides the same members as the default `Global.asax` file, but even better, you can extend the class with additional members, such as custom properties for tracking counters.

Listing 4-4 illustrates one possible custom base class.

Listing 4-4. Creating a Custom Base Class for the Global.asax *File*

```
Imports System.Diagnostics
Public Class apCustomModule
    Inherits System.Web.HttpApplication
```

```
    Private m_Counter As Integer

    Public Property MyCounter() As Integer
        Get
            MyCounter = m_Counter
        End Get
        Set(ByVal Value As Integer)
            m_Counter = Value
        End Set
    End Property

    Sub Application_Start(ByVal sender As Object, ByVal e As EventArgs)
        ' Fires when the application is started
        MyCounter = 0
    End Sub

    Sub Application_BeginRequest(ByVal sender As Object, ByVal e As EventArgs)
        ' Fires at the beginning of each request
        MyCounter = MyCounter + 1
    End Sub

    Sub Application_End(ByVal sender As Object, ByVal e As EventArgs)
        ' Fires when the application ends
        Dim Log As New EventLog()
        Log.Source = "ASP.NET 1.0.3705.0"
        Log.WriteEntry("Number of Application Requests: " & MyCounter, _
            EventLogEntryType.Information)
    End Sub

End Class
```

You can find this code implemented in the sample application, AspNetChap4A, which accompanies this chapter. Notice that the class inherits from the HttpApplication class and that it implements selected event handlers. The class provides a property called MyCounter, which is equivalent to the AllRequests counter from Listing 4-2. This property value gets incremented in the Application_BeginRequest() event handler—that is, once for every client request.

The next and final step is to update the @ Application directive in the Global.asax file to inherit from the custom base class instead of from the default Global class:

```
<%@ Application Codebehind="Global.asax.vb"
    Inherits="MyApp.apCustomModule" %>
```

The custom base class resides in memory continuously for as long as the application remains loaded. As a result, the MyCounter property acts like a static variable, such that all application users will share one instance. When the application does unload, the current counter value gets written to the application event log.

One caveat with this approach is that you run the risk of thread blocking issues if ASP.NET fails to manage the user load correctly. ASP.NET does a good job of managing its thread pool and is efficient at managing its pool of HttpApplication instances. You should not encounter problems updating custom properties if they encapsulate simple data types. To be on the safe side, make sure you stress test your Web application and monitor the number of errors the application encounters under heavy load.

In summary, the Global.asax file serves as a central location for efficiently managing application and session state and as a centralized location for managing application-wide tasks. The Global.asax file plays a key role in developing optimal ASP.NET applications.

Choosing the Right ASP.NET State Management Option

State management is a vastly more complicated topic in ASP.NET than it is in classic ASP. The choices you need to make are not as clear-cut as before because you now have different options for accomplishing the same task. ASP.NET *does* allow you to manage state in the most optimal way for your Web application. The burden is on you, the developer, to make the right choices on which approach you need to take.

When considering using session state, ask the following questions:

Does the application require centralized session state management, or can it be managed on individual Web servers? ASP.NET provides StateServer and SQLServer modes for centralized session state. ASP.NET provides InProc, StateServer, and SQLServer modes for server-specific session state.

Does the application require cookie-based or cookieless session state? Most Web clients support cookies, so cookie-based session state is a good approach for the vast majority of Web clients. Cookieless session state requires the application to contain relative links only. Also, the application is more vulnerable to losing a session reference because the ID is stored in plain text in the URL, which can be easily tampered with.

What kind of information needs to be stored? The InProc session state mode stores any data type, although you should be careful not to store objects that could present threading issues. The StateServer and SQLServer session state modes can only store objects that support binary serialization. This includes most of the simple data types (string, integer, Boolean) as well as some specialized objects, including the DataSet object.

Does the application really need a Session object for all information? Session state management is typically more expensive than application state management because the server provides every client with its own copy of the same information. You should only store information in session state that is truly specific to an individual client. Technically, the ap_SalesQueryWithSession.aspx page presented earlier is *not* a good use of session state and would be better suited for caching. This is because the DataSet contents vary by request parameters, not by individual client.

When considering using application state, ask the following questions:

Does the application require permanent application state? Permanent state values are guaranteed to be available as long as the ASP.NET application remains loaded. You can store permanent state values in the Web.config file. This file is suitable for storing configuration values, but it cannot be used to store objects. Permanent state values may also be stored in the HttpApplicationState class, but then they must be compiled with the application, and there is nothing to prevent them from being modified at runtime. Alternatively, you can set up a public shared variable in the Global.asax file and initialize it with a reference value or object. This variable is accessible throughout the application; however, it does not provide concurrency management. You should not set shared variables more than once, and they should be primarily read-only for the application to prevent concurrency problems. Often these variables are set once (initialized) in the Global.asax file and then are treated as read-only throughout the rest of the application.

Does the application require transient application state? The HttpApplicationState class (the Application object) stores a wide range of objects and data types in memory, and it will persist them until a user alters them or until the application unloads. The Cache class provides more granular control over application data, but it does not guarantee that items will remain persistent in memory. Application code that references cached items must have a contingency for re-creating an item that cannot be retrieved from the cache. The Application object avoids this inconvenience, but it provides none of the storage efficiencies of the Cache class.

How frequently will stored items be updated? You should store reference values used throughout an application in the Web.config file because ASP.NET will automatically reload the application when this file changes. You must store reference objects used throughout an application in the Application object. If one or more of these references changes, then you must recompile the application. Alternatively, you can store object references in the Cache class using dependency expiration. For example, a DataSet may be added to the cache, and the cached reference will be used throughout the application as long as its dependency resource remains unchanged.

Does the client need direct access to the item? If the client does not require direct access to an application item, then consider creating a custom base class for the Global.asax file and storing the item using a class property. For example, you can store a request counter in a class property and automatically increment in it the Global.asax Application_BeginRequest() method.

Ultimately, your choice for managing state comes down to the type of item, how it gets accessed, and whether the item must remain persistent or can be re-created. If used correctly, state management is an important factor in developing optimal ASP.NET applications.

Summary

ASP.NET provides new ways to manage session state and application state. In this chapter we discussed session state management using classic ASP and contrasted it with the new capabilities offered by ASP.NET. We reviewed the three modes of managing session state in ASP.NET, which are InProc, StateServer, and SQLServer. Many texts refer to the performance degradation you can expect to see in your application when you manage session state. However, you rarely see performance numbers that back up these statements. To address this issue, we conducted performance stress tests of a Web page using different session state management modes. The results showed that the effect on performance is not clear-cut and that you may actually recognize performance benefits. Next we discussed application state management in ASP.NET. There are effectively two kinds of information that need to be stored at the application level: transient information and permanent information. You can store transient information using the HttpApplicationState class, and you can store permanent information in the Web.config file. After that, we discussed the important role that Global.asax plays in ASP.NET applications. This class provides numerous event handlers and allows you to execute code at various points in the request process. We showed how to extend the functionality of the `Global.asax` file by writing a custom base class. Finally, we ended the chapter with design considerations for implementing session and application state management.

CHAPTER 5

Caching ASP.NET Applications

CACHING ALLOWS ASP.NET applications to store objects and Hypertext Markup Language (HTML) output in memory and then quickly retrieve them for multiple, repetitious client requests. Web applications commonly serve the same response to multiple clients. It becomes more efficient to serve a copy of the initial response, rather than regenerating the same response for every client request. Caching can significantly improve a Web application's performance and scalability, especially if the cached content includes result sets from database calls. Caching may also speed up an application's response time because the server does not have to spend as much (if any) processing time on the request.

ASP.NET provides a sophisticated set of options for caching content, including the ability to cache portions of a Web page, rather than the entire page. In addition, ASP.NET provides a Cache API that enables you to cache individual objects and data. Caching was first discussed in Chapter 3, "Writing Optimized Data Access Code," where we referred to it as *transient application state management.* This term highlights two important aspects about caching: It is temporary, and it is scoped at the application level.

Caching does come with tradeoffs, which are important to understand before you implement this feature into your Web application. In this chapter we discuss how caching works and what the benefits and tradeoffs are with each caching option. We also look at more advanced topics, such as how caching works in Web farms.

NOTE *Caching is a primary factor in your application's design, and you should factor it in from Day 1. It is more difficult to retrofit a mature application for caching, than it is to incorporate caching early in the design. Take full advantage of ASP.NET's caching options because caching can significantly improve the performance and scalability of your Web application.*

Overview of Caching

ASP.NET provides two types of caching:

> **Output caching**: This is the ability to cache an entire Web page or portions of a Web page if they are contained in user controls. ASP.NET can cache multiple versions of the same page if the requests vary by certain parameters. For example, ASP.NET will vary the cache by using a page's HTTP Response headers or by using its posted form parameters. You need to specify which Response headers, or form parameters, these are. Alternatively, you can choose to not vary the cache by any particular parameter. This results in every client request receiving the same cached version of the cached content.

> **Application data caching**: This is the ability to cache individual objects and data in server memory. The Cache API provides this ability by offering programmatic access to the cache. The Page object's Cache property conveniently exposes the application programming interface (API). Application data caching allows very granular control over cached content. It provides an interesting range of expiration policies, including dependency-based expiration, which links cached content to specific data or to a specific file. This enables the cache to persist as long as its dependency remains unchanged.

Each type of caching works on a similar principle. Content gets added to the cache the first time that a user requests it. Subsequent users continue to receive a cached copy of the content until the cache expires. When this happens, the cache gets repopulated with content, and the cycle begins again. Caching saves the server from having to process the same request multiple times. This feature reduces processing costs, which in turn typically improves an application's performance, scalability, and responsiveness.

The two types of caching described may be founded on the same principle, but they behave differently. Output caching is reliable, and the content is guaranteed to persist (be present) in the cache until it expires. Application data caching is more flexible but is less reliable because content is not guaranteed to remain in the cache. This feature is by design and for efficiency purposes. The Cache API uses a process called *scavenging* to clear out cached content that is infrequently used. This process frees up server resources while impacting a relatively small percentage of clients. The overall application gains in terms of performance because the cache uses server resources in the most optimal way.

By definition, cached content is a copy of the original, which means that it can always be re-created. This point may seem obvious, but it has an interesting implication—namely, that it is perfectly acceptable for cached content to expire and to be scavenged without your specific consent. This approach is much better than one that guarantees cache persistence above all else, even at the expense of efficiency and memory usage. Cached content can be re-created, often without the client even realizing it. But poor application performance and responsiveness is not so easy to hide. ASP.NET caching provides a range of options for satisfying different kinds of caching requirements.

Output Caching

Output caching provides the ability to cache entire rendered Web pages, either on the server or on the client. Output caching is suitable for pages that contain relatively static content and that are served the same way for multiple clients. Often, a Web page will contain a mix of content that combines dynamic content with more static content. *Fragment caching*, or *partial-page caching*, is a special type of output caching that is appropriate for mixed content pages. Fragment caching enables you to cache the static portions of the page once they have been broken out into separate user controls. You can then set individual cache policies for each of the user controls in the page.

Enabling Output Caching

ASP.NET provides two ways to enable output caching:

- **Declarative**: Using the @ OutputCache directive at the top of an *.aspx page. This directive provides several attributes for setting the page cacheability, including Location, which specifies where the page should be cached.

- **Programmatic**: Using the HttpCachePolicy object, which is conveniently exposed via the Page object's Cache property.

The HttpCachePolicy object is the programmatic counterpart to the @ OutputCache directive, meaning that you can configure the same cache settings using either approach. Cache settings are actually stored using several HTTP headers, the most important of which is the Cache-Control header. ASP.NET simply provides two different APIs for accessing the same set of headers. In fact, you could even bypass ASP.NET and configure the cache settings directly using the Internet Information Server (IIS) Administrative utility. However, you would miss out on the more granular control that ASP.NET provides for setting cache policies. The header settings in IIS apply to all pages in the Web application, whereas ASP.NET allows you to set the cache policy on a per-page basis.

The location of the cached page has a lot of significance for the caching behavior. ASP.NET unfortunately sets the default location to "Any," which puts no constraints on where the page may be cached. The other possible locations include the following:

- **Server**: The server where the page originates.

- **Client**: The client machine that requests the page.

- **Proxy servers**: Servers that sit between the client and the server. Proxy servers will cache pages for all the clients to which they route. This shared cache may prevent individual clients from receiving cached pages tailored to their specific request.

An interesting thing about caching is that it was originally intended to occur only on client and proxy servers downstream of the origin server. The HTTP Cache-Control header provides a cache policy for downstream clients. ASP.NET allows for server-side caching, which goes above and beyond the original caching specification. ASP.NET manages output caching using an HttpModule called OutputCacheModule. This module is responsible for the range of server-side caching options that ASP.NET provides. In addition, this module enables specialized features such as sliding expiration.

 NOTE *The term* proxy servers *is becoming outdated with today's newest generation of intermediary servers, such as Microsoft Internet Security and Acceleration Server (ISA Server). These so-called "caching intermediaries" act as both firewalls and as smart caching administrators. The "Caching with ISA Server" section discusses this further.*

You will usually want to cache pages on the Web server because this allows pages to be served to multiple clients from a centralized cache. ASP.NET will typically choose the server as the cache location, but you do not want to leave this issue to chance. You especially do not want to allow proxy servers to cache pages for a group of clients. The recommended setting for the HTTP Cache-Control header is "no-cache," which means that the page may still be cached on the server, but it will never get cached on any downstream client or proxy server. For example, the following page sets the no-cache header and also varies the cache by the client's Accept-Language header:

[Declarative Code]

```
<%@ OutputCache Duration="60" VaryByParam="None" VaryByHeader="accept-language"
    Location="Server"%>
```

[Programmatic Code]

```
With Page.Response.Cache
    .SetLastModified(DateTime.Now)
    .SetExpires(DateTime.Now.AddSeconds(60))
    .SetCacheability(HttpCacheability.Server)
    .SetValidUntilExpires(True)
    .VaryByHeaders.UserLanguage = True ' Equivalent syntax on next line
    .VaryByHeaders("Accept-Language") = True ' Equivalent to .UserLanguage
End With
```

Incidentally, when you set the @ OutputCache Location attribute to "Downstream," this is equivalent to setting the HTTP Cache-Control header to "public." This setting enables content to be cached on any machine that receives the HTTP response, including the client or proxy servers.

Let's look in detail at how to enable output caching at both the page and partial-page levels. This discussion will focus exclusively on using the @ OutputCache directive for enabling output caching. The "Enabling Caching Using the HttpCachePolicy Object" section describes how to accomplish the same task programmatically with the HttpCachePolicy object.

Enabling Page-Level Output Caching

You can declare the cache policy using the @ OutputCache directive at the top of an *.aspx page. For example, use the following syntax to specify that a page should be cached on the server for 20 seconds and for all requests:

```
<%@ OutputCache Duration="20" VaryByParam="None" Location="Server"%>
```

Table 5-1 summarizes the @ OutputCache directive's attributes for page-level output caching only. The @ OutputCache directive provides an additional attribute called VaryByControl, which is specific to user controls. The "Fragment Caching Using the VaryByControl Attribute" section discusses this attribute in more detail.

Table 5-1. @ OutputCache *Attributes for Page-Level Output Caching*

ATTRIBUTE	DESCRIPTION
Duration	(Required.) The expiration policy for the HTTP response, specified in seconds. In other words, this is the length of time that the page will be cached.
Location	(Optional.) The location of the output cache. The values for this attribute come from the OutputCacheLocation enumeration, which is a member of the System.Web.UI namespace. These values are as follows:
	None: The output cache is disabled for the request.
	Server: The output cache is stored on the Web server where the request is processed.
	Client: The output cache is stored on the client that makes the actual request, not on an intermediate proxy server (if present). In addition, this setting allows the client's browser settings to override the server's caching instructions in the HTTP response.
	Downstream: The output cache is stored on the client or proxy server where the request originates.
	Any: The output cache may be stored on any server or client that is involved with the request. This attribute is not required, and will default to "Any" if it is not specified. However, you should always specify the Location and set the value to "Server," unless you specifically want the page to be cached elsewhere.
VaryByParam	(Required.) A semicolon-delimited list of GET and POST parameters used to vary the cache. If multiple parameters are specified, then the cache will vary when any individual parameter value differs from a previous request. The cache does not vary based on a unique combination of parameter values; it varies on individual parameter values. The allowable values for VaryByParam are:
	None: The output cache does not vary based on GET and POST parameters.
	{Asterisk} *: The output cache will vary by all GET and POST parameters.
	{List}: The output cache will vary by a specified semicolon-delimited list of GET and POST parameters.

(continued)

Table 5-1. @ `OutputCache` *Attributes for Page-Level Output Caching (continued)*

ATTRIBUTE	DESCRIPTION
VaryByHeader	(Optional.) A semicolon-delimited list of HTTP request headers that are used to vary the cache. If multiple headers are specified then the cache will vary when any individual header value differs from a previous request. The cache does not vary based on a unique combination of header values; it varies on individual header values.
VaryByCustom	(Optional.) A custom string that is used to vary the cache. If this attribute is set to "browser," then the output cache will vary based on the browser name and its major version information. For example, the cache will vary between Internet Explorer 4.0, Netscape Navigator 4.6, and Internet Explorer 6.0. Any other attribute value is treated as a custom string.
	To use the VaryByCustom attribute with a custom string requires an additional implementation step: You must open the `Global.asax` file and override the `GetVaryByCustomString()` method of the HttpApplication class. For example, you can use VaryByCustom to vary the output cache by the minor version of the browser.

Note that the Duration and VaryByParam attributes are always required for page-level caching. Let's look at some examples that illustrate page-level output caching using the VaryByParam and VaryByHeader attributes.

Output Caching Using the VaryByParam Attribute

Figure 5-1 shows a simple page, `ap_OutputCaching.aspx`, that illustrates page-level output caching. The page provides a text input field called `txtUserName` and a Label control that displays the system time and posted username. The label updates every time the page is submitted.

The page's output cache varies by the posted value of `txtUserName`, using the following directive:

```
<%@ OutputCache Duration="60" Location="Server" VaryByParam="txtUserName"%>
```

You can test this page by opening it in side-by-side browser windows. Enter a different username on each page and then click the Submit buttons repeatedly. Both pages will cache, but they will display different server timestamps for each unique username. This indicates you are receiving multiple cached versions of the same page.

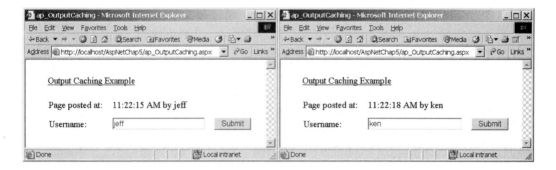

Figure 5-1. Page-level output caching using VaryByParam

Now let's consider an example that illustrates how to use the VaryByHeader attribute.

Output Caching Using the VaryByHeader Attribute

Figure 5-2 shows a simple page, ap_OutputCaching2.aspx, that serves customized content based on the Accept-Language HTTP request header. The page will display a different language string to users with the following header values: us-en, fr, and de-lu.

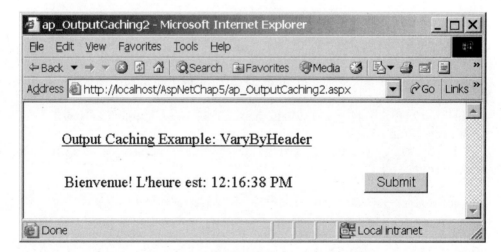

Figure 5-2. Page-level output caching using VaryByHeader

The page simulates multiple international users by auto-assigning a different Accept-Language header value every 20 seconds. For example, a client is assigned "fr" if they request the page between 20 and 39 seconds after the minute. (The alternative was a coordinated international effort to ping the same page!) The code-behind file for doing this is shown in Listing 5-1.

Listing 5-1. Using the Accept-Language Header

```
Private Sub Page_Load(ByVal sender As System.Object, _
    ByVal e As System.EventArgs) Handles MyBase.Load
    Dim dtNow As Date = Now
    ' Cycle through 3 languages every 20 seconds
    With dtNow
        If .Second > 0 And .Second < 20 Then
            Response.AddHeader("Accept-Language", "us-en")
            Me.lblDateTime.Text = "Welcome! The time is: " & dtNow.ToLongTimeString
        ElseIf .Second > 20 And .Second < 40 Then
            Response.AddHeader("Accept-Language", "fr")
            Me.lblDateTime.Text = "Bienvenue! L'heure est: " & .ToLongTimeString
        Else
            Response.AddHeader("Accept-Language", "de-lu")
            Me.lblDateTime.Text = "Wilkommen! Die Zeit ist: " & .ToLongTimeString
        End If
    End With
End Sub
```

In addition, the page will cache for a 30-second period following the initial request and will vary only by the Accept-Header value. You set this cache policy using the following directive:

```
<%@ OutputCache Duration="30" Location="Server" VaryByParam="None"
    VaryByHeader="Accept-Language"%>
```

Notice that the VaryByParam attribute is still specified because it is a required attribute for page-level output caching. It is set here to "None" so that it does not interfere with the VaryByHeader cache policy. You can test this page by opening it in a browser window and clicking the Submit button several times over a 30-plus second interval. For example, the following is one possible sequence of strings you can get if you click the Submit button every 10 seconds:

```
Welcome! The time is: 12:16:08 PM     {Submit button was clicked at 12:16:08 PM}
Welcome! The time is: 12:16:08 PM     {Submit button was clicked at 12:16:18 PM}
Welcome! The time is: 12:16:08 PM     {Submit button was clicked at 12:16:28 PM}
Bienvenue! L'heure est: 12:16:38 PM   {Submit button was clicked at 12:15:38 PM}
```

This wraps up our discussion of output caching using the @ OutputCache directive. Now turn your attention to *fragment caching*, also known as *partial-page caching*.

Enabling Fragment Caching (Partial Page-Level)

Fragment caching provides the ability to set different cache policies within the same page. This approach is suitable for pages that mix dynamic content with static content. The dynamic content cannot be cached and will be regenerated every time the page is requested. You can separate the static content into a user control and then set a specific cache policy. Fragment caching accommodates as many different cache policies as you need. Every user control on a page can have its own unique cache policy. So, you just need to break out one user control per unique cache policy on a page.

You can configure fragment caching for a user control with the @ OutputCache directive. User controls support a limited range of attributes for this directive, as compared to what an *.aspx Page object supports. Table 5-2 summarizes the @ OutputCache directive's attributes for partial page-level output caching only.

Table 5-2. @ OutputCache *Attributes for Fragment (Partial Page-Level) Caching*

ATTRIBUTE	DESCRIPTION
Duration	(Required.) The expiration policy for the HTTP response, specified in seconds. In other words, this is the length of time that the user control will be cached.
VaryByParam	(Optional.) A semi-colon delimited list of GET and POST parameters that are used to vary the cache. If multiple parameters are specified then the cache will vary when any individual parameter value differs from a previous request. The cache does not vary based on a unique combination of parameter values; it varies on individual parameter values. The allowable values for VaryByParam are:
	None: The output cache does not vary based on GET and POST parameters.
	{Asterisk} *: The output cache will vary by all GET and POST parameters.
	{List}: The output cache will vary by a specified semicolon-delimited list of GET and POST parameters.

(continued)

Table 5-2. @ OutputCache *Attributes for Fragment (Partial Page-Level) Caching (continued)*

ATTRIBUTE	DESCRIPTION
VaryByControl	(Optional.) A semicolon-delimited list of user control properties used to vary the cache. VaryByControl also enables the user control to cache based on the values of its own child controls. The cache does not vary based on a unique combination of property values; it varies on individual property values.
VaryByCustom	(Optional.) A custom string that is used to vary the cache. See the full definition in Table 5-1.
Shared	(Optional.) A Boolean value that determines whether user control output can be shared between multiple pages in the same application. Set this value to true in order to create a shared cache. The default attribute value is "False." This attribute is only supported in ASP.NET 1.1 or later.

Fragment caching does not support the Location and VaryByHeader attributes. You will receive a parsing error if you attempt to specify them for the @ OutputCache directive in a user control. In addition, the VaryByParam attribute is not required like it is for page-level output caching, although you must specify either VaryByParam or VaryByControl in the @ OutputCache directive (or both).

A major inefficiency with fragment caching in ASP.NET 1.0 was that user control output was cached on a per-page basis. If multiple pages referenced the same user control, then the server was forced to maintain separate cached versions of the control for each page. ASP.NET 1.1 overcomes this inefficiency by introducing the @ OutputCache directive's Shared attribute. This attribute is a Boolean value that determines whether user control output can be shared. For example, consider a user control that contains a child Textbox control, with an ID of TextBox1. You would implement shared caching for this user control (in its design view) as follows:

```
<%@ OutputCache Duration="60" VaryByControl="TextBox1" Shared="True" %>
```

In this example, the server will continue to hold multiple copies of the control for every unique value entered into the textbox. However, with the Shared attribute value set to "True," the server can now economize its cache by sharing content between multiple pages. Users who enter the same textbox value on different pages will be able to share the same cached copy of the user control.

NOTE *ASP.NET 1.1 introduces the Shared attribute for fragment caching of user controls. This attribute determines whether user control output can be shared between multiple pages. ASP.NET 1.0 does not provide the Shared attribute.*

Fragment Caching Using the VaryByParam Attribute

Figure 5-3 shows a page, ap_OutputCaching3.aspx, that illustrates fragment caching. The page provides a dynamic timestamp that updates every time the page is requested. The page also contains a simple user control, which is bounded with a rectangle frame for clarity. The user control displays its own timestamp and the name of the user who requested the page. The user control's output cache varies by the txtUserName posted value. It can do this because the user control is inserted within the form on the host page. All of the other controls, including the username textbox and the submit button, are contained within the host page.

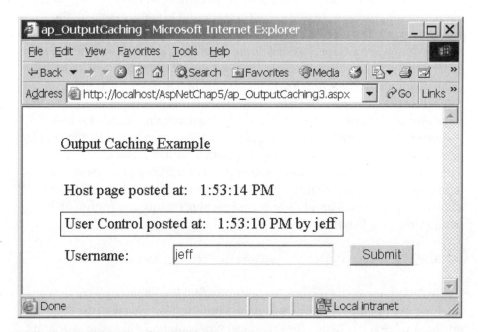

Figure 5-3. Fragment caching using VaryByParam

You design the *.ascx page for the user control as shown in Listing 5-2 (minus the length style attribute values).

Listing 5-2. The `*.ascx` *Page*

```
<%@ OutputCache Duration="10" VaryByParam="txtUserName"%>
<%@ Control Language="vb" AutoEventWireup="false"
    Codebehind="ap_UserControl1.ascx.vb" Inherits="AspNetChap5.ap_UserControl1"
    TargetSchema="http://schemas.microsoft.com/intellisense/ie5" %>
    <asp:Label id="Label2">User Control posted at:</asp:Label>
<asp:Label id="lblDateTime"></asp:Label>
```

Listing 5-3 shows the code-behind file for the user control.

Listing 5-3. The Code-Behind File for the User Control

```
Public MustInherit Class ap_UserControl1
    Inherits System.Web.UI.UserControl
    Protected lblDateTime As System.Web.UI.WebControls.Label

    Private Sub Page_Load(ByVal sender As System.Object, _
        ByVal e As System.EventArgs) Handles MyBase.Load
        Dim dtNow As Date = Now
        If Not Page.IsPostBack Then
            Me.lblDateTime.Text = dtNow.ToLongTimeString
        Else
            If Page.Request("txtUserName") <> "" Then
                Me.lblDateTime.Text = dtNow.ToLongTimeString & " by " & _
                    Page.Request("txtUserName")
            Else
                Me.lblDateTime.Text = dtNow.ToLongTimeString
            End If
        End If
    End Sub
End Class
```

The host page registers the control and inserts it into the form as shown in Listing 5-4.

Listing 5-4. Registering and Inserting the Control

```
<%@ Register TagPrefix="Apress1" TagName="UC1"
        Src="controls/ap_UserControl1.ascx" %>
<%@ Page Language="vb" AutoEventWireup="false"
        Codebehind="ap_OutputCaching3.aspx.vb"
        Inherits="AspNetChap5.ap_OutputCaching3"%>
<HTML>
        <HEAD><!-- not shown --></HEAD>
```

```
<body MS_POSITIONING="GridLayout">
        form id="Form1" method="post" runat="server">
        <asp:label id="Label1">Output Caching Example</asp:label>
        <asp:label id="lblPageDateTime"></asp:label>
        <asp:label id="Label2">Host page posted at: </asp:label>
        <asp:label id="lblUserName">Username:</asp:label>
        <APRESS1:UC1 id="MyUC1" runat="server"></APRESS1:UC1>
        <asp:textbox id="txtUserName"></asp:textbox>
        <asp:Button id="btnSubmit"></asp:Button></form>
    </body>
</HTML>
```

You will notice that the user control specifies a cache policy in its designer code, but the host page does not specify any cache policy. The code-behind file for the host page is extremely simple:

```
Public Class ap_OutputCaching3
    Inherits System.Web.UI.Page
    Protected WithEvents btnSubmit As System.Web.UI.WebControls.Button
    Protected lblPageDateTime As System.Web.UI.WebControls.Label
    Protected txtUserName As System.Web.UI.WebControls.TextBox

    Private Sub Page_Load(ByVal sender As System.Object, _
        ByVal e As System.EventArgs) Handles MyBase.Load
        Dim dtNow As Date = Now
        Me.lblPageDateTime.Text = dtNow.ToLongTimeString
    End Sub
End Class
```

You can test this page by loading it into a browser window and submitting the form repeatedly. The host page's timestamp will update with every page request, and the user control's timestamp will update every 10 seconds. This example is simple, but you can extend the same principles to more complicated user controls that perform sophisticated processing on request parameters. This example shows just one user control, but you can easily add multiple user controls to the page, where each user control specifies its own cache policy.

Let's look at another fragment caching example, this time using the VaryByControl attribute.

Fragment Caching Using the VaryByControl Attribute

The VaryByControl attribute enables the caching of user controls. The purpose of this attribute is to vary the cache based on the values of child controls within the user control.

Figure 5-4 illustrates this behavior. The host page contains a dynamic timestamp and an embedded user control. The user control provides its own timestamp, and it contains a DropDownList control and a Submit button. The cache varies based on the value of the DropDownList control. When a user clicks the Submit button, the host page gets reposted, and the user control either regenerates or is retrieved from the cache. Figure 5-4 shows side-by-side browser windows of the same page. The left window was originally loaded at 10:37:46 A.M., and the right window was originally loaded at 10:37:47 A.M. Both pages were resubmitted again at 10:37:56 A.M., which falls within the 20-second cache window for each page. This indicates you are receiving multiple cached versions of the same page.

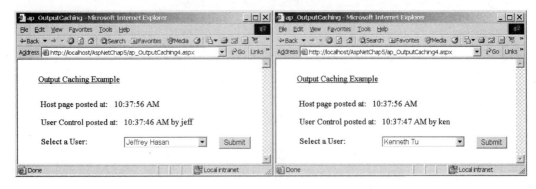

Figure 5-4. Fragment caching using VaryByControl

You design the *.ascx page for the user control as shown in Listing 5-5 (minus the length style attribute values).

*Listing 5-5. The *.axcx Page*

```
<%@ Control Language="vb" AutoEventWireup="false"
        Codebehind="ap_UserControl2.ascx.vb"
        Inherits="AspNetChap5.ap_UserControl2"
        TargetSchema="http://schemas.microsoft.com/intellisense/ie5" %>
<%@ OutputCache Duration="20" VaryByControl="cboUserName"%>
<asp:Label id="Label2" runat="server">User Control posted at:</asp:Label>
<asp:Label id="lblDateTime" runat="server"></asp:Label>
```

```
<asp:Label id="Label1" runat="server">Select a User:</asp:Label>
<asp:DropDownList id="cboUserName" runat="server">
        <asp:ListItem Value="jeff">Jeffrey Hasan</asp:ListItem>
        <asp:ListItem Value="ken">Kenneth Tu</asp:ListItem>
</asp:DropDownList>
<asp:Button id="btnChoose" Text="Submit" runat="server"></asp:Button>
```

Listing 5-6 shows the code-behind for the user control.

Listing 5-6. The Code-Behind File

```
Public MustInherit Class ap_UserControl2
    Inherits System.Web.UI.UserControl
    Protected cboUserName As System.Web.UI.WebControls.DropDownList
    Protected lblDateTime As System.Web.UI.WebControls.Label
    Protected WithEvents btnChoose As System.Web.UI.WebControls.Button

    Private Sub Button1_Click(ByVal sender As Object, _
        ByVal e As System.EventArgs) Handles btnChoose.Click
        Dim dtNow As Date = Now
        Me.lblDateTime.Text = dtNow.ToLongTimeString & " by " & _
            Me.cboUserName.SelectedItem.Value
    End Sub

End Class
```

The host page, ap_OutputCaching4.aspx, registers the control and inserts it into the form as shown in Listing 5-7.

Listing 5-7. ap_OutputCaching4.aspx

```
<%@ Register TagPrefix="Apress1" TagName="UC2"
        Src="controls/ap_UserControl2.ascx" %>
<%@ Page Language="vb" AutoEventWireup="false"
        Codebehind="ap_OutputCaching4.aspx.vb"
        Inherits="AspNetChap5.ap_OutputCaching4"%>
<HTML>
    <HEAD><!-- not shown --></HEAD>
    <body MS_POSITIONING="GridLayout">
        <form id="Form1" method="post" runat="server">
            <asp:label id="Label1">Output Caching Example</asp:label>
            <asp:label id="Label2" runat="server">Host page posted at: </asp:label>
            <asp:label id="lblPageDateTime" runat="server"></asp:label>
            <APRESS1:UC2 id="MyUC2" runat="server"></APRESS1:UC2>
```

```
      </form>
    </body>
</HTML>
```

Finally, you can test this fragment caching example by opening side-by-side browser windows and submitting the form with different users. You will see that each user creates a new version of the cached page.

Enabling Caching Using the HttpCachePolicy Object

The @ OutputCache directive will handle most caching scenarios for you. However, there are times when you will want to set the cache policy programmatically using the HttpCachePolicy object. This API provides more granular control over setting cache policies. In other words, it provides more access to the HTTP headers compared to what the @ OutputCache directive provides.

The HttpCachePolicy object is accessible using the Page.Cache property, and it is a member of the System.Web namespace. The API provides everything the @ OutputCache directive does (and more); however, there is not a one-to-one match between the class members and the directive attributes. You already saw one example that demonstrates how the SetCacheability() and SetExpires() methods configure the same settings as the directive. The following is a variation on the previous example:

[Declarative Code]

```
<%@ OutputCache Duration="60" VaryByParam="UserName" Location="Server"%>
```

[Programmatic Code]

```
With Page.Response.Cache
    .SetLastModified(DateTime.Now)
    .SetExpires(DateTime.Now.AddSeconds(60))
    .SetCacheability(HttpCacheability.Server)
    .SetValidUntilExpires(True)
    .VaryByParams("UserName") = True
End With
```

The API calls are a lot more involved than using the directive, so if your cache policies are straightforward, then you should always use the @ OutputCache directive.

Table 5-3 shows the more interesting members of the HttpCachePolicy class. The close relationship between the API and the HTTP headers is quite apparent from the class member descriptions.

Table 5-3. HttpCachePolicy Class Members

MEMBER	DESCRIPTION
SetCacheability()	Sets the Cache-Control HTTP header to one of the HttpCacheability enumeration values. These values are as follows: NoCache: The output cache is disabled for the request. This value sets the Cache-Control:no-cache header. Server: The output cache is stored on the Web server where the request is processed. This value also sets the Cache-Control:no-cache header; however, the page will still be cached on the origin server. Private: The output cache is stored on the client that makes the actual request, not on an intermediate proxy server (if present). This value sets the Cache-Control:private header. Public: The output cache is stored on the client or proxy server where the request originates. This value sets the Cache-Control:public header.

SetExpires()	Sets the Expires HTTP header to an absolute date and time. If you need to specify a relative duration (for example, 60 minutes), then you must set the date-time to the current date-time plus the duration length. For example, this is how you specify a cache duration of 60 seconds:
	
	`Page.Response.Cache.SetExpires`
	`(DateTime.Now.AddSeconds(60))`

SetValidUntilExpires	Specifies that the ASP.NET cache should ignore any attempts by the client to override the HTTP Cache-Control headers.
SetLastModified	Sets the Last-Modified HTTP header to a specific date-time stamp.
SetSlidingExpiration	Sets the cache expiration to sliding scale. This will renew the page's HTTP headers every time that the server responds to the request.
VaryByHeaders	Gets or sets the list of HTTP headers that will be used to vary the cache.

(continued)

Table 5-3. HttpCachePolicy Class Members (continued)

MEMBER	DESCRIPTION
VaryByParams	Gets or sets the list of HTTP parameters that will be used to vary the cache.
SetNoServerCaching	Stops the origin server from caching items. Once this method is called, caching may not be re-enabled for the remaining duration of the response.

Figure 5-5 shows a page that sets its cache policy using the HttpCachePolicy object.

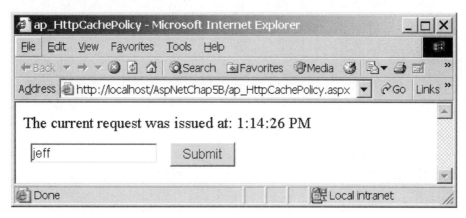

Figure 5-5. Caching with the HttpCachePolicy object

The page displays the timestamp for the current request and varies the output cache by the value of the submitted username. The page will cache for a duration of 60 seconds per unique username. Listing 5-8 shows this page.

Listing 5-8. Caching with the HttpCachePolicy Object

```
Public Class ap_HttpCachePolicy
    Inherits System.Web.UI.Page
    Protected WithEvents TextBox1 As System.Web.UI.WebControls.TextBox
    Protected WithEvents Button1 As System.Web.UI.WebControls.Button

    Private Sub Page_Load(ByVal sender As System.Object, _
        ByVal e As System.EventArgs) Handles MyBase.Load

        With Page.Response.Cache
            .SetLastModified(DateTime.Now)
```

```
        .SetExpires(DateTime.Now.AddSeconds(60))
        .SetCacheability(HttpCacheability.Server)
        .SetValidUntilExpires(True)
        .VaryByParams("*") = True
    End With

    Response.Write("The current request was issued at: " & _
        Me.Context.Timestamp.ToLongTimeString)

  End Sub
End Class
```

The following are some sample responses (without the leading text):

```
1:14:26 PM        {Invoke button was clicked at 1:14:26 PM; txtUser = jeff}
1:14:54 PM        {Invoke button was clicked at 1:14:54 PM; txtUser = ken}
1:14:26 PM        {Invoke button was clicked at 1:14:56 PM; txtUser = jeff}
1:15:28 PM        {Invoke button was clicked at 1:15:28 PM; txtUser = jeff}
1:14:54 PM        {Invoke button was clicked at 1:15:52 PM; txtUser = ken}
```

Application Data Caching Using the Cache API

The Cache API provides a mechanism for caching individual objects, as opposed to Web pages. The Cache object is instanced once per application, and it remains in memory until the application gets restarted. The Cache object is basically a dictionary object that supports specialized Add(), Insert(), and Remove() methods for updating items in the cache.

The Cache object allows for very granular control over cached content because it provides a flexible set of methods for updating objects in the cache. In addition, the Cache object is optimized to persist cache items only for as long as they are needed. The Cache object provides the following useful features:

> **Simple interface:** You can store cache items using a straightforward key-value pair assignment. This makes it easy to add, retrieve, and remove items from the cache. In fact, you must reference cache items using their key name, rather than using an index value. This reflects that items may be shuffled around within the cache for efficiency purposes, or even removed, so indexes have less meaning than actual key names. By comparison, you can reference items stored in Session and Application objects either by name or by index.

Customized expiration: You can assign cache items individual expiration policies. The Cache class supports three kinds of expiration: absolute, sliding, and dependency-based expiration.

Memory management: The Cache class supports a mechanism called *scavenging*, which optimizes memory usage when the available server memory becomes limited. This mechanism automatically removes unused, or infrequently used, items from the cache. The Cache class automatically assigns priority levels to items to determine the order in which items will be scavenged from memory. Underused items will be evicted from the cache before more popular items. In addition, you may override the priority level on any item in the cache.

Concurrency management: The Cache class automatically handles updates from concurrent users. Unlike the Application object, you do not need to explicitly lock the Cache object when performing updates on its items. This does not eliminate the confusion caused when multiple users simultaneously update the same item. However, it does prevent locking problems.

Validation callbacks: The Cache class supports callbacks to delegate functions when items are removed from the cache. This is useful for taking action when an item is (unexpectedly) removed from the cache.

It is inevitable to compare the Cache object against its more familiar counterparts, the Session and Application objects. Each of these three objects has their advantages in certain situations. However, overall, the Cache object provides the flexibility and ease of use that makes it a good choice in a wide variety of situations. (Chapter 4, "Optimizing Application and Session State Management," discusses the Session and Application objects).

Understanding the Cache API

The Cache class is a member of the System.Web.Caching namespace, and it is instanced once per application instance. You can access the Cache object directly via the Page object's Cache property. You can also access it via the Cache property of both the HttpRuntime and HttpContext classes. The Cache class is a dictionary that provides specialized Add(), Insert(), and Remove() methods for updating items. It also supports an IEnumerable interface, which makes it easy to loop through items in the cache. ASP.NET handles the expiration and scavenging mechanisms that help optimize the Cache object's memory usage. Table 5-4 describes important members of the Cache class.

Table 5-4. Cache Class Members

MEMBER	DESCRIPTION
Add()	This method adds an item to the cache with the following parameters:
	`key name [string]` and `value [object]`
	`dependencies`: A CacheDependency object, which specifies a resource that the cache is dependent on. You can set this to "Nothing" if no dependencies exist.
	`absoluteExpiration`: A Date object, which specifies when the item expires and is removed from the cache. Set to the field value: `NoAbsoluteExpiration`, if no expiration policy is required. May not be specified in conjunction with a sliding expiration policy.
	`slidingExpiration`: A TimeSpan object, which specifies the interval over which the item must go unused before it expires and is removed from the cache. Must be no greater than one year from the current date-timestamp. Set to the field value: `NoSlidingExpiration`, if no expiration policy is required. May not be specified in conjunction with an absolute expiration policy.
	`priority`: A CacheItemPriority enumeration value, which sets the item's relative priority in the cache. Objects are assigned a Normal priority by default. Higher priority objects are less likely to be evicted when the cache runs low on resources and starts to scavenge items. Expensive objects (in other words, time-consuming and processor-intensive to create) should be assigned a higher relative priority compared to cheaper objects.
	`onRemoveCallback`: A delegate function that is called when an item is removed from the cache. This serves to notify the application that the item is no longer available in the cache. You can set this to "Nothing" if no delegate is required.
	The `Add()` method is not overloaded, so you must set every parameter. The `Add()` method returns a reference to the item that is being added to the cache.

(continued)

Table 5-4. Cache Class Members (continued)

MEMBER	DESCRIPTION
Insert()	This method inserts an item to the cache using the same parameters as the Add method (see above). This method is overloaded as follows:
	key, value
	key, value, dependencies
	key, value, dependencies, absoluteExpiration, slidingExpiration
	key, value, dependencies, absoluteExpiration, slidingExpiration, priority, onRemoveCallback
	Unlike the Add() method, the Insert() method does not return a reference to the item that is being added to the cache.
Get()	This method retrieves an item from the cache using the key name.
Remove()	This method removes an item from the cache using the key name. The method returns a reference to the item that is being removed from the cache.
GetEnumerator()	This method retrieves an IDictionaryEnumerator object that you can use to iterate through the items in the cache.
NoAbsoluteExpiration	This read-only field may be used in place of an absolute expiration value. The field value is equivalent to the largest possible expiration date: 12/31/9999 11:59:59 PM.
NoSlidingExpiration	This read-only field may be used in place of a sliding expiration value. The field value is equivalent to zero, which means that the absolute expiration policy will be in effect instead.

Understanding Cache Expiration Policies

Before discussing how to add items to the cache, we need to explore the three available Cache expiration policies:

Absolute expiration: This is an absolute date and time when an item expires and is removed from the cache. Absolute expiration is best suited for items that have a well-defined useful lifespan, such as time-sensitive reference information.

Sliding expiration: This is an interval over which the item must go unused before it is expired and removed from the cache. For example, if the interval is set to 30 minutes, then the item will expire if it has not been accessed during the last 30 minutes. Sliding expiration is best suited for items that experience heavy usage initially, followed by declining usage over time.

Dependency expiration: This cached item may be linked to a resource and expired only once this resource changes. Dependency resources may include files, directories, or other items in the cache. For example, an item may link to an XML file. The item remains in the cache until the XML file changes. Dependency expiration is best suited for items that change infrequently.

ASP.NET offers an impressive range of cache expiration policies, which are easy to use and offer few constraints. You cannot set absolute expiration and sliding expiration policies together. You will get an error if you attempt to define them both for the same item. You can set dependency expiration in conjunction with either absolute or sliding expiration policies; however, this defeats the purpose of using it. Dependency expiration is an excellent alternative to using the Application object. This policy automatically updates the cached item when its dependency changes and does not require that the application be restarted.

The Cache object allows you to specify a different expiration policy for every cached item. You can even assign a relative priority to a cached item to influence the sequence in which it gets scavenged. Scavenging is simply the forced expiration of cached items for the purpose of optimizing memory usage. By default, the cache will evict items from the cache based on how frequently they are accessed, so you are not required to set specific priority levels. If server resources become limited, then all Cache items face the possibility of being scavenged and expired from the cache before their assigned expiration time. The best way to ensure your cached item will remain in memory is to specify an expiration policy and to assign it a high priority.

Adding Cache Items

You add items to the cache in three ways:

- **Key-value assignment**: This is the implicit assignment of a key-value pair, in the same way that you would assign an item to a Session object. The value stores an object data type, which means you can assign any .NET data type to the cache.

- **Add() method**: This method adds an item to the cache and specifies its expiration policy, its priority, and a delegate function that notifies the application when the item is removed from the cache. This method returns a reference to the object that is being added to the cache.

- **Insert() method**: This method adds an item to the cache but does not return an object reference to the item. Unlike the Add() method, the Insert() method is overloaded and lets you specify four different combinations of parameters.

Table 5-4 summarizes the Add() and Insert() methods in detail, so this section focuses on code examples.

The simplest way to add an item to the cache is to implicitly assign the value to a key name, in the same way that you would assign a Session variable:

```
Dim sqlDS As DataSet
Page.Cache("MyDS") = sqlDS
```

The disadvantage with this approach is that you cannot specify the expiration policy for the object. This is how you define an absolute expiration using the explicit Add() method:

```
Dim sqlDS As DataSet
Page.Cache.Add("MyDS", sqlDS, Nothing, DateTime.Now.AddMinutes(20), _
    Cache.NoSlidingExpiration, CacheItemPriority.Normal, Nothing)
```

Recall that the Add() method is not overloaded, which means every parameter must be specified, even if you do not require all of them. Alternatively, you can use the Insert() method, which is overloaded and therefore more flexible. This is how you insert an item into the cache with a 20-minute sliding expiration:

```
Dim sqlDS As DataSet
Me.Cache.Insert("MyDS", sqlDS, Nothing, Me.Cache.NoAbsoluteExpiration, _
    New TimeSpan(0, 0, 20))
```

Dependency expiration is almost as easy to implement. Consider Listing 5-9, which shows a Web form that contains a DataGrid control and a Submit button. When the page first loads, a DataSet gets generated from a sales query in the

Northwind database. The DataSet contents also get written out to an XML file called SalesQuery.xml. Next, the DataSet gets added to the cache using the XML file as its dependency resource. The DataSet will remain in the cache as long as this XML file remains unchanged. On subsequent postbacks, the DataSet gets retrieved from the cache. If the dependency file changes, then the DataSet will be regenerated and again added to the cache. Listing 5-9 shows the code for caching with dependency expiration.

Listing 5-9. Caching with Dependency Expiration

```
Imports System.Data
Imports System.Web.Caching
Protected WithEvents DataGrid1 As System.Web.UI.WebControls.DataGrid

Private Sub Page_Load(ByVal sender As System.Object, _
    ByVal e As System.EventArgs) Handles MyBase.Load

    Dim sqlDS As DataSet
    Dim objDependency As CacheDependency

    If Not Page.IsPostBack Then

        ' Generate a DataSet, and write it out to XML
        sqlDS = GenerateDataSet()
        sqlDS.WriteXml("C:\MyCache\SalesQuery.xml")

        ' Insert the DataSet into the Cache, using dependency-based expiration
        objDependency = New CacheDependency("C:\MyCache\SalesQuery.xml")
        Me.Cache.Insert("MyDS", sqlDS, objDependency)

    Else

        ' Retrieve the DataSet from Cache, if it is available
        If IsNothing(sqlDS) Then
            ' Regenerate the DataSet
            sqlDS = GenerateDataSet()
        Else
            sqlDS = Me.Cache.Get("MyDS")
        End If
    End If
```

```
BinDataGrid(sqlDS) ' Bind the DataSet to the DataGrid
sqlDS = Nothing
```

```
End Sub
```

Listing 5-9 uses two helper functions: GenerateDataSet() to retrieve the DataSet and BindDataGrid() to bind the DataSet to the data grid. You can find the code for these functions in the sample project files.

Listing 5-10 shows the SalesQuery.xml file.

Listing 5-10. SalesQuery.xml

```xml
<?xml version="1.0" standalone="yes"?>
<NewDataSet>
  <Table>
    <Country>UK</Country>
    <LastName>Suyama</LastName>
    <FirstName>Michael</FirstName>
    <ShippedDate>1996-07-10T00:00:00.0000000-07:00</ShippedDate>
    <OrderID>10249</OrderID>
    <SaleAmount>1863.4</SaleAmount>
  </Table>
</NewDataSet>
```

You can test dependency caching by altering a value in the SalesQuery.xml file and then stepping through the postback code. For example, alter the <OrderID> value from 10249 to 10248. Repost the page, and you will observe that the compiler bypasses the cached DataSet and regenerates a fresh one.

Finally, you may need to sometimes force a cache item to update. You can add or insert the same key multiple times, and usually the item will update without errors. However, it is safer to first remove the item and then add it to the cache again.

Retrieving Cache Items

You can retrieve cache items individually by their key name using the Get() method. Recall that cached items are not guaranteed to remain in the cache, so you should always test for an item's existence before you attempt to assign it to a reference variable:

```
If Not IsNothing(Page.Cache.Item("MyDS")) Then
     sqlDS = Page.Cache.Get("MyDS")
Else
     sqlDS = GenerateDataSet() ' Regenerate the DataSet
End If
```

The Cache object supports an enumeration interface that allows you to iterate through all of the items in the cache:

```
Dim enmKeys As IDictionaryEnumerator = Me.Cache.GetEnumerator
While enmKeys.MoveNext
    If enmKeys.Value.GetType.ToString = "System.String" Then
        Response.Write(enmKeys.Key & " = " & enmKeys.Value & "<BR>")
    End If
End While
```

Recall that the value property actually holds an object reference, which may not cast to a string or to any renderable data type. The `Response.Write()` method will error out for such items, so you should always check the data type of the object before you attempt to write out its value.

Removing Cache Items

You can remove cache items individually by their key name using the `Remove()` method. This method returns a reference to the item being removed. If the item is not found, then the method will return "Nothing":

```
Dim MyDS As DataSet
MyDS  = Page.Cache.Remove("MyDS") ' Evaluates to True
MyDS  = Page.Cache.Remove("MyDS2") ' Method returns Nothing
```

Cache items will also be removed automatically based on their expiration policies.

Callback Notification

We have pointed out several times that cache items are not guaranteed to remain in the cache. An item may be evicted from the cache if server resources become limited or if an item is being underused. The Cache object supports a callback mechanism that enables it to notify the application if an item gets removed. The callback is handled by one or more delegate functions that you can specify when an item gets added to the cache. The callback mechanism is especially useful in situations where the application needs to monitor items that are removed unexpectedly.

Listing 5-11 shows you how to set up callback notification. This listing is a variation of Listing 5-10. The callback function is called `ItemRemovedCallback()`, which channels the key name, the value, and a variable of type `CacheItemRemovedReason`. This type is an enumeration that indicates the reason the item was removed from the cache. The listing generates a DataSet and assigns it to the cache with an absolute expiration of five seconds. When the user posts the page back, the listing attempts to retrieve the cached item. Assuming that five or more seconds have passed, the compiler will immediately jump to the `ItemRemovedCallback()` function. Once this function executes, the compiler returns to the next line in the postback section, and the code proceeds uninterrupted.

Listing 5-11. Setting Up Callback Notification

```
Private Sub Page_Load(ByVal sender As System.Object, _
    ByVal e As System.EventArgs) Handles MyBase.Load

    If Not Page.IsPostBack Then

        Dim sqlDS As DataSet
        sqlDS = GenerateDataSet() ' Generate the DataSet

        ' Insert object to cache with absolute expiration and a callback function
        Dim MyCallbackFunction As System.Web.Caching.CacheItemRemovedCallback
        MyCallbackFunction = New CacheItemRemovedCallback( _
            AddressOf Me.ItemRemovedCallback)
        Me.Cache.Add("MyDS", sqlDS, Nothing, DateTime.Now.AddSeconds(5), _
            Cache.NoSlidingExpiration, CacheItemPriority.Low, MyCallbackFunction)

    Else

        ' Retrieve the DataSet from Cache, if it is available
        sqlDS = Me.Cache.Get("MyDS") ' Delegates to callback function if applicable
        If IsNothing(sqlDS) Then
            sqlDS = GenerateDataSet() ' Regenerate the DataSet
        End If
        BindDataGrid(sqlDS) ' Bind the DataSet to the DataGrid

    End If

End Sub
```

```
Public Sub ItemRemovedCallback(ByVal strKey As String, ByVal objValue As Object, _
    ByVal r As CacheItemRemovedReason)

    Dim strJSScript As String
    Dim strReason As String = "The item [" & strKey & "] expired."
    If r <> CacheItemRemovedReason.Expired Then _
        strReason = "The item was underused or evicted."
    Response.Write(strReason)

End Sub
```

By definition, cache items can be re-created, so your application should never encounter an unrecoverable error in the event that an item is unexpectedly evicted from the cache. Still, the callback mechanism is useful when the timing of an eviction has the potential to cause problems for the application.

Caching Web Services

Most Web service calls today are done using a Simple Object Access Protocol (SOAP) envelope within the body of a Hypertext Transfer Protocol (HTTP) POST request. Clients and proxy servers cannot intelligently interpret SOAP requests, so they will not automatically instate HTTP caching for Web service responses. (They can do so for regular POST responses, unless the origin server explicitly forbids downstream caching.) The good news is that caching is extremely simple to implement in Web services.

The WebService() attribute class provides a property called CacheDuration, which specifies the number of seconds that a response should be cached. The Web service cache automatically varies by request, and it is always stored on the origin server. The CacheDuration property sets an absolute expiration policy on cached responses by adding the specified duration to the timestamp of the initial. As with any kind of caching, the Web service cache is not guaranteed to persist responses indefinitely. However, unlike with page-level caching, you do not need to write special code in the client for handling this outcome. The Web service takes care of interpreting its own cache contents and will service a request using the cache if it can. Otherwise, it will automatically regenerate the response.

Web Service Caching Using a Proxy Browser Interface

The following code illustrates a Web service method that returns the timestamp of the current HTTP request. The GetDateTimeStamp() method accepts a string argument in order to illustrate how the cache stores multiple versions of the response for varying requests. The Web service implements a 60-second cache policy:

```
<WebMethod(CacheDuration:=60)> Public Function GetDateTimeStamp( _
        ByVal strUser As String) As String
        Return (Me.Context.Timestamp.ToLongTimeString.ToString())
End Function
```

Web services will not cache responses if they are compiled within a Web application project, so you should compile this Web service as a stand-alone project. This Web service is compiled from the ApressWS1 project, which is included with the sample code for this chapter. The Web service filename is apNorthwind.asmx.

Once you have compiled the Web service, you can then invoke the GetDateTimeStamp() method using a proxy browser interface, as shown in Figure 5-6.

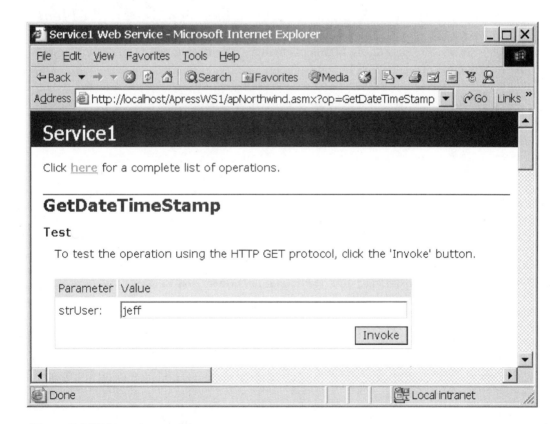

Figure 5-6. Web services caching

The method returns the following SOAP output:

```
<?xml version="1.0" encoding="utf-8" ?>
<string xmlns="http://tempuri.org/">2:47:51 PM</string>
```

The return timestamp will continue to read 2:47:51 P.M. for 60 seconds following the initial request, as long as the strUser argument value remains the same. If
the value changes, then the Web service will return a different cached response
with an alternate timestamp. The following are some sample responses:

```
2:47:51 PM        {Invoke button was clicked at 2:47:51 PM; strUser = jeff}
2:47:51 PM        {Invoke button was clicked at 2:48:21 PM; strUser = jeff}
2:48:31 PM        {Invoke button was clicked at 2:48:31 PM; strUser = ken}
2:47:51 PM        {Invoke button was clicked at 2:48:41 PM; strUser = jeff}
2:48:31 PM        {Invoke button was clicked at 2:48:51 PM; strUser = ken}
```

Web Service Caching Using a Web Application Client

Listing 5-12 illustrates a Web service method that generates a DataSet and implements a 60-second cache policy.

Listing 5-12. Web Service Caching Using a Web Application Client

```
<WebMethod(CacheDuration:=60)> Public Function GenerateDataSet( _
    ByVal BeginningDate As Date, ByVal EndingDate As Date) As DataSet

    Dim sqlDS As DataSet
    Dim strConn As String
    Dim arrParams() As String
    Dim objDB As Apress.Database

    Try
        ' Step 1: Retrieve the connection string from Web.config
        strConn = ConfigurationSettings.AppSettings("ConnectionString")

        ' Step 2: Instance a new Database object
        objDB = New Apress.Database(strConn)

        ' Step 3: Execute [Employee Sales By Country]
        arrParams = New String() {"@Beginning_Date", BeginningDate, _
                                  "@Ending_Date", EndingDate}
```

```
        sqlDS = objDB.RunQueryReturnDS("[Employee Sales By Country]", _
                                        arrParams)
    Catch err As Exception
        ' Implement error-handling code here
    Finally
    End Try


    Return (sqlDS)


End Function
```

This Web service is also compiled in the ApressWS1 project. The Web service manages its own cache and ensures that a response will be delivered to the Web client page, whether or not the response originates from the cache. The client does not need to check for the existence of a response.

The sample project AspNetChap5B contains a Web page, ap_OutputCache3.aspx, that is a client for the ApressWS1 Web service. The client application must first set a dynamic Web reference to the Web service. Follow these steps:

1. Compile the ApressWS1 project.

2. Switch over to the AspNetChap5B project. In Solution Explorer, right-click the project file and select Add Web Reference from the pop-up menu.

3. In the dialog box, type in the Uniform Resource Indicator (URI) for the Web service—for example: http://localhost/ApressWS1/apNorthwind.asmx.

4. The contract details will appear in the left pane of the dialog box.

5. Click the Add Reference button.

6. In Solution Explorer, open the properties page for the Web reference.

7. Change the URL behavior from Static to Dynamic. This adds the URI to the Web.config file.

This is the URI that gets added to a new application setting in the Web.config file:

```
<appSettings>
        <add key="AspNetChap5B.localhost.Service1"
                value="http://localhost/ApressWS1/apNorthwind.asmx"/>
</appSettings>
```

The Web client calls the GenerateDataSet() Web service method as shown in Listing 5-13.

Listing 5-13. Calling GenerateDataSet()

```
Private Sub Page_Load(ByVal sender As System.Object, _
    ByVal e As System.EventArgs) Handles MyBase.Load

    Dim sqlDS As DataSet
    Dim objWS As localhost.Service1

    Try

        ' Step 1: Generate the DataSet, using a Web Service call
        objWS = New localhost.Service1()
        objWS.Url = ConfigurationSettings.AppSettings( _
                "AspNetChap5B.localhost.Service1")
        sqlDS = objWS.GenerateDataSet(Me.ap_txt_beginning_date.Text, _
                Me.ap_txt_ending_date.Text)
        ' Step 2: Bind the DataSet to the DataGrid
        BindDataGrid(sqlDS)
    Catch err As Exception
        Response.Write(err.Message)
    Finally
        sqlDS = Nothing
    End Try

End Sub
```

As with the previous example, the GenerateDataSet() Web service method will cache responses for 60 seconds and will vary the cache based on the request. Users who request the same date range will receive the same cached response.

NOTE *You should be careful in deciding whether to imple-*
ment Web service caching simply because you have so little
control over the behavior of the cache. You should not imple-
ment caching in Web services that handle widely varying
requests and that consistently generate large responses. This
scenario could result in a cache that is populated with mul-
tiple versions of large responses. The cache will optimize its
memory usage, but you cannot guarantee that it will do so
effectively enough such that the Web service performance
level remains consistent.

Caching in Web Farms

Caching is inherently incompatible with a multiserver environment such as
a Web farm. The cache mechanism is specific to an individual application
instance, which cannot be shared between multiple servers. Cached items may
have application-level scope, but they are limited to a single server. Whether this
is an issue or not depends on two main factors:

- The Web Application architecture

- The type of information being stored in the cache

Internet Protocol (IP) redirectors, such as Cisco's LocalDirector and F5
Network's BIGIP, are popular components for managing requests to servers in
a Web farm. IP redirectors can ensure that a client's requests get routed to the
same server for the duration of their session if you enable the option for so-called
sticky sessions. However, if that server happens to crash, or become unavailable,
then the user will be routed to another server that will have no record of their
cached information. This should not really be a problem if you consider the phi-
losophy behind cached content. As pointed out earlier, cached content is, by
definition, re-creatable. The Application object, and the Web.config file, store
information that must be available at all times for the application to function
correctly. The Cache object, however, stores transient information and improves
performance. Cached items are not guaranteed to remain in the cache, so the
application should never assume that they will always be there. This point was
clearly illustrated in the code examples for the Cache API: An application may
attempt to retrieve a DataSet from the cache before making a database call. But
the code must run a null check on the existence of the cached item before automatically referencing it.

On a side note, keep in mind that SQL Server provides its own caching mechanism that is independent of ASP.NET. SQL Server caches data pages in memory in order to speed up its response to queries. For example, if multiple users execute the same query, then SQL Server will attempt to return the resultsets by assembling data pages from the cache. This approach can have significant performance benefits. Cached data pages may be served on the order of nanoseconds, whereas disk reads may take on the order of milliseconds. It is not uncommon to run a SQL trace on a stored procedure call and to observe a response time of zero milliseconds. Of course, the exact response times depend greatly on the type and amount of information you are retrieving.

Regardless of how fast SQL Server may be, the important point is this: SQL Server typically plays a central role in a multiserver Web farm environment. Effectively, SQL Server *is* a centralized cache. Multiple servers may run their own application instances, but they retrieve their information from a central SQL Server database. The database server maintains a cache that is influenced by all user requests, not just those that originate from a single server. Essentially, Web farm architectures that are built around a centralized database already benefit from a centralized cache. (We are not intentionally ignoring other, non-Microsoft database servers, many of which provide similar benefits).

For those readers who prefer to centralize their cache using ASP.NET, you can design a centralized cache using a Web service component, as follows:

1. Determine what kind of information needs to be cached. For example, let's say your application generates a large DataSet to assemble the same start page for every user.

2. Create a Web service that contains a method for generating the common DataSet.

3. Compile the Web service and install it on a server that is accessible to the Web farm. Ideally, this server should be in the same domain, and on the same physical network, in order to minimize communication time.

4. Add a Web reference to the application code to retrieve the DataSet from the Web service.

Keep in mind that this approach only works for individual cached items, which are managed using the Cache API. Page-level output caching cannot be centralized in a Web service because the Page object cannot be marshaled using a SOAP envelope. There is a cost associated with marshaling large SOAP envelopes across the wire and with serializing the data, especially for complex data. On the positive side, SOAP envelopes are, after all, just text, so the envelope would have to be very large to generate a significant number of bytes.

The critical part of this workaround approach is installing the Web service in close proximity to the Web servers to minimize response times. (Alternatively, you could write a .NET component in place of the Web service and communicate with it using binary formatting over TCP. This approach would eliminate the parsing penalties associated with calling a conventional Web service. However, you also lose the flexibility of a Web service, which may be called from a wider variety of consumers.)

This chapter has presented much of what you need to develop the Web service and to plug it in to the Web client. The next step is for you to run performance tests on your application to determine if the resulting performance is acceptable. Chapter 7, "Stress Testing and Monitoring ASP.NET Applications," provides a detailed discussion for how to run application performance tests.

In summary, you have three options for implementing caching in a Web farm environment:

- **Take no action**: You can allow each server to maintain its own cache.

- **Use an IP Redirector**: You can do this to handle user sessions on the same server.

- **Implement a workaround**: You can use a Web service to maintain a centralized cache for every application instance in the Web farm.

Caching with ISA Server

Microsoft ISA Server is a firewall system that also provides sophisticated caching capabilities for speeding up access to Web content. ISA Server acts as a secure intermediary between an internal network and the external Internet. Its caching capabilities provide accelerated access to information on both sides of the firewall. Specifically, ISA Server provides two broad types of caching:

> **Forward caching**: This is for internal clients that are accessing information on the Internet. ISA Server maintains a local cache of frequently cached pages, which reduces the access time significantly for internal clients. In addition, the system administrator can schedule ISA Server to scan the Internet for specific content so that it will already be available in the cache the first time that it is accessed.

Reverse caching: This is for external clients that are accessing information on internal, published servers. ISA Server impersonates the internal servers for external clients and fulfills requests directly from its cache. ISA Server will redirect the request directly to the internal server only if the external client's request cannot be fulfilled from the cache.

ISA Server stores cached content locally both on disk and in memory. This mechanism will obviously consume resources on the server, so ISA Server provides two complementary caching mechanisms for reducing this burden:

Distributed caching: ISA Server will cache content across an array of servers, but it will organize the content as a single logical cache. Essentially, ISA Server is distributing the caching burden across multiple servers. It accomplishes this using the Cache Array Routing Protocol (CARP).

Hierarchical caching: ISA Server extends the distributed caching mechanism by administering multiple server arrays (essentially a supergroup of multiple groups of servers). ISA Server will route client requests to the most available server array.

The performance improvements with ISA Server can be dramatic. Internal clients will experience reduced response times for retrieving Internet content. In addition, bandwidth usage on the Internet connection will be reduced, which will result in a potentially faster Internet connection for all clients.

Microsoft recommends that the ideal deployment scenario for .NET Web applications is to use nondistributed deployment with ISA Server. This means you should install your application in a Web farm (in other words, on multiple servers) and use ISA Server for load balancing and caching services. It is *not* ideal to manually distribute components across multiple servers and have them communicate using .NET remoting.

NOTE *You can read more about ISA Server at* http://msdn.microsoft.com/library/ default.asp?url=/library/en-us/isa/isaabout_0sdz.asp. *You can read more about non-distributed deployment with ISA Server at* http://msdn.microsoft.com/library/ default.asp?url=/library/en-us/dwamish7/html/ vtconNon-DistributedDeploymentWithISAServer.asp.

This concludes our discussion of caching in ASP.NET.

Summary

Caching is a feature that allows ASP.NET applications to store frequently accessed items in memory for better responsiveness. ASP.NET provides two types of caching: output caching and application data caching. Output caching provides the ability to cache partial or full-page responses on the Web server. We discussed how to implement output caching, both declaratively and programmatically. Output caching can vary by parameters, which allows flexible caching for groups of requests for the same page. The @ OutputCache directive provides declarative caching setup and configuration. The HttpCachePolicy object provides programmatic caching setup and configuration. Next, we discussed Application data caching using the Cache API. This is a highly flexible and optimized way to store frequently accessed items. The Cache API provides a number of features that make it an excellent alternative to using the Application object, including memory management, concurrency management, and dependency-based expiration. Next, we reviewed caching in Web services. Finally, we closed with a discussion on design considerations for caching in Web farms.

CHAPTER 6

Writing Optimized Web Services

WEB SERVICES **ARE DISTRIBUTED** components that communicate using standard pro-
tocols such as Simple Object Access Protocol (SOAP) and Hypertext Transfer
Protocol (HTTP) over Transmission Control Protocol/Internet Protocol (TCP/IP).
Web services are flexible and robust because they operate in a loosely coupled
environment using reliable, industry-standard communication mechanisms.
Web services are self-documenting because they publish details of their interface
using an Extensible Markup Language (XML) vocabulary called *the Web Services
Description Language* (WSDL). In addition, you build Web services with bindings
to documented namespaces that serve as a point of reference for the Web service
methods. These technologies enable Web service components to evolve over time
in a self-documenting manner that minimizes the adverse impacts of these
changes on consumers. Web services are platform and language agnostic, and
they may be consumed by any client on any platform, as long as that client is
capable of exchanging XML. In short, the technologies that Web services are built
on enable these remote components to operate in a full-disclosure manner,
which removes the mystery of how to call and communicate with them.

ASP.NET provides a special project type and a number of high-level classes
for building Web services. Visual Studio .NET (VS .NET) provides excellent
productivity benefits for building Web services by encapsulating many of the
low-level infrastructure details that are required when building Web services. For
example, it will automatically generate the XML-based WSDL file that describes
the interface for your Web service. This is enormously beneficial, especially when
your Web service interface is evolving in the early stages of development. If you
have ever looked at the complexity of a WSDL file, then you will immediately
appreciate why you do not want to have to generate these files manually! Finally,
VS .NET allows you to avoid having to handle SOAP responses and requests
directly. Instead, you can generate a proxy class that handles the SOAP interaction details for you.

Much attention has been given to the fact that XML Web services are
platform-independent, meaning that they can respond to requests that originate
from any source. Although this is certainly true in concept, it is not always easy to
write platform-agnostic Web services. This is mainly because different vendors
support a wide range of complex data types (such as the Microsoft ADO.NET

DataSet) that may not be equally supported by every platform. In theory, complex data types should be a non-issue, as long as they can serialize to XML and be represented in a SOAP packet. The Web service WSDL file completely documents its interface and the XML namespaces that it references. For example, any Web service built using ASP.NET should reference the XML-MSDATA namespace, which documents complex data types such as the ADO.NET DataSet. Even so, you should be prepared to do some integration work if your project requires you to invoke Web services built on a different platform from the one you are using.

There is a lot of marketing hype surrounding Web services, which we avoid in this chapter in favor of a more pragmatic perspective. In the spirit of this book, we highlight the important aspects of Microsoft-based Web services technology and then look at how you use the technology optimally. Our position on Web services is clear: They are a mind-opening, revolutionary way to bring business logic to the Internet. ASP.NET enables you to build them, and we spend most of this chapter discussing how to build them in the most optimal way.

A Web Services Technology Primer

Acronyms abound in the world of Web services. SOAP, WSDL, and Universal Discovery, Description, and Integration (UDDI) are three key technologies that play a role in building, consuming, and discovering Web services. Let's summarize each of the important technologies:

> **Standard Object Access Protocol (SOAP)**: SOAP is a communications protocol and an XML-based specification for messages. SOAP is the protocol of choice for communicating with Web services, although HTTP-POST and HTTP-GET are viable (but limited) alternatives. SOAP messages are usually transmitted over HTTP, although they may also be transmitted over TCP/IP, SMTP, and assorted other protocols.

> **Web Services Description Language (WSDL)**: WSDL is an XML-based vocabulary that describes the set of SOAP messages that a Web service supports. Every Web service has an associated WSDL file that documents the Web methods, including their arguments and return type. VS .NET uses the WSDL file for generating a proxy class that ASP.NET consumer applications can use for communicating with the Web service. VS .NET also provides a default Service Description screen that summarizes the WSDL information in a readable format. You can view the service description when you navigate directly to a Web service and append the ?WSDL query string to the URL entry.

Universal Discovery, Description, and Integration (UDDI): UDDI is a registered XML file that publishes information about a Web service in a centralized, browsable location. A UDDI directory enables third parties to locate and research your Web service. For more information, visit http://uddi.microsoft.com.

In this chapter we explore in greater detail the roles of SOAP and WSDL in building and consuming Web services. We also discuss how ASP.NET and VS .NET use these technologies out of the box. Typically, you do not need to alter the WSDL file that ASP.NET generates for your Web service. And usually you do not need to interact with SOAP requests and responses directly. This shielding translates directly into productivity gains as you build Web services. Still, there are times when you will need to do a little work under the hood to optimize your Web service. We spend some time discussing how to work with SOAP extensions for added functionality.

Building Web Services Using ASP.NET

ASP.NET makes it easy to build Web services because it provides a special project type and targeted framework classes for constructing and implementing Web service methods. VS .NET provides even more productivity gains because it handles most of the complex infrastructure issues for you that are required to communicate with the Web service. For example, VS .NET will automatically generate a proxy class from the Web service's WSDL document. Recall that a proxy class enables managed code to call a Web service much like a standard component, without directly assembling and interpreting SOAP request and response envelopes. VS .NET automatically generates a proxy class when you add a Web reference to the Web service directly from the consumer application.

Web service projects are a specialized type of ASP.NET project. Although you can build Web services without ASP.NET and VS .NET, we do not discuss this approach because the productivity benefits are too powerful to ignore. The entry point file for the Web service ends with an .asmx extension and contains the @ WebService directive with attributes that describe the code-behind assembly. For example:

```
<%@ WebService Language="vb" Codebehind="wsNorthwind.asmx.vb"
        Class="WebService6A.Northwind" %>
```

The Web service's code-behind assembly class should derive from the WebService base class, which also provides access to the ASP.NET intrinsic objects. The WebService class is a member of the System.Web.Services namespace, which also provides the WebServiceAttribute and WebMethodAttribute classes. These classes provide members for exposing assembly functions as callable Web service methods. Table 6-1 summarizes the important members of this namespace.

Table 6-1. Important Members of the System.Web.Services *Namespace*

MEMBER	DESCRIPTION
WebServiceAttribute	Sets and retrieves descriptive properties for a Web service assembly class, including the following:
	Namespace: The default XML namespace to which the Web service belongs. The namespace is the first part of the XML qualified name for the Web service.
	Name: The name of the Web service. The name is the second part of the XML qualified name for the Web service. The name displays in the Service Description page for the Web service.
	Description: A description of the Web service. The description displays in the Service Description page for the Web service.
WebMethodAttribute	Exposes an assembly function as a callable Web service method. It provides properties for controlling the behavior of the Web method, including the following:
	MessageName: The name of the Web method used in messages to and from the Web service method.
	Description: A description of the Web method.
	CacheDuration: The number of seconds to cache response output. This form of output caching varies by parameter—in other words, a non-cached response is generated if the input parameter values for the current response vary from the cached response.
	TransactionOption: Sets the level of transaction support by the Web method. Note, Web methods may initiate new root transactions, but they may not participate in existing ones.
	EnableSession: Indicates whether the Web method enables session state management.

(continued)

Table 6-1. Important Members of the `System.Web.Services` *Namespace (continued)*

MEMBER	DESCRIPTION
WebService	Sets the base class from which a Web service assembly class should derive. This base class is optional, but it does provide access to the ASP.NET intrinsic objects. This includes the User object, which may be used for authentication purposes.
WebServiceBindingAttribute	Attaches a Web method to an XML binding, which is a collection of related Web methods, similar to an interface.

The programming syntax for using these namespace classes is different from the traditional code-behind approach of creating object instances. Instead, the classes are referenced as annotated attributes directly on the Web service assembly methods. The following code, which uses wire frame code for a Web service with one method, illustrates this:

```
Imports System.Data
Imports System.Web.Services
<WebService(Namespace:="http://tempuri.org/")> _
Public Class Northwind
    Inherits System.Web.Services.WebService
    <WebMethod(Description:="Generates a DataSet of Employee Sales By Date", _
            CacheDuration:=60)> _
    Public Function GetEmployeeSales(ByVal BeginningDate As Date, _
            ByVal EndingDate As Date) As DataSet
    End Function
End Class
```

Of course, the beauty of the .NET Framework is that its classes are available to any .NET project type, including ASP.NET Web services. So, while coding a Web service, you can continue to leverage useful namespaces such as `System.Data` for accessing data and `System.Xml` for manipulating XML.

Generating a Proxy Class Using WSDL

Web services include associated Service Description files that describe the interface that the Web service supports. VS .NET uses the WSDL file to automatically generate a proxy class for accessing the Web service. This proxy class assembles the requests and responses in the correct format and enables the consumer code to focus on the input and output values, without worrying about formats.

You can view the WSDL code directly when you navigate directly to a Web service `*.asmx` file in the browser and append the `?WSDL` query string to the Uniform Resource Locator (URL) entry. Alternatively, you can navigate to the default Service Description file that VS .NET provides, as shown in Figure 6-1.

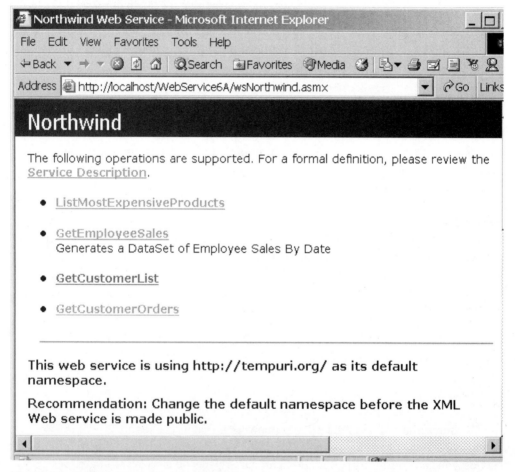

Figure 6-1. Default Service Description File

You can click any of the Web method hyperlinks to execute the method and view the output directly in the browser, as shown in Figure 6-2.

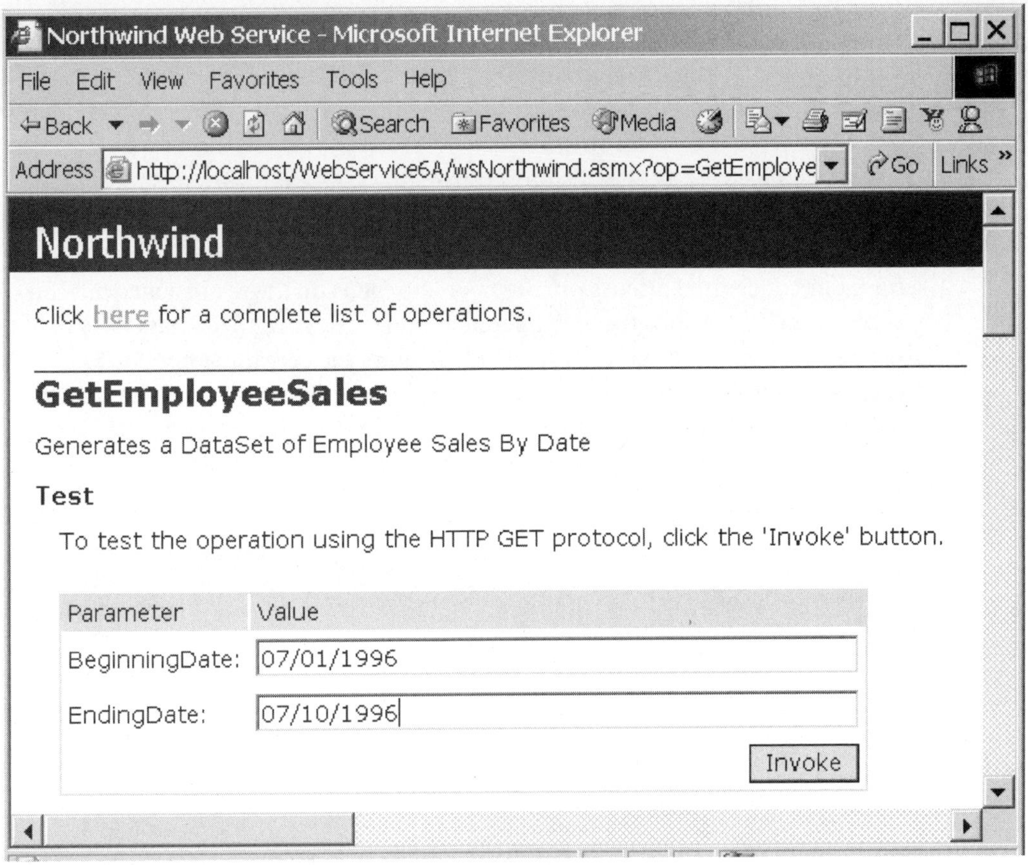

Figure 6-2. Using the default Service Description file

The response will be returned directly to the browser window as a SOAP response envelope because this Web service uses SOAP as its communication protocol. The following code shows a small section of the response XML:

```
<diffgr:diffgram xmlns:msdata="urn:schemas-microsoft-com:xml-msdata"
    xmlns:diffgr="urn:schemas-microsoft-com:xml-diffgram-v1">
<NewDataSet xmlns="">
        <Table diffgr:id="Table1" msdata:rowOrder="0">
                <Country>UK</Country>
                <LastName>Suyama</LastName>
                <FirstName>Michael</FirstName>
                <ShippedDate>1996-07-10T00:00:00.0000000-07:00</ShippedDate>
                <OrderID>10249</OrderID>
```

```
                    <SaleAmount>1863.4</SaleAmount>
        </Table>
    </NewDataSet>
    </diffgr:diffgram>
```

You create proxy classes using VS .NET simply by adding a Web reference to the ASP.NET application that will consume the Web service. We outline the exact steps later in the "Consuming the Web Service" section so as not to get distracted from our conceptual discussion. For now, let's focus on the result. Once the consumer application adds the Web reference, you can switch to its Class View to review the proxy class interface. Figure 6-3 shows the consumer application's Class View once a Web reference has been set to the Northwind Web service on the localhost server.

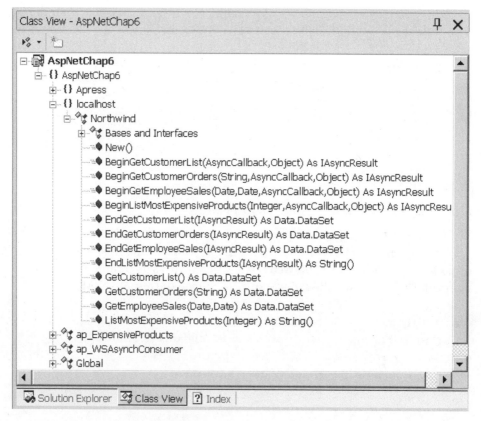

Figure 6-3. Web service proxy class interface

Notice that the proxy class automatically creates three proxy methods for every Web method. One proxy method is for accessing the Web method synchronously. For example, the GetCustomerList() proxy method is for synchronous access to the GetCustomerList() Web method. In addition, the proxy class contains a Begin[MethodName] and End[MethodName] pair that handles asynchronous access to the GetCustomerList() Web method. We will see examples of each later in the chapter.

Web Service-Supported Data Types

Web services exist to exchange data, which poses a challenge because supported data types may vary between platforms. Microsoft-based Web services support a number of the data types that are outlined in the XML Schema Definition Language (XSD). This includes a mix of primitive and simple data types. Table 6-2 summarizes the supported XSD data types and their equivalent .NET Framework data types.

Table 6-2. Web Service–Supported Data Types

XSD DATA TYPE	.NET FRAMEWORK DATA TYPE
boolean	Boolean
Byte	Byte
decimal	Decimal
enumeration	Enum
Float	Single
Short	Int16 (unsigned version also available: UInt16)
Int	Int32 (unsigned version also available: UInt32)
Long	Int64 (unsigned version also available: UInt64)
String	String
timeInstant	DateTime
Qname	XmlQualifiedName (a .NET class that represents an XML name and its reference namespace)

Microsoft-based Web services support additional complex data types such as the ADO.NET DataSet, which serializes to XML and can be represented in a SOAP response. In fact, the DataSet is represented in XML using a combination of several XSD-standard data types, including the schema and sequence data types. Data type construction is beyond the scope of our discussion, but suffice it to say that Web services may support any data type, including both customer-defined and user-defined data types, as long as they serialize to XML and can be described in an XML specification document.

Building and Consuming Web Services

ASP.NET allows you to build and compile a Web service directly into an ASP.NET Web application. Alternatively, you can build a stand-alone Web service (in its own project). We take the second approach because it provides a more realistic approach. Web services operate remotely, so it does not make sense to compile them together with a client application, even for demonstration purposes. ASP.NET lets you easily set a reference to the Web service from a client application, such as an ASP.NET Web application.

Examples of Web Services and Consumers

The best way to continue our discussion on Web services is to jump right in and show how they are built and consumed. The sample code that accompanies this chapter contains two projects: a Web service application and a consumer Web application:

> **WebService6A**: A Web service application for Northwind.asmx, which provides the following Web methods:

- GetEmployeeSales(): Executes the [Employee Sales By Country] stored procedure in the Northwind database. It accepts beginning and ending dates.

- ListMostExpensiveProducts(): Executes the [Ten Most Expensive Products] stored procedure. It accepts a product count, specifying how many records should be returned.

- GetCustomerList(): Executes a custom stored procedure called [CustomerList], which returns the full listing of customers in the Northwind database.

- GetCustomerOrders(): Executes the [CustOrderHist] stored procedure, which returns all orders for a specific customer. It accepts a customer ID.

AspNetChap6: A client application for the Northwind.asmx Web service:

- ap_WSConsumer1.aspx: The client page for the GetEmployeeSales() Web method. This page calls the Web method from server-side code.

- ap_WSAsynchCustomer1.aspx: A client page that displays a list of customers and their associated orders using both the GetCustomerList() and GetCustomerOrders() web methods. This page demonstrates how to call Web methods asynchronously.

- ap_ExpensiveProducts.aspx: The client page for the ListMostExpensiveProducts() Web method. This page calls the Web method from client-side code.

Each of the three consumer pages represents a different way of accessing Web service methods. The Web service code on its own is fairly simple, but the picture gets more interesting when you look at how the methods get consumed. In summary, we look at three types of Web service consumption:

- Synchronous server side: Synchronous access from a code assembly

- Asynchronous server side: Asynchronous access from a code assembly

- Asynchronous client side: Asynchronous access using the WebService DHTML behavior

Let's look at each client application in turn and discuss the associated Web service methods while working through the clients. We hope you will find this approach to be effective and intuitive because the concepts will be presented by example and will be grounded in useful code that you can apply to real-world challenges.

Building a Web Service for a Server-Side Consumer

Figure 6-4 shows the ap_WSConsumer1.aspx client page.

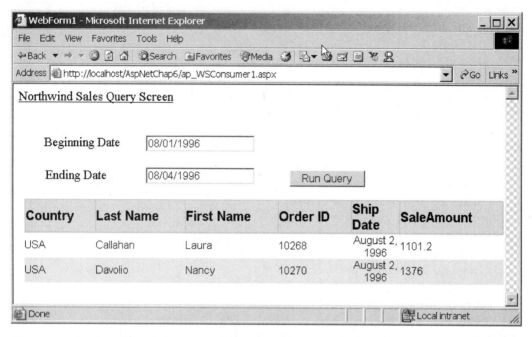

Figure 6-4. Consuming a Web service synchronously

The page accepts beginning and ending dates, and it returns a listing of employee sales by country for the specified date range. The Run Query button posts the form to the server, which in turn calls the `GetEmployeeSales()` Web method. This method returns a DataSet that gets bound directly to the DataGrid control on the client page.

Listing 6-1 shows the code for the `GetEmployeeSales()` Web method.

Listing 6-1. `GetEmployeeSales()`

```
Imports System.Data
Imports System.Data.SqlClient
Imports System.Configuration
Imports System.Xml
Imports System.Web.Services
Imports System.Web.Services.Protocols

<WebService(Namespace:="http://tempuri.org/")> _
Public Class Northwind
    Inherits System.Web.Services.WebService
```

```
<WebMethod()> Public Function GetEmployeeSales(ByVal BeginningDate As Date, _
                                ByVal EndingDate As Date) As DataSet
    Dim sqlDS As DataSet
    Dim strConn As String
    Dim arrParams() As String
    Dim objDB As Apress.Database

    Try
        ' Step 1: Retrieve the connection string from Web.config
        strConn = ConfigurationSettings.AppSettings("ConnectionString")

        ' Step 2: Instance a new Database object
        objDB = New Apress.Database(strConn)

        ' Step 3: Execute [Employee Sales By Country]
        arrParams = New String() {"@Beginning_Date", BeginningDate, _
                            "@Ending_Date", EndingDate}
        sqlDS = objDB.RunQueryReturnDS("[Employee Sales By Country]", _
                        arrParams)
    Catch err As Exception
        Throw err
    Finally
    End Try
    Return (sqlDS) ' Return the DataSet
End Function
End Class
```

The following points are interesting to note:

- The Web service is assigned to the http://tempuri.org namespace by default.

- The code-behind file for this Web service is encapsulated by the Northwind class, which in turn inherits from the System.Web.Services class.

- The Web method retrieves its database connection string from the local Web.config file.

- The Web method uses a custom database access class called Apress.Database, which you can review in the sample project.

Aside from the Web method attributes and some of the imported classes, Listing 6-1 looks unremarkable.

Consuming the Web Service

The client application must set a Web reference to the Web service before any Web methods can be invoked. The steps for setting a Web reference are as follows:

1. Compile the WebService6A Web service project.

2. Switch over to the AspNetChap6 project. In Solution Explorer, right-click the project file and select Add Web Reference from the pop-up menu.

3. In the dialog box, type in the Uniform Resource Indicator (URI) for the Web service: `http://localhost/WebService6A/wsNorthwind.asmx`.

4. The contract details will appear in the left pane of the dialog box (as shown in Figure 6-5).

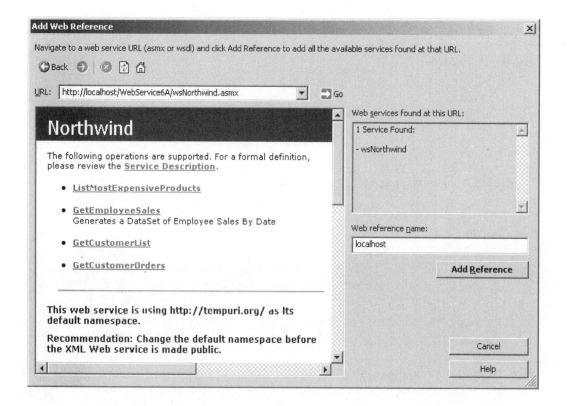

Figure 6-5. Setting a Web reference to a Web service

5. Click the Add Reference button.

6. In Solution Explorer, click the localhost server node in the Web References folder to open its property page.

7. Change the URL behavior property value from "Static" to "Dynamic." This step automatically adds the URI to the Web.config file, which makes it easy for you to update the Web service location should it change in the future.

This URI gets added to a new application setting in the Web.config file:

```
<appSettings>
    <add key="AspNetChap6.localhost.Northwind"
            value="http://localhost/WebService6/wsNorthwind.asmx"/>
</appSettings>
```

The client page can now call the GetEmployeeSales() Web service method as shown in Listing 6-2.

Listing 6-2. Calling GetEmployeeSales()

```
Private Sub btnRunQuery_Click(ByVal sender As System.Object, _
        ByVal e As System.EventArgs) Handles btnRunQuery.Click
    ' Purpose: Load a Sales Query DataSet using the beginning and ending dates
    ' provided by the user
    Dim sqlDS As DataSet
    Dim objWS As localhost.Northwind

    Try
        ' Step 1: Generate the DataSet, using a Web service call
        objWS = New localhost.Northwind()
        objWS.Url = _
            ConfigurationSettings.AppSettings("AspNetChap6.localhost.Northwind")
            sqlDS = objWS.GetEmployeeSales(Me.ap_txt_beginning_date.Text, _
                Me.ap_txt_ending_date.Text)

        ' Step 2: Bind the DataSet to the DataGrid
        BindDataGrid(sqlDS)
    Catch errSoap As System.Web.Services.Protocols.SoapException
        Response.Write("SOAP Exception: " & errSoap.Message)
    Catch err As Exception
```

```
            Response.Write(err.Message)
        Finally
            sqlDS = Nothing
        End Try
    End Sub
```

Exception Handling in Web Service Methods

In general, you have three main options when it comes to raising exceptions from a Web service method:

- **Return exceptions**: You can build exception messages into the return argument. For example, if your Web service returns an array of strings, then you could have the first array element indicate the success or failure of the call.

- **Implied exceptions**: You can imply that an exception occurred by returning empty or null values. For example, if your Web service returns a DataSet, then you could intentionally return "Nothing" if an exception occurs. This approach is appropriate if the client does not need to know details of why the exception occurred.

- **SoapException exceptions**: The SoapException class is a specialized exception class that is generated by a Web service method when it throws an exception back to the calling client. The client must be able to interpret a SOAP response to interpret the SOAP exception.

The first two options are both acceptable approaches for exception handling. But the third option, using the SoapException class, is the only good choice when the client needs to receive meaningful exception information from the Web service method. Let's explore this approach in further detail.

Exception Handling Using the SoapException Class

The SoapException class inherits from the standard System.Exception class, but the similarity ends there. The SoapException class is tailored toward delivering exception messages inside of a SOAP Response envelope. As such, it provides an overloaded constructor that optionally accepts an XML document. This feature is useful for many reasons. If a malformed SOAP request causes the exception, then the Web service could return the offending splice of the SOAP request packet back to the user for remediation. Alternatively, the Web service could return exceptions as XML documents using a standard schema. The client could then in turn transform the exception document into a standard, stylized exception Web page. Table 6-3 lists the properties used in constructing a SoapException class.

Table 6-3. Properties for the SoapException Class Constructor

PROPERTY	DESCRIPTION
Message	[Required] The Message property describes the exception.
Code	[Required] SOAP fault codes that indicate what type of exception has occurred. The values are as follows:
	ClientFaultCode: The client call was malformed, could not be authenticated, or did not contain sufficient information. This fault code indicates that the client's SOAP request must be remedied.
	ServerFaultCode: The server encountered an exception while processing the client request, but it was not because of any problems with the client's SOAP request. If the code raises a standard exception, then it is automatically converted to a SoapException, and the default setting for Code is ServerFaultCode.
	VersionMismatchFaultCode: An invalid namespace was found somewhere in the SOAP envelope and must be remedied.
	MustUnderstandFaultCode: Indicates that every SOAP element must be successfully processed. The Web service may successfully process a request even if certain SOAP elements have minor issues. However, no issues will be allowed if MustUnderstandFaultCode is set.
Actor	[Optional] The URI of the Web service method that experienced the exception.
Detail	[Optional] An XML node that represents application-specific exception information. The information here should refer to exceptions that are related to processing the body of the SOAP request. Issues with the SOAP headers should be raised using the SoapHeaderException class.
InnerException	[Optional] An Exception class that references to the root cause of the Web method exception.

The GetEmployeeSales() Web service method, as it is currently written, will throw back a standard exception, but it will not return meaningful information about problems with the SOAP request. The Web service automatically converts a standard thrown exception to a SoapException class instance. The client does not have to trap for the SoapException class specifically. Instead, the client can retrieve some exception details, such as the exception message, by trapping for the standard Exception class. This approach is adequate if your client application does not anticipate having problems with the structure of its SOAP request. But sophisticated Web services should always implement the SoapException class because one cannot anticipate the mistakes that outside users will make in compiling their SOAP requests. You will do them a big favor by returning detailed information about the nature of their exception.

There is really no correct way to raise a SOAP exception; however, it must return Message and Code parameters at a minimum. The power of the SoapException class lies in its flexibility. Let's look at one way of raising a detailed SOAP exception using the GetEmployeeSales() Web method.

Raising a SOAP Exception Server Fault Code

You can simulate a server-side exception inside the GetEmployeeSales() Web method by manually raising an exception right before the exception handler:

```
' Simulate a server-side exception
err.Raise(vbObjectError + 512, "wsNorthwind.GenerateDataSet", _
    "The SOAP request could not be processed.")
Catch err As Exception
            ' Exception handling code goes here
```

You can add code inside the Web method's exception handler to build a SoapException:

```
Catch err As Exception

    ' Step 1: Build the detail element of the SOAP exception.
    Dim doc As New System.Xml.XmlDocument()
    Dim node As System.Xml.XmlNode = doc.CreateNode(XmlNodeType.Element, _
    SoapException.DetailElementName.Name, _
            SoapException.DetailElementName.Namespace)

    ' Step 2: Add a child detail XML element to the document
    Dim details As System.Xml.XmlNode = doc.CreateNode(XmlNodeType.Element, _
            "ErrDetail", "http://tempuri.org/")
```

```
details.InnerText = "An exception occurred while processing the dates: " & _
        BeginningDate & " and " & EndingDate
node.AppendChild(details)

' Step 3 Assemble the SoapException class and throw the exception
Dim errSoap As New SoapException(err.Message, _
        SoapException.ServerFaultCode, "wsNorthwind.asmx", node)
Throw errSoap ' Throw the SOAP Exception
```

On the client application side, you can trap for both the general and the detailed exception messages as follows:

```
Catch errSoap As System.Web.Services.Protocols.SoapException
    ' Writes out the general SOAP exception message
    Response.Write("SOAP Exception1: " & errSoap.Message & "<BR>")
    ' Writes out the full SOAP exception details (from an XML details node)
Response.Write("SOAP Exception2: " & errSoap.Detail.InnerText)
```

The resulting exception gets posted as follows:

```
SOAP Exception1: System.Web.Services.Protocols.SoapException:
                The SOAP request could not be processed
SOAP Exception2: An exception occurred while processing the dates:
                7/10/1996 and 7/10/1996
```

Clearly, SOAP exception handling is not a trivial undertaking because there are many possibilities for both creating and consuming SOAP exceptions.

Building a Web Service for a Server-Side Consumer with Asynchronous Calls

Asynchronous Web method calls are useful for calling methods that require a long time to execute. In synchronous calls, the calling thread must wait until the method call is complete. This becomes a problem if the calling thread must wait around for a long-running method call to complete. Recall that the ASP.NET worker process maintains a thread pool for servicing all application requests. Every thread that gets tied up in waiting for a long-running method to complete is unavailable to participate in the finite thread pool. This has the potential to block the ASP.NET worker process so that new application requests get queued up, rather than serviced immediately.

Asynchronous Web method calls free up the calling thread and return it to the thread pool where it can continue servicing other requests. In asynchronous calls, the HttpContext for the current request does not get released until the call is completed, so the details of the request are preserved. Once the asynchronous call completes, any available thread in the pool can pick the request up again and finish executing it.

In practical terms, asynchronous Web method calls may improve the scalability of your Web application because the ASP.NET worker process can continue to handle new application requests, even while it is handling pending requests.

It is not just other applications that may benefit. The current application instance may require a number of lengthy operations. It may be beneficial to handle some of these operations asynchronously so that other, synchronous operations can start earlier. The net result of this mix of synchronous and asynchronous operations is that the Web application's responsiveness and scalability may improve. This will result in better real and perceived performance for the user.

The previous Web service examples all used synchronous method calls, which are the simpler to code compared to asynchronous method calls. Web services do not require any special compilation options to support asynchronous methods calls. This is because the proxy class is automatically built with methods for asynchronous invocation. A Web method such as GetEmployeeOrders() is compiled as three methods in the proxy class:

- **GetEmployeeOrders**(): For synchronous method invocation

- **BeginGetEmployeeOrders**(): To begin asynchronous method invocation

- **EndGetEmployeeOrders**(): To end asynchronous method invocation

VS .NET creates the proxy class automatically when you add a Web reference to the Web service. When you call the Begin<Method> function, .NET automatically spawns a separate thread and dispatches the method call to this new thread. The main ASP.NET worker thread is then free to continue working on other things.

Asynchronous method invocation used to be a difficult task best left for expert level programmers; but with the release of the .NET Framework, this is no longer the case. The .NET Framework handles the infrastructure for asynchronous programming, which lifts a considerable burden off the developer. The .NET Framework defines a design pattern for asynchronous method invocation that makes this a relatively straightforward task. The Web service proxy classes integrate into the design pattern and do not require any special programming steps.

Consuming the Web Service

Figure 6-6 shows the ap_WSAsynchConsumer1.aspx client page.

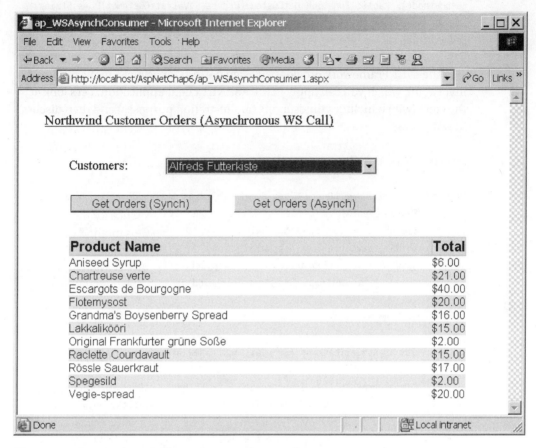

Figure 6-6. Consuming a Web service asynchronously

The client page provides a list of all customers in the Northwind database along with their associated orders. The Customers list is generated from the GetCustomerList() Web service method using a synchronous call. The "Get Orders" buttons load the order details for the currently selected customer using the GetCustomerOrders() Web service method. The left button invokes the Web service method synchronously, and the right button invokes the method asynchronously.

The code listings for the Web service methods are straightforward: They execute stored procedures and return DataSet objects. You need only look at the interface code for the purposes of this discussion:

```
<WebMethod()> Public Function GetCustomerList() As DataSet
End Function
```

```
<WebMethod()> Public Function GetCustomerOrders(ByVal strCustomerID As String) _
    As DataSet
End Function
```

The .NET Framework provides a design pattern for asynchronous method invocation, which you can apply in the ASP.NET client application. Let's look at the code (which includes timestamps for illustration purposes) and then discuss how it works:

```
Imports System.Threading

Private Sub btnRunAsynchQuery_Click(ByVal sender As System.Object, ByVal e As _
        System.EventArgs) Handles btnRunAsynchQuery.Click
        Dim objWS As localhost.Northwind
        objWS = New localhost.Northwind()
        objWS.Url = ConfigurationSettings.AppSettings( _
                "AspNetChap6.localhost.Northwind")

        strTime = "1. Asynch Request Begins: " & Now.TimeOfDay.ToString

        Dim asynchCallback As AsyncCallback = New AsyncCallback(AddressOf _
            HandleOrderDetails)
        Dim asynchResult As IAsyncResult = objWS.BeginGetCustomerOrders( _
            Me.cboCustomers.SelectedItem.Value, asynchCallback, objWS)

        strTime &= "2. Asynch Request ends: " & Now.TimeOfDay.ToString

        strTime &= "3. Main Thread Sleep Begins: " & Now.TimeOfDay.ToString

        ' Suspend the main thread for 3 seconds to simulate a long operation
        ' Note, the asynchronous operation will complete during this time, and the
        ' main thread will be interrupted when this happens
        Thread.Sleep(3000)

        strTime &= " 4. Main Thread Sleep Ends: " & Now.TimeOfDay.ToString
        'Response.Write(strTime) ' Uncomment to print execution times to the screen

End Sub

Private Sub HandleOrderDetails(ByVal asynchResult As IAsyncResult)
        ' Purpose: Callback function for asynch web method call
        Dim sqlDS As DataSet
        Dim objWS As localhost.Northwind = asynchResult.AsyncState
```

```
Try
    ' Step 1: Retrieve the DataSet
    sqlDS = objWS.EndGetCustomerOrders(asynchResult)

    ' Step 2: Populate the data grid with Customer data
    With Me.DataGrid1
        .DataSource = sqlDS
        .DataBind()
    End With

Catch err As Exception
    Response.Write(err.Message)
Finally
    sqlDS = Nothing
    objWS = Nothing
    strTime &= " 5. Asynch Result Delivered: " & Now.TimeOfDay.ToString
End Try

End Sub
```

The .NET Framework Design Pattern for Asynchronous Method Invocation

The asynchronous method call to GetCustomerOrders() is initiated when the user selects a new customer in the drop-down list and then clicks the "btnRunAsAsynchQuery" button (which triggers its _Click() event handler). The design pattern for asynchronous method invocation works as follows:

1. The _Click() event handler sets a reference to the Web service.

2. The _Click() event handler defines a callback method (HandleOrderDetails()) to respond to the end of the asynchronous method call. The callback method is a type-safe function pointer.

3. The _Click() event handler calls a special implementation of the Web method for asynchronous method invocation, called BeginGetCustomerOrders(). This method call includes a reference to the callback method, which will trigger when the method call is complete.

4. The main thread continues executing. The _Click() event handler contains a sleep function that simulates three seconds of activity. It is likely that the asynchronous call will complete during this sleep period.

5. At some point the asynchronous call completes, which invokes the callback method, HandleOrderDetails(). This method retrieves the Web service output from a special implementation of the method called EndGetCustomerOrders().

6. The DataSet that is retrieved from the Web method call gets bound to the DataGrid, which leaves the main thread to complete execution.

Now let's study the embedded timestamps. If the method invocation had been synchronous, the timestamps would have returned in the following order:

```
1. Asynch Request Begins: {timestamp}
5. Asynch Result Delivered: {timestamp}
2. Asynch Request ends: {timestamp}
3. Main Thread Sleep Begins: {timestamp}
4. Main Thread Sleep Ends: {timestamp}
```

Instead, the method invocation is asynchronous, and the timestamps return as follows:

```
1. Asynch Request Begins: 22:00:43.9156588
2. Asynch Request ends: 22:00:43.9156588
3. Main Thread Sleep Begins: 22:00:43.9156588
5. Asynch Result Delivered: 22:00:43.9356882
4. Main Thread Sleep Ends: 22:00:46.9200688
```

Of course, some Web service methods are not suitable for asynchronous method invocations. If the resultset is needed before the worker process can continue working, then you will have to call the Web service synchronously.

Building a Web Service for a Client-Side Consumer

Traditional interactive Web applications are usually designed to use form POST operations to exchange information between the client and the server. From the client's perspective, this action essentially puts the Web application out of commission for the time it takes to post the form to the server and to receive a response back. The form POST approach may be an effective communication channel for most purposes; however, it can also be a restrictive one. There are times when the client needs to exchange information with the server without having to use a full form POST operation.

Classic ASP addressed this issue using *remote scripting*, which enabled client-side scripts to send requests directly to the Web server and to receive responses without requiring a form POST operation. But remote scripting proved to be limiting because it supported a very narrow range of primitive data types and had a 2KB maximum on the size of communicated data.

Now that you can build Web services, it is a logical next step to ask if you can invoke Web methods from client-side script. The answer is "yes," and the WebService DHTML behavior provides this capability.

Overview of the WebService Behavior

The WebService behavior allows client-side scripts to call methods on remote Web services using SOAP. The behavior is implemented as an HTML Control (HTC) file that can be attached to a Web page and called directly from client-side script. The behavior encapsulates all of the SOAP request and response details, and it supports most of the data types outlined in Table 6-2. The WebService behavior provides a simple method for sending requests to a Web service, and it exposes the generated response as a scriptable result object that provides the following information:

- The raw XML of the generated response

- Direct access to the response data values

- Exception information

The one limitation with the WebService behavior is that it cannot invoke Web services on remote servers—in other words, on servers that are on a different domain from the Web server that hosts the client-side script. As a workaround you could configure a Web server in your domain to act as a proxy for a remote server. This approach requires complicated configuration and may incur significant performance costs.

Let's look at how to attach the WebService behavior to a page and then use it to call Web service methods.

NOTE *The WebService behavior may only be used with Microsoft Internet Explorer 5.5 or greater. You can find articles, documentation, and download instructions for the WebService behavior under MSDN Home ➢ MSDN Library ➢ Behaviors ➢ WebService Behavior or at* http://msdn.microsoft.com/library/default.asp?url=/workshop/author/webservice/overview.asp.

Using the WebService Behavior

The WebService behavior is implemented in a file called WebService.htc, which is available for download at http://msdn.microsoft.com/downloads/samples/internet/behaviors/library/webservice/default.asp.

You must include the WebService behavior file in the ASP.NET client application, typically within the same directory as the Web form *.aspx pages. You only need one copy of the file per application instance. Once the file is installed, you can use it to call a Web service method as follows:

1. Attach the WebService behavior to a Web page.

2. Identify the Web service you want to use.

3. Call a method on the Web service.

4. Handle the results of the method call in a callback function.

Let's show each of these steps by example, using a page in the sample client project.

Consuming the Web Service

The AspNetChap6 sample project contains a client page called ap_ExpensiveProducts.aspx, which illustrates how to call a Web service from client-side script. The following code listings come from the ap_ExpensiveProducts.aspx page.

Before proceeding, let's take a quick look at the client-side page, as shown in Figure 6-7.

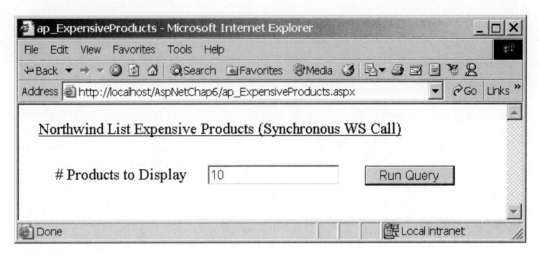

Figure 6-7. Using the WebService behavior

The page simply queries the Northwind database for up to 10 of the most expensive products every time the Run Query button is clicked. Listing 6-3 shows an abbreviated version of the ListMostExpensiveProducts() Web method.

Listing 6-3. The Shortened ListMostExpensiveProducts()

```
<WebMethod()> Public Function ListMostExpensiveProducts(ByVal nProductCount _
        As Integer) As String()
        Dim strConn As String
        Dim objDB As Apress.Database
        Dim sqlDR As SqlDataReader

        Dim i As Integer = -1
        Dim arrResult(0) As String ' 1-D array
        Dim nReturnCount As Integer

        ' Retrieve the connection string from Web.config
        strConn = ConfigurationSettings.AppSettings("ConnectionString")

        ' Set nReturnCount between 1 and 10
        nReturnCount = IIf(nProductCount > 10, 10, nProductCount)
        nReturnCount = IIf(nReturnCount = 0, 1, nReturnCount)
```

```
Try
    objDB = New Apress.Database(strConn)
    Dim arrParams() As String = New String() {} ' No arguments
    sqlDR = objDB.RunQueryReturnDR("[Ten Most Expensive Products]", _
                  arrParams)

    While sqlDR.Read()
        i += 1
        'Filter # of returned records, using nReturnCount
        If i + 1 > nReturnCount Then Exit While
        ReDim Preserve arrResult(i)
        arrResult(i) = sqlDR.GetValue(0)
    End While
    sqlDR.Close()
Catch err As Exception
    ' Exception handling code goes here
Finally
End Try

Return (arrResult)


End Function
```

The "Run Query" button invokes the `ListMostExpensiveProducts()` Web service method, using the WebService behavior. The products are returned from the Web service as an array of strings. The client page does not repost when the button is clicked, and the results get displayed in a pop-up dialog box over the page.

Implementing and Using the WebService Behavior

To attach the WebService behavior to a page, simply add a `<div>` tag with a behavior style as follows:

```
<body MS_POSITIONING="GridLayout" onload="Initialize();">
        <!-- Attach the web service behavior to a div element -->
        <div id="service" style="BEHAVIOR: url(webservice.htc)"></div>
        <!-- End Attach -->
        <form id="Form1" method="post" runat="server">
                <--Form Elements go here -->
        </form>
</body>
```

This code assumes that the `WebService.htc` file lives in the same directory as `ap_ExpensiveProducts.aspx`.

Notice that we call a client-side function called `Initialize()` in the `<body>` tag's `onLoad()` event. This function initializes the behavior as follows:

```
function Initialize() {
// Create an instance of the web service and call it svcNorthwind
service.useService("http://localhost/WebService6A/wsNorthwind.asmx?WSDL", _
                                    "svcNorthwind");

    }
```

The WebService behavior provides the `useService()` method for attaching to a Web service WSDL document and for creating an alias for the Web service *instance*.

To actually call the Web service method, you need to use the behavior's `callService()` method. The following code is a JavaScript function called `getProductList()` that gets called by the Run Query button's `onClick()` event:

```
function getProductList() {
    // Note: This function may be called from any JS event, e.g, onClick or onBlur
    var iCallID;
    var txt1 = document.forms[0].ap_txt_product_count;
    var nProductCount = txt1.value;
    // Code to invoke the wsNorthwind : ListMostExpensiveProducts() method
    // Note: onProductListResult() is the callback function for the return result
    iCallID = service.svcNorthwind.callService(onProductListResult,
        'ListMostExpensiveProducts', nProductCount);
    return false;
    }
```

The `callService()` function requires the following arguments:

- **Callback function**: This optional argument represents the name of a call-back function for handling the result of the method call. If you do not specify a callback function, then the behavior will automatically send the result to a generic function called "onresult," which you are then required to implement.

- **Web service method name**: This required argument represents the name of the Web service method being called.

- **Web service method parameters**: This required argument represents a comma-delimited array of parameters that are required by the Web service method.

The result object gets passed off to a callback function that implements a standard interface (it must accept the result object). This callback function gets called regardless of the outcome of the Web service request. Listing 6-4 shows the custom callback function, called onProductListResult():

Listing 6-4. The onProductListResult() *Custom Callback Function*

```
function onProductListResult(result) {
// Handles the result for wsNorthwind : ListMostExpensiveProducts()
var strProductList = '';
if (result.error) {
            // exception handling code goes here
            }
else {
            // Assign the result string to a variable
            var text = result.value;
            // Loop through the return array
            n = text.length;
            for (var r = 0; r < n; r+=1) {
                            strProductList = strProductList + text[r] + ' : '
                            }
            // Display the data
            alert("The Most Expensive Products are: " + strProductList);
            // Display the raw SOAP packet
            alert(result.raw.xml);
            }
    }
```

Listing 6-4 omits the exception handling code, although the function does check the value of the result.error object. The return array of products is exposed directly via the result object's value property as follows (for a product count of two):

```
The Most Expensive Products are: Côte de Blaye : Thüringer Rostbratwurst
```

The raw XML of the SOAP response is exposed via the result object's raw.xml property:

```
<soap:Envelope xmlns:soap=http://schemas.xmlsoap.org/soap/envelope/
        xmlns:xsi=http://www.w3.org/2001/XMLSchema-instance
```

```
        xmlns:xsd="http://www.w3.org/2001/XMLSchema">
        <soap:Body><ListMostExpensiveProductsResponse
            xmlns="http://tempuri.org/"><ListMostExpensiveProductsResult>
            <string>Côte de Blaye</string>
            <string>Thüringer Rostbratwurst</string>
            </ListMostExpensiveProductsResult></ListMostExpensiveProductsResponse>
        </soap:Body>
</soap:Envelope>
```

JavaScript is very versatile and will allow you to insert the result data anywhere in the page. Client-side Web service method calls are often used to
populate linked combo boxes—in other words, to repopulate one combo box
when the selected item changes in the other. Client-side validation moves to the
next level with Web services because you can perform sophisticated server-based
validation directly from the client. Client-side calls to the server are obviously not
as fast as local script functions, so you need to design for this. For example, we
typically disable all buttons on a client form until the Web service method call
has completely finished. We typically re-enable the buttons at the end of the callback function.

Finally, it is important to note that the callService() function invokes an asynchronous Web method call by design (it does not execute synchronous Web method
calls). This means that the script interpreter will make the callService() function call
and then immediately move to the next line in the JavaScript function. The callback
function (onProductListResult(), in this case) will fire whenever the Web method
call is complete. So, if you are executing dependent code, such as populating linked
combo boxes, then you must make the second call at the end of the callback function
and not following the callService() method call.

This important point is perhaps easiest to understand by example.
Listing 6-5 is pseudo-script for populating linked DropDownList controls using
Web method calls. Combo2 will only populate if Combo1 has first been successfully
populated.

*Listing 6-5. Pseudo-Script for Populating Linked DropDownList Controls Using
Web Method Calls*

```
function Initialize() {
    // Create an instance of the Web service and call it svcMyWS
    service.useService("http://localhost/WebService1/wsMyWS.asmx?WSDL",
        "svcMyWS");
}


function FillCombo1() {
```

```
        var iCallID = service.svcMyWS.callService(onFillCombo1Result,'FillCombo1');
    }


function onFillCombo1Result() {
    if (result.error) {
        // exception handling code goes here
        }
    else {
        // Step 1: Populate Combo1 with data from the Web service
        // Code Goes Here
        // Step 2: Call FillCombo2() to populate the dependent combo
        }
    }

function FillCombo2() {
    // Populate Combo2 based on the currently selected value in Combo1
    var intCombo1Value = document.forms[0].iq_cbo1.value;
    var iCallID = service.svcMyWS.callService(onFillCombo2Result,'FillCombo2',
        intCombo1Value);
    }

function onFillCombo1Result() {
    if (result.error) {
        // exception handling code goes here
        }
    else {
        // Step 1: Populate Combo2 with data from the Web service
        // Code Goes Here
        }
    }
```

Now, turn your attention to the important topic of exception handling using the Web service behavior.

Exception Handling Using the WebService Behavior

The WebService behavior provides reasonable support for processing SOAP exceptions. The actual exception details are encapsulated in an object called errorDetail, which is undefined if the value of result.error is "False." The errorDetail object provides three properties that expose exception information:

- **Code**: SOAP fault codes that indicate the type of exception that occurred. These are the same fault codes described in Table 6-3. Possible values include Client, Server, VersionMismatch, and MustUnderstand.

- **Raw**: The raw SOAP response packet that was returned from the Web service method.

- **String**: The exception message.

The errorDetail object is easy to use, as shown here:

```
if (result.error) {
    // Retrieve exception information from the event.result.errorDetail
    // properties
    var xfaultcode   = result.errorDetail.code;
    var xfaultstring = result.errorDetail.string;
    var xfaultsoap   = result.errorDetail.raw.xml;
    // Add custom code to handle specific exceptions
    }
```

This is how a simple exception would be returned back to the client:

```
[xfaultcode] soap:Server
[xfaultstring] System.Web.Services.Protocols.SoapException:
Server was unable to process request.
System.Exception: The SOAP request could not be processed.
[xfaultsoap]
<soap:Envelope xmlns:soap="http://schemas.xmlsoap.org/soap/envelope/">
    <soap:Body>
        <soap:Fault>
            <faultcode>soap:Server</faultcode>
                <faultstring>System.Web.Services.Protocols.SoapException:
                Server was unable to process request.>;
                System.Exception: The SOAP request could not be
                processed.</faultstring>
            <detail/>
        </soap:Fault>
    </soap:Body>
</soap:Envelope>
```

It is much more difficult to process SOAP exceptions in client-side JavaScript compared to ASP.NET code because you do not have the benefit of the SoapException class. The full SOAP exception does get returned to the client via the errorDetail object's `raw.xml` property, so with a little perseverance, you can retrieve whatever detailed exception information you need. Our design approach with client-side Web service calls is to use defensive programming to never allow an exception to occur. This means implementing as much validation as possible before actually issuing the method call. It also means ensuring that exception alert dialogs provide just enough information for the user either to research the issue further or to report it, but not enough information to overwhelm them. Of course, defensive programming is not a substitute for server-side exception handling in the Web method itself.

Setting Web Services Security

Web service security and authentication is a difficult topic to tackle because the industry leaders are still defining the best approach for handling this task. As of this writing, Microsoft, IBM, and VeriSign have jointly released the WS-Security specification, which is a set of SOAP extensions that essentially define security tokens that accompany SOAP messages. This approach embodies the concept of *federated security*, which states that if a message comes from a trusted party and has not been tampered with, then it is a "secure" message. At a high level, this approach follows the successful path of the HTTPS approach. The HTTPS protocol uses certificates and tokens to provide "security" in two ways: by vouching for the integrity of the transmission—in other words, by ensuring that the message has not been tampered with in transit—and by vouching for the identity of the sending party. We are greatly oversimplifying federated security with this comparison, but it does begin to give you an idea about the technology.

> **NOTE** *You can read more about Microsoft's Federated Security and Identity Roadmap at* `http://msdn.microsoft.com/library/default.asp?url=/` `library/en-us/dnwebsrv/html/wsfederate.asp`.

Web services are special ASP.NET project types, so they can fully leverage the standard authentication schemes that ASP.NET provides, including Forms Authentication and Windows Authentication. We do not discuss this approach here because you can get whatever information you need from a standard discussion on ASP.NET security options. Instead, we are more intrigued by the possibilities that SOAP extensions provide for authenticating SOAP messages. This approach is particularly relevant given the role that SOAP extensions play in the WS-Security model.

SOAP headers are extensions to a SOAP envelope that are independent of the individual Web method messages. SOAP headers are useful for passing application-level information, such as authentication information, in a way that is independent of a specific Web method but instead applies to the entire Web service. ASP.NET makes it easy to work with SOAP headers, by providing a specialized SoapHeader base class, which is a member of the `System.Web.Services.Protocols` namespace. The steps for implementing a SOAP header in a Web service are as follows:

1. Create a custom class in the Web service that derives from the SoapHeader base class.

2. Add to the class one public property for each SOAP header being added.

3. Add a `SoapHeaderAttribute()` to the Web method, which will process the SOAP header. This attribute includes a reference to the custom class. It also sets the direction of the SOAP header and whether it is required.

4. Process the SOAP header inside the Web method.

Let's move straight into an example that demonstrates how SOAP headers can play a role in authenticating Web service requests. We have written a Web method that returns the most expensive product in the Northwind database. Assume that this is restricted information and that the client must provide an access code to receive the name of the most expensive product. The access code is stored in the `Web.config` file so that it can be updated easily.

Listing 6-6 is the abbreviated code for this Web service, which is called `SecureNorthwind.asmx`. You can find the full code in the WebService6B project in the sample code that accompanies this chapter. Note that the actual database retrieval code has been omitted for brevity.

Listing 6-6. The Abbreviated `SecureNorthwind.asmx`

```
Imports System.Configuration
Imports System.Web.Services
Imports System.Web.Services.Protocols

Public Class APSoapHeader
    Inherits SoapHeader
    Public AccessCode As String
End Class
```

```
<WebService(Namespace:="http://tempuri.org/")> _
Public Class SecureNorthwind
    Inherits System.Web.Services.WebService

    Public objCSH As WebService6B.APSoapHeader

    <WebMethod(), _
        SoapHeaderAttribute("objCSH", Direction:=SoapHeaderDirection.In, _
            Required:=True)> _
    Public Function GetMostExpensiveProduct() As String

        Dim m_strAccessCode As String = ""
        Dim m_strMostExpensiveProduct As String = ""

        ' Retrieve the AccessCode value that is passed in the SOAP Header
        m_strAccessCode = objCSH.AccessCode.ToString()

        Try
            If m_strAccessCode = ConfigurationSettings.AppSettings( _
                        "WSAccessCode") Then
                ' Make a database call for the most expensive product
                ' Note, this detailed code listing is not shown
                m_strMostExpensiveProduct = <Retrieved from the database>
            End If
        Catch err As Exception
        Finally
        End Try

        Return (m_strMostExpensiveProduct)

    End Function

End Class
```

Listing 6-6 includes a custom public class that defines the SOAP header, called APSoapHeader. This class defines a public member called AccessCode, which represents one collection element in the XML for the SOAP header. The Web method is called GetMostExpensiveProducts(), and it contains an instance of the custom class, APSoapHeader. The Web method also includes a SoapHeaderAttribute that sets the SOAP header as being input only and required. Notice that the full SOAP class itself is required and not just one member of the class. By extension, every member of the class that is defined must be passed in. (In this case, we have only one member, so we are technically implementing every available class member).

Now let's look at an ASP.NET client that calls this Web service (see Listing 6-7). The client page is called ap_WSGetMostExpensiveProduct.aspx and is included in the sample project AspNetChap6, which we worked with earlier. This listing makes use of a second Web reference to SecureNorthwind.asmx.

Listing 6-7. ap_WSGetMostExpensiveProduct.aspx

```
Private Sub Page_Load(ByVal sender As System.Object, _
        ByVal e As System.EventArgs) Handles MyBase.Load
    Dim strProduct As String
    Dim objWS As localhost1.SecureNorthwind
    Dim objCSH As localhost1.APSoapHeader

    Try
        ' Step 1: Instance the Web service and set its URL
        objWS = New localhost1.SecureNorthwind()
        objWS.Url = _

        ConfigurationSettings.AppSettings("AspNetChap6.localhost1.SecureNorthwind")

        ' Step 2: Instance the Soap Header, and set its AccessCode property
        objCSH = New localhost1.APSoapHeader()
        objCSH.AccessCode = _
            ConfigurationSettings.AppSettings("WebServiceAccessCode")

        ' Step 3: Assign the SoapHeader object to objWS.APSoapHeaderValue
        objWS.APSoapHeaderValue = objCSH

        ' Step 4: Retrieve the most expensive product
        strProduct = objWS.GetMostExpensiveProduct()
    Catch errSoap As System.Web.Services.Protocols.SoapException
        Response.Write("SOAP Exception: " & errSoap.Message)
    Finally
    End Try

End Sub
```

The code is more complicated than it appears. Quite simply, you have to set the access code property to a valid setting before you can submit a request to the Web method. The proxy class exposes a property on the Web service called AccessCodeValue (a variation of the original property name). The catch is that this property is of type `APSoapHeader`. So, you cannot just set a value and be done. Instead, you must create a new instance of `APSoapHeader`, populate it, and assign it to the Web service's `AccessCodeValue` property.

Accordingly, the client page must instance two separate objects. The first, `objWS`, references the Web service. The second, `objCSH`, references a new instance of the custom SOAP header class. The access code gets retrieved in the `Web.config` file and assigned to the `objCSH.AccessCode` property. Next, the object reference itself, objCSH, is assigned to the Web service's `AccessCodeValue` property. Finally, the actual target Web method is finally called.

If you fail to set the SOAP header, then you will receive the following exception message:

```
Required field/property SecureNorthwind.APSoapHeaderValue of SOAP header
APSoapHeader was not set by the client prior to making the call.
```

If you set the SOAP header value correctly, then you will successfully receive the product name:

```
Côte de Blaye
```

It does not take much imagination to extend this approach to a more full-fledged security implementation. You could add separate input SOAP headers for username and password information and then validate it on the Web service side. You could also implement HTTPS transmission between the Web server and the Web service to ensure the privacy and integrity of the transmission. (Without HTTPS, a hacker with a network sniffer could discover the header contents and render them meaningless.) Of course, this approach assumes that the Web server and the remote Web service will stay synchronized with their authentication settings. There are many implications that we cannot begin to tackle here. Our point is simply to open your eyes to the possibilities that SOAP extensions provide for authenticating Web service requests. In the long run, the future of Web services security lies in federated security and the WS-Security specification mentioned earlier. You should make sure to stay informed on this important and evolving security specification.

.NET Remoting vs. ASP.NET Web Services

The .NET Framework provides the infrastructure for remote object invocation across application domains, otherwise known as .NET *remoting*. This technology is a successor to the Distributed Component Object Model (DCOM) technology, which has traditionally handled distributed application logic. .NET remoting is a powerful technology because it encapsulates many of the complex infrastructure (a.k.a. *plumbing*) details required for remote object invocation. The .NET Framework classes for remoting simplify the implementation with a straightforward application programming interface (API). This capability naturally raises the question of whether .NET remoting is a viable alternative to ASP.NET Web services. To answer this question, you need to examine the similarities and differences between each technology.

ASP.NET Web Services

The highlights of this technology are as follows:

- ASP.NET integrates with Internet Information Server (IIS) to provide an infrastructure for Web services that is based on industry standard technologies, including HTTP, XML, SOAP, and WSDL.

- ASP.NET Web services are interoperable across any platform that provides support for WSDL, SOAP, and HTTP. The Web service consumer does not need to be running on a platform that supports the .NET Framework.

- ASP.NET integrates with IIS to provide authentication for all incoming requests, including for Web services. IIS supports a number of authentication mechanisms, including Basic, Digest, .NET Passport, and digital certificates.

- ASP.NET Web services use HTTP as the exclusive transport protocol and can therefore use SSL to secure transmissions over the wire.

- ASP.NET Web services are stateless, so they will not maintain client state information between requests.

- ASP.NET Web services are easy to create, configure, and consume.

- ASP.NET Web services are robust because they execute in the ASP.NET worker process (which will restart automatically if it is terminated).

.NET Remoting

The highlights of this technology are as follows:

- .NET remoting supports several transport protocols, including TCP, HTTP, and custom protocols.

- .NET remoting supports several serialization formats, including binary, SOAP, and custom formats.

- .NET remoting requires a host process, which can be a .NET executable or IIS.

- .NET remoting provides the fastest communication using binary formatting over a TCP channel. The TCP channel is more efficient than HTTP because it uses raw sockets to transmit data. This design provides high performance but is not interoperable across different platforms unless they are running the .NET Framework.

- .NET remoting provides several modes for creating objects and specifying their lifetime. These modes are as follows:

  - **SingleCall**: Objects are created for single requests from individual clients. The objects are stateless, so they will not persist state between requests and they will not share information between multiple client requests.

  - **Singleton**: Objects are persisted for multiple client requests. This enables the objects to share state between multiple client requests. This mode is useful for sharing data between clients and for invoking objects that are expensive to create.

  - **Client-Activated**: Objects are invoked using an intermediate proxy object on the client. This proxy enables the objects to maintain state on a per-client basis.

- .NET remoting is more complicated to configure than ASP.NET Web services, depending on the host process.

- .NET remoting may be less robust than ASP.NET Web services, depending on the host process.

Choosing .NET Remoting over ASP.NET Web Services

.NET remoting can only be compared to ASP.NET Web services in a restricted sense because .NET remoting provides a wider level of functionality than

ASP.NET Web services. For example, .NET remoting allows you to invoke objects in Singleton mode so that they persist between multiple client requests. However, ASP.NET Web services are not designed to even address this scenario. In absolute terms, there is no faster invocation design than using .NET remoting with binary formatting over a TCP channel. However, this design requires that both the object and the client be installed on a platform that runs the .NET Framework. This lack of interoperability means that it is not even useful to compare Web services against .NET remoting using binary-TCP.

ASP.NET clients can in fact use .NET remoting (with SOAP over HTTP) almost as easily as they can use Web services, although the client-side code is more involved. ASP.NET clients can only use the SingleCall .NET remoting mode, which in a sense approximates the stateless nature of Web service calls. ASP.NET clients cannot use the Client-Activated mode; however, they can approximate this mode with separate ASP.NET session management in conjunction with the SingleCall mode. In terms of performance, you may be surprised to learn that standard Web service calls actually outperform .NET remoting calls using SOAP over HTTP. The reason is that ASP.NET is more efficient at serializing SOAP compared to .NET remoting. (Serialization in .NET remoting is handled by dedicated serialization formatters.) In addition, standard Web service calls have comparable performance to .NET remoting calls using binary over HTTP.

NOTE *For more information on performance issues, see the MSDN Architectural Topics article entitled "Performance Comparison: .NET Remoting vs. ASP.NET Web services" at* http://msdn.microsoft.com/library/default.asp?url=/ library/en-us/dnbda/html/bdadotnetarch14.asp.

In theory, you can use .NET remoting to expose an object as an XML Web service if it is hosted in IIS and if it uses SOAP formatting over an HTTP channel. In reality, this is not equivalent to a standard ASP.NET Web service, mainly because .NET remoting does not generate the same kind of WSDL descriptions as Web services. Web service WSDL relates all interface information to XSD schemas. In contrast, .NET remoting WSDL encodes interface details purely as SOAP, without reference to XSD schema information. This will not be a problem if the object supports simple data types. But for complex data types, such as the DataSet object, this lack of schema information can prevent some clients from communicating with the object. For example, ASP.NET clients that interact with a Web service will expect the WSDL to contain XSD schema references for all data types. On the other hand, a .NET remoting client will not need these XSD schema references when it interacts with a Web service that is also built on .NET remoting infrastructure.

In a roundabout way, you thus come to a set of simple answers to the question of how to choose between ASP.NET Web services and .NET remoting. If you require interoperability with different platforms, then you should expose your components as ASP.NET Web services. If you do not require this level of interoperability, then you can invoke your components using .NET remoting. ASP.NET clients can invoke IIS-hosted components using .NET remoting as long as the WSDL provides enough descriptive information for all of the object's data types. Finally, if you have an ASP.NET client and you must use SOAP formatting, then you should use standard Web services rather than using .NET remoting with SOAP.

 NOTE *For more information on .NET remoting, refer to* Advanced .NET Remoting *(VB .NET Edition) by Ingo Rammer (Apress, 2002). C# developers should refer to* Advanced .NET Remoting *(C# Edition) by Ingo Rammer (Apress, 2002).*

Optimizing Web Service Design

Web services are always called remotely and are typically invoked using a SOAP request. This architecture by design creates a process boundary that automatically degrades the responsiveness of the Web service. In addition, Web services and their consumers are forced to take the extra processing step of assembling and parsing SOAP requests. By their nature, Web services will not respond as fast as locally installed components, so it is extra important that you take steps to maximize the performance of your Web service. You can do so with a few simple design optimizations:

- **Use asynchronous Web method calls where possible**: Asynchronous calls are ideal for intensive Web methods that take a significant time to process and where the consumer application has the flexibility to work on other things while it waits for a response from the Web service.

- **Use timeouts for synchronous calls**: Web methods should contain built-in timeouts in case the Web method hangs or takes an unusually long time to execute. This will prevent the client application from hanging indefinitely while it waits for the Web service call to return. In addition, you can set the Timeout property explicitly on the Web service client proxy class. Web service proxy classes implement a common base class called WebClientProtocol, which in turn provides a Timeout property. For example:

```
Dim objWS As localhost.Northwind = New localhost.Northwind() ' Proxy Class
objWS.Timeout = 15000 ' Set the Web method call timeout to 15 seconds
```

- **Use output caching for responses**: Output caching will improve the responsiveness and performance of a Web method. The `WebMethod()` attribute provides a `CacheDuration` property that specifies the number of seconds to cache an output response. Web service output caching varies by parameter, so users with different requests parameters will not receive the same cached response. Chapter 4, "Optimizing Application and Session State Management," discusses output caching in great detail and includes a section on Web services.

- **Minimize traffic**: Cross-process calls are expensive, so you should minimize the amount of traffic that flows between a Web service and its consumer. Use fewer Web methods that return more information vs. more Web methods that return limited, granular information. Avoid multiple consecutive Web method calls if you can accomplish the same result using a single Web method that returns more information.

- **Minimize use of complex data types**: Complex data types such as the ADO.NET DataSet provide a sophisticated level of information but come with a performance price. The DataSet object, for example, serializes to a large chunk of XML that requires intensive processing to serialize and to parse. By all means use these complex types if they make the most sense. But if they are not needed, then you are better off using simple types. For example, in our Web methods we typically map the contents of a DataSet to an array of simple types, such as an array of strings. This creates a smaller footprint than a serialized DataSet object.

- **Use SOAP Headers for global information**: If your Web service uses SOAP as its communication protocol, then you should consider using SOAP headers for passing certain types of information. SOAP headers are included within a SOAP envelope, but they are not tied to a specific Web method message. SOAP headers are useful for passing global values that apply to all Web methods. They generate a small footprint and do not clutter the WSDL definitions for individual Web methods. In addition, SOAP headers are useful for passing authentication information between a Web service and a consumer.

- **Use client-side invocation**: You have seen techniques for invoking Web services from client-side script using the WebService DHTML behavior. Client-side invocation minimizes server postbacks and may be the most efficient way to process user input, especially on pages with large view state or pages that accept input but do not display much information. For example, we typically design form input screens to process the update with a Web service. This design updates the information quickly and the form can be refreshed quickly using a client-side script.

- **Code intelligently**: Web services are simply another type of .NET application, so you should follow the same smart coding conventions that you use in other kinds of .NET applications. The conventions include, but are not limited to, the following: use early binding for object references, release object references as soon as you are done with them, and use casting to convert object references from one data type to another.

- **Compile intelligently**: ASP.NET automatically leverages the .NET Framework's optimized runtime system, which uses Just-In-Time (JIT) compilation to keep components loaded in memory only for as long as they are needed. Keep your Web services small and ensure that your Web methods remain logically partitioned between several Web services rather than in one large Web service. There is no quantitative measure to guide you here, besides stress testing results. Qualitatively, you can keep your Web services more responsive if they are smaller and can be loaded quickly by the JIT compiler. Remember to always switch the project's Build Configuration from Debug to Release before deployment. This will result in a smaller, faster executable that implements all of the chosen optimizations from the project property pages.

As a final thought, you may want to consider using .NET remoting as an alternative to Web services. .NET remoting is a technology for distributed programming that uses SOAP as one available protocol choice, in addition to binary remoting over TCP/IP. .NET remoting is a useful technology for passing binary objects across process boundaries, and it is usually much more efficient than Web services if you are generating complex objects and do not need to use SOAP. The .NET Framework provides efficient design patterns for .NET remoting solutions that provide sophisticated functionality with relatively little code. You can read more about .NET remoting in the .NET Framework Software Development Kit (SDK).

Summary

Web services are powerful applications that are easy to build using ASP.NET and VS .NET. You can invoke Web methods from server-side assemblies or from client-side scripts using the WebService DHTML behavior. In addition, you can call Web methods in either synchronous or in asynchronous modes. Web services are called remotely, so it is important that they be designed for maximum responsiveness. Finally, Web services currently have no standard, established method for authentication and security. A group of industry leaders have proposed a federated security system that uses SOAP extensions. This approach contains elements that have been successfully applied in HTTPS. This chapter also extended the discussion by showing how to use SOAP headers for implementing a simple authentication system.

CHAPTER 7

Stress Testing and Monitoring ASP.NET Applications

PERFORMANCE TESTING IS an important component of testing any Web application. In this chapter, we discuss the concepts behind performance testing and its role in the development and testing cycles. We cover performance testing fundamentals and general methodologies for testing a Web application. We also describe the features of the Microsoft Application Center Test (ACT) tool and provide a step-by-step tutorial on how to utilize the tool on an ASP.NET application.

Understanding Performance Testing Concepts

Performance testing is the process of measuring and understanding how the application responds under different user loads. Determining how your ASP.NET application performs under different user loads is an important process to creating a mission-critical application. Besides getting a qualitative analysis of the application's performance, it is also important to get quantitative measurements. The measurements will help you analyze problems and even determine how to fix them properly.

During the performance testing process, it is important to monitor the application for certain errors or performance issues that may occur only under user loads. This helps to identify subtle bugs within the application that you might not otherwise catch until you deploy the application. Monitoring also helps to identify the effects of application changes during the process.

An important step in the performance testing process is identifying the targeted user load. Also, you must account for the load variance in the testing. Most applications do not have a constant load. For example, an expense reimbursement application may experience heavier load at the end of the month when the expense reports are due. In these cases, the performance test must simulate the peak user load rather than the average user load.

Performance tuning is the process of modifying the application to improve its performance and is a natural extension of performance testing. You can modify application design and logic to improve performance. You can adjust system settings, as well as the hardware. During the tuning process, make sure you change only one parameter or piece of logic at a time. Maintain a consistent user load when adjusting system parameters or application logic. Collect and compare the performance results for each test under each setting. Repeat the process until you improve the performance of the application to the desired level.

Using Performance Metrics

When you can measure what you are speaking about, and express it in numbers, you know something about it; but when you cannot measure it, when you cannot express it in numbers, your knowledge is of a meager and unsatisfactory kind: it may be the beginning of knowledge, but you have scarcely in your thoughts advanced to the state of science.

—Lord Kelvin (William Thomson)

You can measure the performance of an ASP.NET application by its latency, throughput, and utilization metrics. All performance metrics (measures of performance) are based on system behavior over time.

Latency

Latency, or response time, measures the delay between initiating or requesting some action and the arrival of the result. You measure latency in units of (elapsed) time. The definition of a specific latency metric must specify both a start and stop event: when to begin measuring the delay and when to stop. Some examples of latency metrics include the following:

- The time between sending a page request from a Web browser and the time the requested page is completely displayed

- The time a network router holds a packet before forwarding it

- The delay between receiving an order for an item at an online store and updating the inventory amount that is reported to other customers

In ASP.NET applications, latency is the delay between the start and end of an operation (or between the request and the response). An application that exhibits a lower latency is always desired. In many Web performance tools, latency is represented by the metric Time to Last Byte (TTLB), which measures the delay between sending out a page request and receiving the last byte of the page response. Another important metric is the Time to First Byte (TTFB), which measures the delay between sending a page request and receiving the first byte of the response. Both the size of the page response and the network latency affect TTFB.

In most applications, latency is linearly proportional to the user load within a range of user loads. In this range, as the user load increases, the latency will proportionally increase. This occurs when the application is in a *steady-state*, where performance techniques such as connection pooling and caching are in full swing with a set of multiple users. When the application is running with a small user load (one to five users), you do not exercise the same performance-improving techniques, thereby actually increasing the latency at these low user loads.

Figure 7-1 shows a representative graph of an application's latency behavior vs. user load. As shown, latency has a tendency to increase slowly at low levels of user load, but at a certain user load level, latency will increase exponentially. Note the graph begins at a user load where the application has already reached a steady-state.

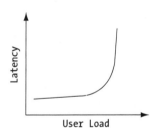

Figure 7-1. General characteristics of latency vs. user load

Typically, the sudden increase in latency is an indication of the system meeting a performance limit on one of its resources. Web servers commonly encounter this scenario when the number of requests exceeds the maximum number of concurrent sessions available. When this maximum is met, any additional requests will be placed in a queue and handled as sessions become available. The time spent in the queue contributes to the increase in latency.

You can divide the latency factors in an ASP.NET application into two categories: network latencies and application latencies. *Network latencies* refer to the time it takes data to transfer between servers. *Application latencies* refer to the time the server takes to process the data. An ASP.NET application typically has several different instances of both latency types. Figure 7-2 shows the various latencies in the processing of a Web request.

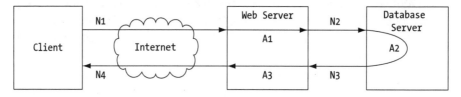

Figure 7-2. Latencies affecting a typical Web application

The latencies in Figure 7-2 represent the following:

- **N1, N4**: Network latencies from the client browser to the Web server across the Internet

- **N2, N3**: Network latencies within the production environment between the Web servers, application servers (if applicable), and database servers

- **A1, A2, A3**: Application latencies inherent in the server applications

You figure out the total latency of the Web application with the following:

Total Latency = $\Sigma\, N_n + \Sigma\, A_n$

where $N_n = n^{th}$ Network Latency and $A_n = n^{th}$ Application Latency

Network latencies across the Internet are a fact of life for Web applications. Client access can vary from high-speed T1 to intermediate Digital Subscriber Line (DSL) to traditional dial-up access. An option to minimize these latencies is to host the Web servers within major Internet hosting providers that have redundant high-speed connections to major public and private Internet exchange points. This will minimize the number of network hops within the Internet "cloud."

Network latencies within the production environment can be another issue. These latencies can be affected by the physical network layout as well as by network equipment and configuration. Whenever possible, you should configure servers on the same subnet for optimal performance. Also, you should configure servers with fixed IP addresses to prevent a down or unavailable DHCP server from disabling the servers. When equipment performance becomes a factor in the overall latency of an application, consider upgrading to higher performing network equipment (routers, switches, and so on).

Application latencies are another matter entirely. Many factors affect the processing time an application requires to complete a task. To minimize these factors and lower the application latency, keep in mind the following when developing the application:

- **Application design**: Minimize tasks that produce high latency such as making roundtrips between servers and using a transaction when none is required. Keep page response sizes down.

- **Code efficiency**: Implement code efficiently. Cache data that is used frequently or is expensive to calculate. For quicker content loads, implement both client-side and server-side caching.

- **Database efficiency**: Perform database optimization and tuning. Optimize stored procedures and implement indexes to improve database performance.

- **Server hardware**: Verify that the hardware meets the system requirements and expected user load of the application.

Throughput

Throughput, or capacity, measures the amount of work done per unit time, or the rate at which responses arrive. Throughput is the rate at which requests can be serviced. You measure throughput metrics in units of inverse time. Some examples of throughput are as follows:

- Transactions completed per minute

- Gigabytes of data written to tape per hour

- Memory accesses per second

- Megabits of data transmitted per second

In ASP.NET applications, throughput is the number of GET or POST requests per second, or simply the requests per second (RPS). Throughput is one of the more useful metrics, playing an important role in helping to identify performance bottlenecks. Figure 7-3 illustrates the typical characteristic of throughput vs. user load.

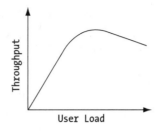

Figure 7-3. General characteristics of throughput vs. user load

Throughput tends to increase at a linear rate as the user load increases. However, at a certain user load, the maximum throughput for the system will be reached, as defined by the peak throughput in Figure 7-3. Additional users on the system will decrease the number of requests serviced, resulting in a decreased throughput. An application must support the maximum number of users serviced while still providing adequate performance to meet the business requirements.

Throughput metrics are highly dependent on the complexities of an application. A highly dynamic Web application would have different throughput metrics than a Web application serving static Hypertext Markup Language (HTML) pages. As such, comparing throughput metrics between different Web applications does not provide much information. However, comparing throughput metrics for the same application will provide valuable information about how changes in the application have affected its performance.

Utilization

Resource utilization, or simply *utilization*, is a measure of the percentage of available resources (system components, such as the CPU, memory, or data link) consumed by the application. Utilization is a percentile between 0 and 100 percent. When a system component reaches 100-percent utilization, it can no longer perform any additional tasks and will therefore become the performance bottleneck for the system. As a practical matter, latency increases rapidly as utilization approaches 100 percent so that many systems are designed to keep utilization below some threshold such as 70 percent or 80 percent.

Utilization increases proportionally to user load. At a certain limit, the maximum utilization will be reached, and it will stay at this limit as the user load increases. Figure 7-4 illustrates the typical utilization characteristic for a system vs. user load.

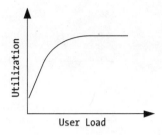

Figure 7-4. General characteristics of utilization vs. user load

If a system component's utilization becomes the performance bottleneck, then an option to improving performance is to upgrade the system component to a higher capacity. You can upgrade most hardware components to a higher capacity. Another option is to distribute the utilization across additional servers using network load balancing. These options, known as *vertical* and *horizontal scaling*, are discussed in more detail in the "Exploring Common Performance Testing Approaches" section. Apart from hardware, you need to analyze the aspects of the application (storing session information, data access, caching techniques) discussed in the earlier chapters that may decrease the high utilization.

Performance Metrics Relationships

Monitoring only one of the described metrics does not tell the whole performance story for an application. You must monitor and analyze all three metrics—latency, throughput, and utilization—to truly understand an application's performance. In the previous sections, we generalized their characteristics vs. user load. However, the relationships between the metrics provide valuable information about an application's performance.

Take the relationship between latency and utilization. Latency tends to increase as the inverse of unutilized capacity. When a system component reaches a maximum utilization, it will cause a dramatic increase in latency. Because utilization is a metric of each component, gathering test information can be a painstaking task. A major system component such as the CPU or memory may not reach its maximum utilization before the latency becomes unacceptable, as shown in Figure 7-5.

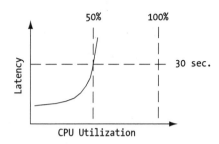

Figure 7-5. Latency vs. utilization for a sample application

In this example, the latency has reached a level of 30 seconds while the CPU utilization has only reached 50 percent. In cases like this, comparing other system component utilizations to the latency metric will help determine which component is the performance bottleneck.

Throughput and latency are different approaches to thinking about the same problem. In general, an application that exhibits high latency will have low throughput (if the delay in fulfilling a request is high, then the number of requests the application can handle will be low). The same criteria used to reduce latency in an application will also increase the throughput. Just as utilization must be analyzed and related to latency, analyzing throughput without consideration for latency is misleading. Latency often rises under load before throughput peaks. Like the sample regarding latency and utilization, the peak throughput may occur at a latency that is unacceptable from an application usability standpoint.

Exploring Common Performance Testing Approaches

You use different performance tests to gather the various performance metrics. The three most common performance tests are as follows:

- Load/stress

- Scalability

- Transaction Cost Analysis (TCA)

The *load*, or stress, test is the most common performance test because it is the most versatile. The load test allows you to measure the latency, throughput, and resource utilization at varying user loads. The goal of load testing is not only to gather metrics to describe the performance characteristics of the application but also to determine the limit of its performance. In essence, the goal is to crash the application by increasing the user load past performance degradation until the application begins to fail because of resource utilization or the occurrence of errors. Analyzing the results of the stress test will help to uncover bugs that would otherwise go undetected until the application was deployed. Because performance bugs are typically the result of design flaws, stress testing should begin early in the development phase on each area of the application.

Scalability testing is a series of stress tests with different hardware configurations. The goal of scalability testing is to determine the best scaling strategy to support an increased user load. The scalability options are vertical scalability or horizontal scalability.

Vertical scalability, or scaling up, refers to increasing the component capacity of a system onto a bigger and/or faster system. Typical vertical scaling options include increasing the number of CPUs on the server or adding more memory to the server. To test for vertical scalability, run stress tests with a different number of CPUs. An application is termed *vertically scalable* if its performance increases linearly in relation to the component capacity of the server—in our sample case, the number of CPUs. A useful feature of the Windows operating system is the ability to specify the number of CPUs to run in the boot.ini file. To enable multiple processors, set the NUMPROC parameter in the [operating systems] section to the number of processors to use:

```
[operating systems]
/NUMPROC=2
```

Horizontal scalability, or scaling out, refers to increasing the number of servers available to help run the application. A typical horizontal scaling option is to increase the number of load-balanced servers in a Web farm. To test for horizontal scalability, set up a server cluster using Windows 2000 Network Load Balancing or a hardware load balancer. Then run the same stress test with a different number of servers active in the cluster. Finally, analyze the results of all the tests. The results will show whether the application will scale linearly with additional servers.

Transaction Cost Analysis (TCA) is not exactly a type of test but is more a method to formulate the relationship between throughput and utilization. TCA calculates a resource cost to a transaction. To use TCA, you gather test performance metrics for a specific transaction. The transaction can be a unique feature, such as keyword search, or a specific task within the application, such as adding an item to the shopping cart. Using the test metrics, it is possible to calculate the unit cost of a resource per unit of throughput for a particular transaction. TCA is commonly used for capacity planning. For example, if you calculate that the CPU TCA for a keyword search was 20MHz per requests per second, then you could plan to require at lease a 500MHz CPU if you wanted to handle 25 simultaneous requests per second.

Best Practices for Performance Testing

The fundamental goal of performance testing is not only to identify the limitations within the application but also to resolve and push the application beyond these limitations. The performance metrics gathered allow you to determine which changes to make and quantify how well those changes advance toward that goal. The process of performance testing is in many ways more an art form than a science. One checklist will not apply to every application. However, there are some best practices that will help you get started.

The first step is to design the performance test to gather the correct metrics. An ASP.NET application has some general counters and measurements that should always be part of the performance metrics gathered during a test (see Table 7-1). You can find the Web application counters in the Microsoft Application Center Test (ACT) tool, not within any defined objects in Performance Monitor.

Table 7-1. Basic Performance Counters

OBJECT	PERFORMANCE COUNTER	DESCRIPTION
Processor	%Processor Time/_Total Instance	Processor utilization.
Memory	Available Bytes	Amount of memory on the server.
Network Interface	Bytes Total/Sec	Network traffic from the client to the server.
Active Server Pages	Requests Queued	Number of requests queued.
Web Application	Avg. Requests/sec	Average number of requests per second. This value is an average over the duration of the test.
Web Application	Avg. Time to First Byte (TTFB)	Average time between sending the request and receiving the first byte of the response.
Web Application	Avg. Time to Last Byte (TTLB)	Average time between sending the request and receiving the last byte of the response.
Web Application	HTTP Errors	Sum of all responses with HTTP result codes in the 400–499 and |500–599 ranges.

It is a good practice to gather baseline performance metrics by running control (performance) tests. You can then compare subsequent tests to the baseline to determine any improvements or to identify changes that have no effect or an adverse effect on performance.

You must design performance tests to be reproducible. A test is valid only if it can be reproduced. If it is not reproducible, you would not be able to correlate performance test results to application changes. When solving performance issues, make changes in a controlled manner, such that subsequent tests are a result of the changes only and not because other factors that invalidate the test. Resist the urge to make many changes at once; instead, make one change at a time.

Performance Tuning

To tune an application for performance, run an initial test against the application and save a base performance metric. Analyze the initial performance to determine if any modifications are needed to resolve any bottleneck issues. After you make the changes, repeat the test and save a second performance metric. Comparing the two metrics will help determine if the changes have improved the application's performance. The cycle continues with application changes and performance retests until the performance requirements are met. This cycle is known as *performance tuning*.

Using the Application Center Test Tool

Microsoft's stress testing tool is Application Center Test (ACT). ACT is included in the Visual Studio .NET Enterprise Developer and Architect Editions. ACT stress tests Web servers and analyzes performance and scalability problems with Web applications. ACT is a successor to the original Web Application Stress Tool (WAS), informally referred to as *Homer*. ACT supports many of the features left out of WAS by providing greater control in the test scripting interface and a more robust feature list.

Understanding ACT Features

ACT provides many features that help to perform capacity planning and stress testing on ASP.NET applications. ACT provides the following distinct features:

- Simulates a large group of users by opening multiple connections to the server and rapidly sending Hypertext Transfer Protocol (HTTP) requests.

- Supports programmable dynamic testing, which allows for robust functional testing.

- Supports several different authentication schemes and the Secure Sockets Layer (SSL) protocol, making it ideal for testing personalized and secure sites.

- Tests can be scripted, allowing for reproducible performance testing and tuning.

- Compatible with all Web servers and Web applications that adhere to the HTTP protocol.

ACT collects and summarizes all of the response times for each test request. Metrics such as TTFB, TTLB, and RPS are useful in analyzing the throughput and latency of an application. Also, ACT integrates with the system's performance counters to simplify correlation analysis between utilization and the other metrics.

Understanding ACT Test Architecture

To accurately measure performance, you should run the tests in an environment that matches as closely as possible with the production environment. Because many production environments are comprised of server farms, it is unlikely you can duplicate the server numbers in the test environment. The ideal test environment would be to run the tests in production if it does not interfere with business usage. However, it is feasible to gather useful data and optimize an application's performance in a scaled-back environment. Gains in performance on a single server will translate to similar performance gains in a server farm environment.

At a minimum, the Web server and Web client should be on separate machines so that you can isolate the resource utilization to specific tasks. Use ACT on the client machine to simulate HTTP requests and to measure client metrics such as TTLB and RPS. At the same time, use either ACT on the client machine or the Windows Performance Monitor on the Web server to measure the resource utilization.

For all the examples used in this chapter, the hardware is as follows:

- The Web server is an IBM PL300 with a Pentium III 733MHz processor, 512MB RAM, and 10GB available hard drive space.

- The Web client is an IBM ThinkPad A20M with a Pentium III 700MHz processor, 512MB RAM, and 6GB available hard drive space.

Setting Up a Test

You can create and run ACT tests from two user interfaces:

- **Visual Studio .NET (VS.NET) shell integration**: Enables you to create and run tests and view performance data while developing the application from within VS.NET

- **Stand-alone user interface**: Enables you to create and run tests and provides more in-depth reporting information and graphs

The ACT stand-alone user interface (UI) provides much more detailed reports than the VS.NET integrated version. The test scripts live in project folders that you can open from either interface. To add a test project through the VS.NET integrated development environment (IDE), follow these steps:

1. From the menu, select File ➤ Add Project ➤ New Project.

2. In the Add New Project window, expand the Other Projects node.

3. Select the ACT Projects node. Available templates will be displayed in the right panel.

4. Highlight the ACT Project template, set the Name and Location for the project, and click the OK button.

To add a test project with the ACT stand-alone UI, follow these steps:

1. Start Act.exe from the menu. The default menu path is Programs ➤ Microsoft Visual Studio .NET ➤ Visual Studio .NET Enterprise Features ➤ Microsoft Application Center Test.

2. Within the UI, select File ➤ New Project. A dialog box will display.

3. Within the dialog box, set the Name and Location for the project and click the OK button.

Recording a Browser Session

The easiest way to set up a test is by recording a browser session. The browser session will be automatically scripted to a VBScript (.vbs) file.

To record a browser session from the VS IDE, follow these steps:

1. Right-click the ACT project and select Add New Item.

2. Select the Browser Recorded Test (.vbs) Template from the Add New Item dialog box.

3. When the browser opens, direct the browser to the Web application and record the sequence of operations to execute.

4. When finished, click Stop on the recorder dialog box.

To record a browser session from the ACT UI, follow these steps:

1. From the Actions menu, choose New Test to start the New Test Wizard. Click Next to open the Test Source dialog box.

2. Select the Record a New Test option, click Next twice to accept the VBScript language default, open the Browser Record dialog box, and click Start Recording to open an instance of Internet Explorer (IE).

3. Replace "about: blank" with your starting URL in the Address textbox and record the sequence of operations to execute.

4. Return to the wizard, click Stop Recording, close IE, and click Next.

5. In the Test Properties dialog box, type the name of the test, click Next and then Finish to dismiss the wizard.

For simplicity, our ACT test script samples in this section will be from the ACT UI, which provides more detailed information than running ACT from the VS.NET IDE. We use the Duwamish 7.0 sample site included in the `Visual Studio Samples` package as the sample Web application.

To install the Duwamish site, run the self-installation package `Duwamish.msi` located in `C:\Program Files\Microsoft Visual Studio .NET\Enterprise Samples\Duwamish 7.0` VB. A C# version is also available in the `Duwamish 7.0 CS` directory. This will extract the Web application files as well as the Duwamish SQL database.

In the AspNetChap7ACTTest project, we have created a test script by recording a browser session on the Duwamish site. This session captures a user logging in to the site, adding several books to their shopping cart, and completing the checkout process. Figure 7-6 illustrates how the ACT UI will appear after the session has been recorded.

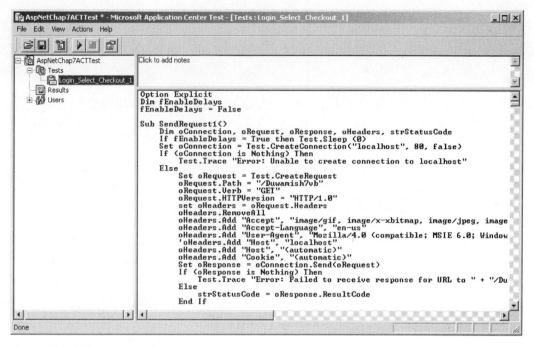

Figure 7-6. ACT user interface

Note that we have named our test "Login_Select_Checkout_1," as shown below the Tests category. The right panel displays the test script.

Defining a Dynamic Test

Another type of test you can run in ACT is the dynamic test. In the dynamic test, you can script the content and logic for the test in VBScript. To create an empty dynamic test from the VS.NET IDE, follow these steps:

1. Right-click the ACT project and select Add New Item.

2. Select the generic Test (.vbs) Template from the Add New Item dialog box.

3. A new .vbs file will be added to the project under the test project with the initial script line `Test.SendRequest("http://localhost")`.

To create an empty dynamic test from the ACT UI, follow these steps:

1. In the New Test Wizard, choose the Create an Empty Test option and then click Next.

2. Select a scripting language from the list and then click Next.

3. Type a name in the Test Name box and then click Next.

4. Click Finish to add the empty test file to the project.

Similar to the layout shown in Figure 7-6, the script for a dynamic test is editable in the large script window on the right portion of the ACT UI.

Scripting the test requests and responses in a dynamic test requires using the Application object and Test object models, which are covered in the "Using the ACT Test Object Model" section.

Saving a Test

Whether the test is a browser-recorded session or a dynamic test, the information required to run the test resides in the test script file. Saving the test script file allows you to reuse the test later. You can copy a self-contained test script from one project to another.

Customizing a Test

After you have created the test script, you can customize it to meet the application's performance requirements. You can access the test properties by right-clicking a test and selecting Properties from the stand-alone user interface. If using the VS.NET integration user interface, the properties of a test are available in the Properties window when a test is selected in Solution Explorer. You can customize the following test properties:

- Test load level

- Test duration

- User groups

- Performance counters

- Reporting level

Test Load Levels

The test load level controls the number of simultaneous browser connections the tool will employ during the test. This number is equal to the number of copies of the test script that will be running simultaneously during the test. You can equate this number to the number of users simultaneously using the site. You can configure the test load level from the test's Properties dialog box.

To set the test load level, follow these steps:

1. Open the test's Properties dialog box by right-clicking the test script and selecting Properties.

2. Select the General tab if it is not enabled.

3. In the Test Load Level section, set the value for the Simultaneous Browser Connections to the required level for the test.

Figure 7-7 shows the Properties dialog box for the Login_Select_Checkout_1 test script . In the sample, we have set the value to 10, such that ACT will generate 10 simultaneous connections during the test. If more than one Connection object is used in the script, then the actual number of simultaneous connections will be higher than the defined value.

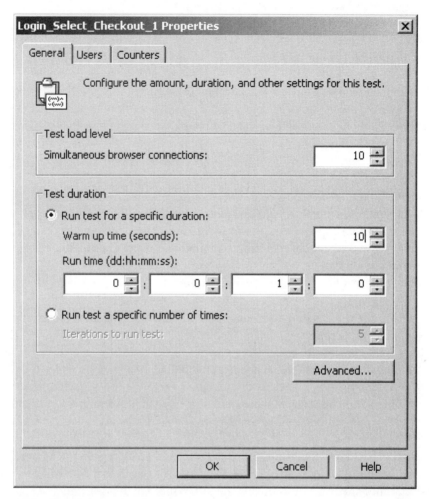

Figure 7-7. Sample Properties dialog box

Test Duration

You can set the duration of a test as a specific length of time or when a specific number of requests have occurred. The test duration section of the test properties allows customization of either parameter to control the duration of a test. Figure 7-7 shows the Test Duration section in the test's Properties dialog box. Depending on the test requirements, select either the time duration or the number of iterations as the test duration setting.

To run the test for a specific length of time, select the Run Test for a Specific Duration option, and enter the length of time in days, hours, minutes, and seconds to run the test. A test duration of one to five minutes is more than adequate in capturing the basic performance features of an application. However, the size and complexity of the test script may require a longer duration to exercise the application completely. Characteristics such as memory or other resource leaks will require a longer duration to reveal.

To run the test for a number of iterations, select the Run Test a Specific Number of Times option, and enter the iteration value. Bear in mind that the number of iterations and the number of simultaneous connections are interrelated. Setting the number of iterations to 5 for this sample would in essence set the test to simulate 10 simultaneous connections five times, or 50 overall connections during the test duration.

Note the Warm Up Time (Seconds) field. This is the setting that instructs ACT to ignore the performance metrics for an initial x number of seconds to account for the warm-up time needed to start the application, initialize components, and set caching. Although this setting is within the Run Test for a Specific Duration section, the Warm Up Time (Seconds) field applies to either test duration setting. A 10-second warm-up time is sufficient for most applications.

Setting User Groups and Users

Most Web applications require distinct user information in their performance testing. You can generate users dynamically by ACT or pull them from a set of predefined users. ACT can automatically generate users during the test on an as-needed basis. Automatically creating users can fulfill the specific load level for a test run. If the predefined user population is small, then potential problems can be generated when the specific load level exceeds this user population. If user authentication is required, or you want to view or reuse the user-specific cookies, you can create users and user groups and then select them in the test's Properties dialog box.

You define a user group on a per-project basis under the Users node in ACT. Highlighting the Users section will display the user groups defined for the project, including the Default Users Group. To add a new user group, right-click Users and select Add. You can assign each user in the group a username, password, and domain. To define a domain, it is necessary to define it in the form of domain\username. Figure 7-8 shows the custom user group SampleUserGroup1 with five defined users.

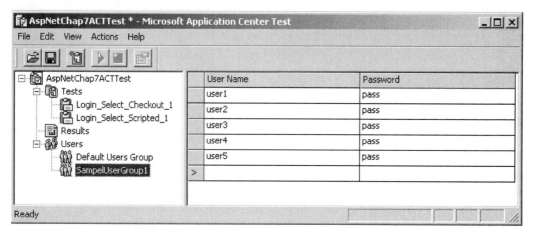

Figure 7-8. Defining users in a user group

You can add users to a user group with three methods:

- Adding a user individually

- Generating a set number of users

- Importing users from a data file

To add users individually, click each entry in the panel to the right and enter the appropriate data. To generate a set of users, select Actions ➤ Generate Users. In the Generate Users dialog box, enter the number of users to generate, the user-name prefix, and the password for the users. In this sample we want to generate five users with the name prefix of "user" and a password of "pass." Figure 7-9 shows the results of our entries.

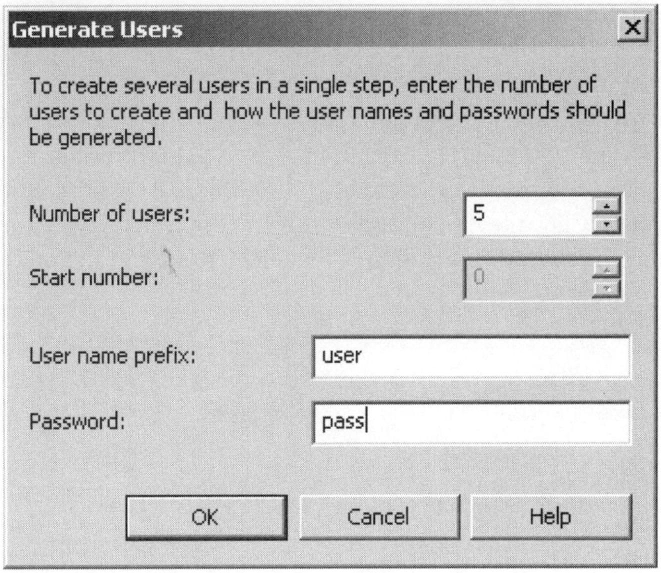

Figure 7-9. Generate Users dialog box

To import the users from a data file, select the Import Users command from the Actions menu. Browse to the data file, select it, and then click Open. ACT will parse the file and add the users to the group, along with any password information. ACT ignores parsing errors, so you should verify the resulting list of users for accuracy and completeness.

The format for each line in the data file should be as follows:

```
name, password
```

You must assign a user group to a specific test script to be used during the test run. To assign a test group to a test script, open the test's Properties dialog box and select the Users tab. Then select the appropriate user group and click OK.

Setting Up Performance Monitor Counters

One of ACT's features is the ability to integrate performance counters into its test report data. Select the Counters tab from the test's Properties dialog box to view the counter properties. You can specify how often the counter data is collected within the Counters window. Enter the interval value in the Counter Collection interval box. Keep in mind that a small interval value may reduce the ACT client performance because resources are required to collect the counters.

To add performance counters to a test script, click the Add button to open the Browse Performance Counters dialog box. Use this dialog box to add the appropriate counters to be monitored during the test run. A nice feature of ACT is the ability to monitor counters from remote servers. This allows you to monitor both the client and server performance counters in a single resultset. To add a counter, select the appropriate computer, performance object, counter, and counter instance. Click the Add button to add it to the test. Clicking the Explain button displays a detailed description of the selected counter in the Explain Text dialog box, as shown in Figure 7-10.

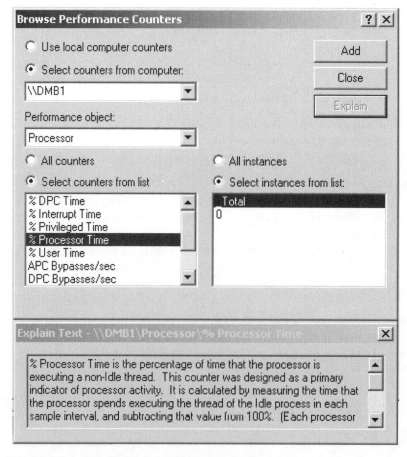

Figure 7-10. Browse Performance Counters dialog box

Setting the Reporting Level for a Test

You set the reporting level in the Advanced Settings dialog box, which you open by clicking the Advanced button in the test's Properties dialog box. The reporting level controls the amount of information generated and saved during a test run. Using the less-detailed reporting option will decrease the amount of time it takes to create a report, especially for tests that request a larger number of unique paths.

If detailed results are used, reports will include information for each page that was requested in the test. If detailed results are not used, then average values for the test run will be calculated and saved, but the page-level information will not be stored in the report.

Running a Test

Once a test script and test properties are ready, it is time to run the test. You can run the test manually or as a scheduled task. To run a test manually, select the test script and click Start Test on the toolbar. Alternatively, right-click the test and select the Start Test command.

Once the test starts, you can view the test status as it progresses. The test status window shows a summary of the test results, as illustrated in the upper section of Figure 7-11. Click Details to display more information about the test as it runs (as shown in the lower section of Figure 7-11). The Graph tab displays a colored graph of the RPS, total requests, socket errors, and HTTP errors for the test. The Status tab displays information about when the test has reached a certain stage—in other words, when the test is initialized and when the test is gathering information at the end of the test.

This summary provides an initial analysis of the test to determine if the test is valid or needs to be modified. If the initial metrics show an issue with the test, such as HTTP errors or socket errors, then the test may be invalid or not performing properly. You can stop the test prematurely by clicking the Stop Test button. ACT will then compile the metrics from the test up to its stopping point.

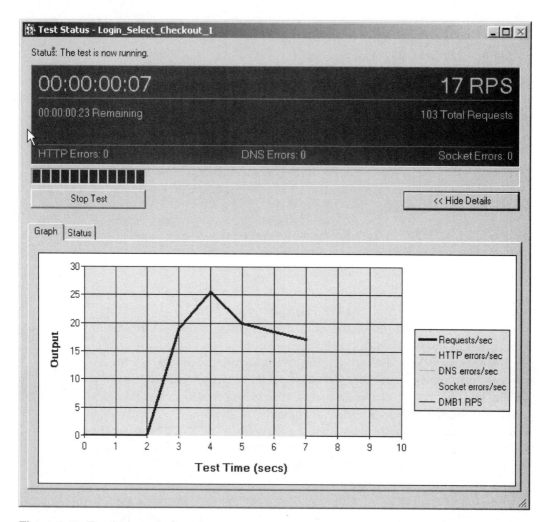

Figure 7-11. Test Status window

To run a test as a scheduled task, you must use a Windows Script Host file. Because the ACT executable Act.exe does not accept command-line arguments, the script file needs to call the Application object model to programmatically initialize and execute a test script. The script file ScheduleTaskRunScript1.vbs provides an example of how to execute a test script programmatically. You can set up the script as a scheduled task using the Scheduled Task Wizard.

Using the Report Interface

Once the test completes, you can view results of the test in the Results node within ACT. Once you select the Results node, the Test Runs panel displays the test runs related to each test script. In our sample project, we recorded a script to test the performance of the category pages in the Duwamish sample site.

Figure 7-12 shows the Overview Report for four test runs of varying simultaneous connections (15, 25, 50, and 75). Expanding the test in the Test Runs panel allows you to view each test run report. The Report panel contains a drop-down list with Overview, Graphs, and Requests. The Overview summary shows many basic performance counters that you can use to get a general idea of the test's performance.

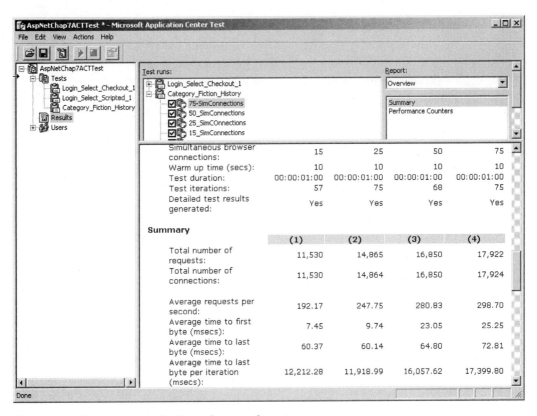

Figure 7-12. Summary results from the sample test

Checking Basic Performance Counters

You need to check some basic performance counters after a test run to verify the test was valid. They include the following:

- **Web server processor usage**: To obtain an upper limit on the application's performance, the Web server's processor use should reach at least 80 percent. If it does not, try increasing the load by increasing the number of simultaneous browser connections.

- **ACT client processor usage**: If it is at maximum usage (near 100 percent) and the Web server is not, the client machine might not be able to create enough load to determine the server's maximum capacity.

- **HTTP errors**: Verify that there are no excess HTTP 403, 404, or 500 errors. Encountering these errors would invalidate the test.

You can compare a test run report against another test run from either the same test or a different test. You can view multiple test runs simultaneously by selecting the check box preceding each run. In Figure 7-12, we have selected the four test runs for viewing.

You can do a basic test analysis from these counters. For example, the metrics for throughput (RPS) and latency (TTLB) are included in the set of basic counters. From Figure 7-12, you can deduce a trend of the TTLB increasing as the number of requests increases (60.37, 60.14, 64.80, and 72.81). You can also see the beginnings of a bottleneck between the third and fourth tests, which has a TTLB increase much greater than that between the second and third tests.

Saving Test Reports

Once you have generated test reports, the test data lives in an Extensible Markup Language (XML) file in the ACT project directory. The name of the file is comprised of the name of the test script and a date timestamp of when the test was run. The XML file format makes it flexible to transform the data into any other custom format. Saving the test project will save the test scripts as well as the test run data.

One of the features of ACT is the ability to create custom graphs from the test data. To generate a custom graph, select Graphs from the Reports drop-down menu. Select a source for the Y-axis from the Source list and a source for the X-axis from the Measured Against drop-down list. This will generate and display the graph using the two selected values.

Two commonly used graphs available in ACT are the latency vs. user load and throughput vs. user load. In ACT you can measure latency as TTLB, throughput as RPS, and user load as the number of simultaneous connections. For the Category_Fiction_History test runs, Figure 7-13 shows the RPS vs. browser connections graph, and Figure 7-14 show the TTLB vs. browser connections graph. Note that the relative curvature of the two graphs is comparable to the theoretical graphs (Figures 7-1 and 7-2) discussed in the "Understanding Performance Testing Concepts" section.

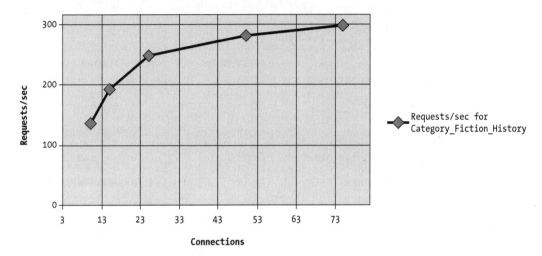

Figure 7-13. Custom graph of RPS vs. browser connections

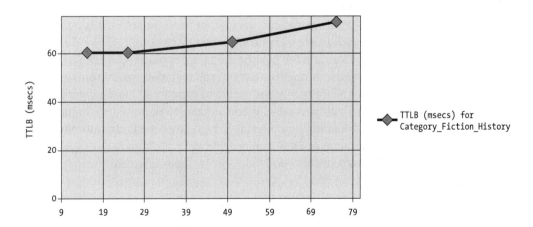

Figure 7-14. Custom graph of TTLB vs. browser connections

A limitation of the ACT version from VS.NET 1.0 is that any custom graphs will not be saved in the project. You need to set up graphs each time you reopen an ACT project.

Analyzing the Test Results from ACT

ACT provides an abundance of metrics within the test run reports. The real science is analyzing the results to identify key performance issues in the application. Table 7-2 describes the key metrics to consider in the test run reports.

Table 7-2. ACT Test Run Key Metrics

METRIC	MEASURED ON	DESCRIPTION
Browser Connection	Client	Measures user load
Requests per Second	Server	Measures throughput
TTLB	Client	Measures latency
% Processor Time /_Total instance	Server	Measures utilization
Available Bytes (Memory)	Server	Measures utilization

These metrics allow you to quantify your application's performance and determine if there are any performance bottlenecks.

Throughput vs. User Load

Graphing the throughput against the user load provides a useful measurement of the throughput limitations of an application. Take, for example, Figure 7-13, which depicts the graph for the tests run against the category pages in the Duwamish sample site. Although the throughput has not yet degraded, the increase in the level of RPS becomes non-linear as the user load increases. This is a common behavior and is usually associated with beginnings of a performance bottleneck in the application. In this example, analyzing this graph allows you to identify the performance of the category pages and provide an upper limit to its throughput. Graphs such as these provide a good indication of areas to investigate for performance gains.

Latency vs. User Load

Graphing latency against the user load provides a useful measurement of the critical effects of overutilization. In our example, shown in Figure 7-14, the latency increases steadily as the user load increases. At our upper user load limit of 75 simultaneous connections, TTLB still had not reached a critical increase, so you can conclude that the performance limitation on the application will not be latency.

Response Code Results

The test results from our sample test script were from user loads of five up to 75 simultaneous connections. We could not go higher than 75 because we began to encounter a large number of unsuccessful page requests. When this occurs, the metrics can get skewed. The HTTP response code of 200 denotes a successful request. Take, for example, a test where 20 percent of the page requests returned a non-200 error (unsuccessful request); these request errors could potentially reduce the performance of the Web server and make the test results less accurate. Common error responses include the following:

- **500 (Internal Server Error)**: This indicates that the server encountered errors in attempting to fulfill the request. This is usually caused by the application's inability to handle the user load.

- **404 (Not Found)**: This indicates Internet Information Server (IIS) is not responding to the request in a timely manner. This is likely caused by IIS not being able to handle the user request because of a tag that references a missing image or source file.

- **403 (Server Too Busy)**: This indicates that the server understood the request but is refusing to fulfill it.

These response codes commonly occur when the number of concurrent browsers is too high for the Web server to handle. A good practice is to invalidate any test run that generates page request errors greater than 2.5 percent of the total page requests. In other words, a meaningful test generates a response code of 200 (successful request) for greater than 97.5 percent of the total number of requests.

Utilize Percentiles

ACT provides the test report data in subdivided percentiles. These provide a better measurement of how the response times are distributed, whereas an average can sometimes be misleading. For example, if 99 responses have a TTLB of 50 milliseconds, but just one response in this group took 1 second, the average would be skewed to 59 milliseconds. Percentiles lessen this issue by providing a distribution to represent the metrics of the majority of the request. A percentile represents a value in which a percentage of the requests are greater and the remaining percentage is less. The values within the 25th and 75th percentiles are the best indication of response time. These values represent the response time of the majority of the page requests.

Performance Tuning

The user load tests ran against the Duwamish sample site provide a base performance metric. Reviewing the metrics showed an increasing number of socket errors after the 75 simultaneous connections mark. What you can ascertain from the test results is that the limitation of 75 simultaneous connections is most likely caused by the Web server's hardware capability as it started to overload and reject page requests.

To performance tune the application, you would attempt to increase the capacity of the server, either with more memory or a faster CPU, run the tests again, and take note of the changes in the RPS value, TTFB, and TTLB. You would check the Web server's processor use levels again, and, if necessary, increase the load for the next test run. If the processor use does not increase to 80 percent or more, you may need use performance counters to investigate bottlenecks other than processor speed.

Using the ACT Application Object Model

The ACT Application object model programmatically automates ACT to start and stop tests, analyze reports, and execute other tasks available from the ACT user interface. You can instantiate the objects within the ACT Application object model within scripts using either VBScript or JScript. Table 7-3 describes the major objects in the ACT Application object model.

Table 7-3. Major ACT Application Object Model Objects

OBJECT	DESCRIPTION
Project	Represents an ACT project. The Project object is the main object in the Application object model and provides references to all aspects of the ACT project, including the Tests and Properties collections.
Test	Represents an ACT test script. The Tests collection represents the collection of tests in the ACT project and is a property of the Project object. Each test object represents one of the test scripts in the project.
Controller	The Controller object represents the ACT server and includes methods that allow tests and applications to start and stop any test in an ACT project.

The code to create the Project object in VBScript is as follows:

```
Dim oProject
Set oProject = CreateObject("ACT.Project")
```

Table 7-4 summarizes the basic methods for the Project object.

Table 7-4. Project Object Basic Methods

METHOD	DESCRIPTION	CODE SAMPLE
Open()	This method opens the project.	oProject.Open(strPath, strProjectFileName, bPrompt)
Close()	This method closes the project.	oProject.Close

As mentioned earlier, you can set the properties of a project programmatically through the Project Properties collection. Each property is in the format "Component:Name," where the component string is equal to "Project." The code to reference the Properties collection and to set a property value is as follows:

```
Dim oProperties
Set oProperties = oProject.Properties
oProperties.Item("Project:LogEnable").value = False
```

Similarly, the same format of "Component:Name" applies for Test Properties, except the component string is equal to "TestProperties." You can find the complete list of project and test properties in the .NET documentation.

The code in VBScript to reference a Test object is as follows:

```
Dim oTest
Set oTest = oProject.Tests.Item(strTestName)
```

Table 7-5 summarizes the useful methods and properties for the Controller object.

Table 7-5. Controller Object Main Methods and Properties

METHOD/PROPERTY	DESCRIPTION	CODE SAMPLE
StartTest()	This method starts a test.	oController.StartTest(oProject, oTest, bWaitForCompletion)
StopTest()	This method stops a test.	oController.StopTest
TestIsRunning	This property checks if a test is running.	bIsRunning = Controller.TestIsRunning

The file ScheduleTaskRunScript1.vbs includes an example using the Application object model. Note the usage of the object methods and properties in the following code snippet from the file:

```
' Procedure to run the specified test from the ACT project.
Sub RunTest(oProject, strTestName, oController)
    Dim oTest
    ' check if test is already running
    If oController.TestIsRunning Then
        WScript.Echo("ACT is already running a test.")
    Else
        ' get a reference to the specific test and start the test
        Set olest = oProject.Tests.Item(strTestName)
        Call oController.StartTest(oProject, oTest, False)
    End If
End Sub
```

Using the ACT Test Object Model

The ACT Test object model provides an interface to the HTTP client that ACT uses to send requests. You use it in the test scripts to control the actions of the HTTP client, allowing for full control of the details of a test. Whereas the ACT Application object model focuses on running a defined test script programmatically, the ACT Test object model provides the application programming interface (API) to define a customized test script. Bear in mind this difference because certain objects with the same name in both models will represent different objects.

The Test Object

The Test object is the main object in the Test object model, and it controls the test session. This Test object should not be confused with the Test object from the Application object model. This Test object is the root object that allows access to the other objects including the Request object, Connection object, User object, and Response object. A built-in Test object named "Test" is available in all dynamic tests, so there is no need to explicitly create a new Test object. Table 7-6 summarizes the main methods of the Test object.

Table 7-6. Test Object Main Methods

METHOD	DESCRIPTION
CreateConnection()	Creates a new Connection object representing the connection between the client and the server
CreateRequest()	Creates a new Request object that can be used to send a request using the Connection object's Send method
SendRequest()	Sends a simple URL request to a Web server and returns the server response in a Response object
Trace()	Writes an entry to the ACTTrace.log file
GetCurrentUser()	Returns the User object for the current user
GetNextUser()	Returns the User object for the next user in the Users group and sets the next user as the current user

The Request Object

The Request object represents the HTTP request to be sent to the test server. The VBScript code to get a reference to the Request object is as follows:

```
Dim oRequest
Set oRequest = Test.CreateRequest()
```

Table 7-7 summarizes the main properties of the Request object, which can be set before being sent to the server.

Table 7-7. Request Object Properties

PROPERTY	DESCRIPTION	CODE SAMPLE
Body	The HTTP Body	oRequest.Body = "__VIEWSTATE=..."
HTTPVersion	The HTTP version. "HTTP/1.1" is the default value.	oRequest.HTTPVersion = "HTTP/1.0"
Path	The HTTP Path component of the URL.	oRequest.Path = "/Duwamish7vb/secure/checkout.aspx"
Verb	The HTTP Verb for the request. Default is "GET."	oRequest.Verb = "POST"

The Connection Object

The Connection object represents the connection from the client (test script) to the Web server. You create the connection from the Test object and can send multiple requests as long as it is not closed. The following VBScript code shows how to create a connection to Web server web01 using port 80 with no SSL:

```
Dim oConnection
' call CreateConnection method with arguments (strServer, lPort, bUseSSL)
Set oConnection = Test.CreateConnection("web01", 80, false)
```

It is important to note that the connection is implicitly opened when the Test object CreateConnection() method is called. There is no explicit Open() method on the Connection object.

Table 7-8 describes the main methods and properties of the Connection object.

Table 7-8. Connection Object Methods and Properties

METHODS/PROPERTIES	DESCRIPTION
Close()	This method closes the connection.
Send()	This method sends a HTTP request represented by the Request object to the Web server.
IsOpen	This property checks the state of the connection the last time it was tested by the client. Note that if the server subsequently disconnects and the connection is no longer open, the property will still be set to "True."

The following VBScript code shows how to use each method:

```
Sub SendRequest(oRequest)
    Dim oConnection, oResponse
    ' call CreateConnection method with arguments (strServer, lPort, bUseSSL)
    Set oConnection = Test.CreateConnection("web01", 80, false)
    If (oConnection.IsOpen) Then
        Set oResponse = oConnection.Send(oRequest)
        If (oResponse Is Nothing) Then
            Call Test.Trace("Error: host not found or request is invalid.")
        Else
            Call Test.Trace("Status code:" & oResponse.ResultCode)
        End If
    End If
    oConnection.Close
End Sub
```

The User Object

The User object represents the current user in the test. The object exposes three properties: Name, Password, and Cookies, allowing programmatic access to change the user's credentials and view the user's HTTP cookies. The Test object methods GetCurrentUser() and GetNextUser() return the User object.

Table 7-9 describes the main properties of the User object.

Table 7-9. User Object Main Properties

PROPERTIES	DESCRIPTION
Cookies	Gets the Cookies collection from the specified domain for a unique user
Name	Gets or sets the user name
Password	Gets or sets the user password

You must address an important issue when stress testing with a finite set of unique users. Invariably, collisions will occur if multiple test users access the application with the same user credentials. For example, both user 1 and user 2 log in with the same user ID and password. User 1 adds an item to the shopping cart (item added to the database). User 2 deletes the item from the database. If user 1 tries to delete the item, he will encounter an error (item does not exist). Take into account this issue during the design of the test scenarios.

The Response Object

The Response object represents the HTTP response from the Web server. The properties of the Response object are read-only. The object is useful in developing functional test scripts that require programming logic based on the response from the Web server. Table 7-10 describes some useful properties of the Response object.

Table 7-10. Response Object Properties

PROPERTY	DESCRIPTION
Body	Gets the body of the HTTP response from the response buffer. This is useful for checking values returned from the server.
BytesReceived	Gets the number of bytes received by the client in the response.
ResultCode	Gets the HTTP response code. You can use this to check the status of the request.
TTLB	Gets the TTLB of the response was received. The time is in milliseconds.

The Body and ResultCode properties are useful in checking the content and status of the response, and the BytesReceived and TTLB properties are good metrics for analyzing the performance of the response. You can find the complete list of Response object properties, as well as the methods and properties for the other objects in the Test object model, in the ACT documentation.

Scripting Dynamic Tests with the Test Object Model

You can handle several test scenarios by scripting a dynamic test within ACT. Recording a test enables you to repeat a certain test, but it does not allow you to configure disparate test scenarios within a single test script. A dynamic test script allows you to configure every aspect of the test, from the header information sent in the request to the target page to the response from the Web server, as the following sample scripts will demonstrate.

Simulating Browser Compatibility

One of the more important application tests is to test for browser compatibility. You can handle this by scripting a dynamic test to imitate the browser request headers sent by common browsers. The Request object exposes a Headers collection whose values can be set to match those of common browsers. You can find a code sample in the test script BrowserTest.vbs in the AspNetChap7ACTTest project. The function MakeIE60GETRequest(oRequest) shows how to set up the headers to simulate a request from an Internet Explorer 6.0 browser (see Listing 7-1).

Listing 7-1. The MakeIE60GETRequest() *Function*

```
Function MakeIE60GETRequest(oRequest)
    ' function returns a request object with the appropriate header setup
    Dim oHeaders
    If Not (oRequest Is Nothing) Then
        ' set request line
        oRequest.Verb = "GET"
        oRequest.HTTPVersion = "HTTP/1.1"
        Set oHeaders = oRequest.Headers
        With oHeaders
            Call .RemoveAll()
            ' set header fields
            Call .Add("Accept", "*/*")
            Call .Add("Accept-Language", "en-us")
            Call .Add("Connection", "Keep-Alive")
            Call .Add("Host", "(Automatic)")
            Call .Add("User-Agent", _
                " Mozilla/4.0 (compatible; MSIE 6.0; Windows NT 5.0)")
```

```
                      Call .Add("Accept-Encoding", "gzip, deflate")
                      Call .Add("Cookie", "(Automatic)")
              End With
         Else
              Test.Trace("Invalid Request object")
         End If
         Set MakeIE60GETRequest = oRequest
     End Function
```

Listing 7-2 shows the code to send the request and check the result code.

Listing 7-2. The SendRequest() *Function*

```
Const SERVER_NAME = "localhost"
Const PATH = "/Default.asp"
Dim oIE6Request
Set oIE6Request = Test.CreateRequest
Call MakeIE60GETRequest(oIE6Request)
Call SendRequest(oIE6Request)

Sub SendRequest(oRequest)
    Dim oConnection
    Set oConnection = Test.CreateConnection(SERVER_NAME, 80, False)
    If (oConnection Is Nothing) Then
        Test.Trace("Error: Unable to create connection.")
    Else
        If (oConnection.IsOpen) Then
            oRequest.Path = PATH
            Set oResponse = oConnection.Send(oRequest)
            ' check for a bad connection or request
            If (oResponse Is Nothing) Then
                Test.Trace("Error: invalid request or host not found ")
            Else
                Test.Trace("Server response:" & oResponse.ResultCode)
            End If
            Call oConnection.Close()
        Else
            Test.Trace("Connection was closed")
        End If
    End If
End Sub
```

You could simulate various browser requests in this manner by setting the correct header data for each browser type. Note this test script verifies that the server does not generate an error for the browser-specific request header, but it does not verify the server responded in a correct manner for the specific browser. For example, the response may still contain code that renders fine in IE6 but may encounter rendering issues in Netscape 6. Likewise, the script cannot verify if the server lowers the resolution to 240x320 when the client browser is a Pocket IE. To verify these issues, an option is to save each browser response during execution of the test script and then verify each response by loading it into the appropriate browser.

Note the use of the `Test.Trace()` method, which appends a string to the `ACTTrace.log` file. The log file is in `%ProgramFiles%\Microsoft ACT\ACTTrace.log`. The `ACTTrace.log` file is overwritten when a new test is started, so you must manually move or rename it if you want to save the information from each test run.

Configuring a Dynamic Test for Multiple Pages

At one time or another, you must test an application to verify all the pages and components are functional. This requires the tester to run through every page in the application. With ACT, you can automate this function with a dynamically configurable test script. The sample test script `PageTest.vbs` in project AspNetChap7ACTTest demonstrates how to use a text file (`RequestPaths.dat`) to configure the target pages for a test. The text file stores the request paths in the format:

```
/Duwamish7vb/default.aspx
/Duwamish7vb/secure/logon.aspx?ReturnUrl=%2fDuwamish7vb%2fsecure%2faccount.aspx
/Duwamish7vb/categories.aspx?id=830
/Duwamish7vb/viewsource.aspx?path=categories.src
/Duwamish7vb/shoppingcart.aspx
```

where each line defines a unique test request path. The script reads each line and assigns it to the `Request.Path` property before opening a connection, as shown in Listing 7-3.

Listing 7-3. Dynamic Script to Test Multiple Pages

```
Dim strURLPath, arrURLPaths(100)
Dim lCount, lNumberOfItemsInArray
Dim oConnection, oUser, oResponse, oRequest

strURLPath = ""
```

```
lCount = 0
lNumberOfItemsInArray = 0
strURLPath = ""

Set oConnection = Test.CreateConnection(SERVER_NAME, 80, False)
Set oRequest = Test.CreateRequest
lNumberOfItemsInArray = GetDataFromFile( (DATA_FILE_PATH & _
    DATA_FILE_NAME) , arrURLPaths)

For lCount = 0 To (lNumberOfItemsInArray - 1)      ' loop through each URL
    strURLPath = arrURLPaths(lCount)          ' get an element from the array
    oRequest.Path = strURLPath       ' assign Request.Path property
    Set oResponse = oConnection.Send(oRequest)       ' send the request
    If (oResponse Is Nothing) Then       ' check for a bad request or connection
        Call Test.Trace("E: Invalid request or host not found." & VbCrLf)
    Else
        Call Test.Trace("I: Requested '" & strURLPath & "'" & vbCrLf)
        Call Test.Trace("I: Server response: " & oResponse.ResultCode & VbCrLf)
    End If
Next
```

The result code is checked for each response, and the results are written to the Trace log. After the test is run, messages in the Trace log would show the requested page, and the result code from the response for each path is listed in the .dat file:

```
[08/29 - 16:03:44!2880]    1>I: Requested '/Duwamish7vb/default.aspx'
[08/29 - 16:03:44!2880]    1>I: Server response: 200
[08/29 - 16:03:45!2880]    1>I: Requested '/Duwamish7vb/categories.aspx?id=830'
[08/29 - 16:03:45!2880]    1>I: Server response: 200
[08/29 - 16:03:46!2880]    1>I: Requested '/Duwamish7vb/categories.aspx?id=831'
[08/29 - 16:03:46!2880]    1>I: Server response: 200
```

There are a multitude of test scenarios that you can implement using the Test object model. These two samples should have provided a starting point from which will spring many other imaginative test scripts. You can find other interesting test scripts in the ACT Samples directory, located in the ACT installation directory.

Understanding Common Runtime Issues with ACT

The following sections focus on common runtime issues encountered while using ACT. These issues all prevent the user from running the ACT tool with their application. Some issues relate to configuration, and others require workarounds to overcome some shortcomings within ACT:

- Error encountered when using ACT with NTLM authentication

- Provider load failure error message encountered in ACT

- Low percentage of meaningful response codes

- ACT user interface limits test script length

NTLM Authentication Error

During testing of a Web application with NTLM authentication enabled, you may encounter the following error:

```
401 - The requested resource requires user authentication
```

This error occurred because HTTP 1.0 does not support *keep-alive* connections. This error has been known to occur in the ACT, Developer Edition. To resolve this error, set the HTTP version in the test script from this:

```
oRequest.HTTPVersion = "HTTP/1.0"
```

to this:

```
oRequest.HTTPVersion = "HTTP/1.1"
```

Also, using NTLM authentication requires the test users to be valid domain users. The format for the users in the Users node should be as follows:

```
Domain_name\user_name
```

Provider Load Failure Error Message Encountered

The common error message encountered at the start of a test is this:

```
Could not start the test.
Provider load failure (0x80041013)
```

This error is commonly a result of the ACT account ACTUser not having the appropriate rights on the local machine. The ACTUser account requires *batch log on* rights to access the ACT objects through Distributed COM (DCOM).

To verify the rights are set correctly, follow these steps on the local machine:

1. Open Local Security Policy under Administrative Tools.

2. Select the Local Policies node and then double-click User Rights Assignment.

3. Double-click Log On as a Batch Job and then verify that ACTUser is selected in the Local Policy Setting and Effective Policy Setting columns. Add ACTUser if it does not appear on the list.

4. If your server is a domain member, in Local Security Settings of the Microsoft Management Console (MMC), right-click Security Settings and then click Reload.

Both the ACT Controller and ACT Broker programs run under the ACTUser account identity. If the password for the ACTUser account is modified from its original value, you must update the identity of both programs by using the DCOM configuration utility dcomcnfg.exe.

Low Percentage of Meaningful Response Codes

The ACT test results will only be meaningful if a majority of the response codes are successful. An HTTP response code of 200 indicates that the server successfully processed a request. In addition, an overloaded server commonly returns these result codes:

- Response Code 403 indicates that the server understood the request but is refusing to fulfill it.

- Response Code 404 indicates that the server could not find a linked resource, usually an image file or an include file.

- Response Code 500 indicates that the server encountered errors in attempting to fulfill the request.

In our performance testing, we expect to see greater than 97.5 percent of the response codes returned as successful 200 codes. Otherwise, we do not treat the results as meaningful. This percentage is somewhat arbitrary, although it is loosely based on a statistical approach that uses standard deviations as a measure of certainty. You may choose to use an alternative percentage, but make sure that it is a high value and that every test within a group of tests is measured against a consistent value.

ACT Test Script Length Limitation

The ACT user interface for the test script limits the length of the test script to 1024KB. This limitation is strictly a limitation of the ACT script user interface and not a limitation of the ACT test script engine. ACT can execute files larger than 1024KB. A common practice is to edit the test script outside of ACT in your favorite script editor. The VS.NET IDE is more than adequate for this purpose. After the script is complete, simply copy and paste it into the ACT script panel.

> **NOTE**   *The Microsoft newsgroups provide helpful information for resolving issues with ACT. Microsoft developers regularly monitor these newsgroups and will post answers and suggestions to posted questions. The newsgroups for ACT and application performance are at* `microsoft.public.vsnet.enterprise.tools` *and* `microsoft.public.dotnet.framework.performance`.

Summary

As shown in this chapter, performance testing is a necessary task to understand the limits of an application. Latency, throughput, and utilization help to quantify the performance of an application. Analysis of the metrics behind these concepts helps you draw conclusions about the software and hardware performance bottlenecks. The ACT tool provides a means to test, capture, and analyze performance metrics of an ASP.NET application. Its statistical and graphical features help summarize and organize the test run results. The Test object model provides an object-based interface for creating dynamic test scripts to further enhance the available scope of the tests. With the Test object model, you can script performance and functional tests and repeat them under configurable conditions. With its features, ACT is a welcome addition to any developer's performance toolset.

CHAPTER 8

Debugging and Tracing ASP.NET Applications

As APPLICATION DEVELOPERS, we strive to deliver a product that meets requirements and is free from defects. Although we all want to accomplish this goal with one cycle of development, we rarely get this lucky. Application development involves an iterative cycle of creating code and testing it in different environments. The process starts in the development environment, where code is written, compiled, and unit tested. The application then moves into the quality assurance environment for functional and integration testing. Finally, it moves into the production environment where it is deployed in its release version.

The application development cycle is iterative because it takes successive attempts to resolve exceptions in applications. Generally, the exceptions that developers encounter fall into two distinct groups:

Syntax/compilation exceptions: These exceptions prevent code from compiling and include type-referencing issues and incomplete function references. The compiler usually intercepts these exceptions, which do not make it into the build. Dynamic type casting can cause unexpected behavior on the test or production servers because it can introduce issues involving missing or unregistered DLLs or COM components with incompatible versions. This may cause exceptions that you would otherwise catch at compile-time.

Logical/semantic exceptions: These are exceptions where the code syntax is correct, but the logic execution causes problems. Examples include array-referencing exceptions, where the code references an index that is out of bounds; operator overflow exceptions, such as inadvertently dividing by zero; or exceptions caused by inadvertently passing null references into a function.

You routinely have to debug your code and set traces throughout the application development process to find and fix exceptions. *Debugging* is the process of diagnosing the precise nature of a known exception and then resolving it. *Tracing* is the process of tracking and logging the execution of an application at runtime.

You use debugging mostly during the development cycle to identify and correct the logical and semantic errors that prevent your application from running correctly.

You use tracing often during integration testing and in the production environment to gather information on errors that are not easily reproduced in the development and testing environments. A production application essentially runs unattended and may not log enough information about an error for the developer to resolve the issue. Tracing allows you to report information from strategic locations within the application and write it to a log for future reference.

The .NET Framework Software Development Kit (SDK) and Visual Studio .NET (VS .NET) provide an excellent set of tools for diagnosing and resolving application issues. The .NET Framework provides specialized Debug and Trace classes that provide access to a rich amount of information about errors and application state, including detailed call stacks. The Debug and Trace classes help troubleshoot logical and semantic errors not caught by the complier or integrated development environment (IDE). This includes errors due to incorrect logic or unforeseen user input. To find and resolve these types of errors, you must have the ability to monitor specific data and control the application flow during runtime.

ASP.NET has access to the same debugging and tracing functionality that is available to other application types. In addition, ASP.NET supports the TraceContext class, which is a subclass of the Trace class that provides specialized tracing capabilities for ASP.NET Web applications. The capabilities of ASP.NET enable developers to debug and trace applications, as well as to incorporate event logging and performance counters in the application. This ability is commonly referred to as *instrumentation*.

Instrumentation comprises the following features:

- **Debugging**: Diagnosing and resolving programming issues during development

- **Tracing**: Monitoring the execution of an application at runtime by logging informative messages

- **Event logging**: Components that help to track major events in the execution of the application

- **Performance counters**: Components that help track the performance of your application

In this chapter we discuss the tools provided by the .NET Framework SDK and VS .NET that support debugging, tracing, and logging within ASP.NET applications.

Understanding Application Builds

Applications go through a cycle of iterative builds throughout the development process. This cycle continues even after the application has been deployed to production as a release build. The term *build configuration* refers to the settings and configurations incorporated into a specific build. A build configuration controls the application build settings, including the files and components to be built. You can tailor a build configuration to a target platform. In addition, it contains settings that define the level of support for debugging and tracing in the compiled build. You can define two levels of build configuration in VS .NET:

- **Solution build configurations**: These are composed of a set of project configurations where each project entry in the solution build configuration includes the name of the project, the type of build, and the platform supported. The set of entries together specifies how the projects in the solution are to be built and deployed.

- **Project configurations**: These are a set of defined project properties that control how a project is to be built and deployed.

The build configuration is a useful tool during the development process because it helps developers manage the configuration of builds for different targeted platforms, including development, quality assurance, staging, and production. Builds for the development environment do not have the same configuration as builds for the Quality Assurance (QA) environment, and both are in turn different from production environment builds. Development builds, for example, can support debugging symbols, whereas production builds will not. The build created by each associated build configuration is called a *build type*. VS .NET has two default build types: a debug build and a release build.

Debug Builds vs. Release Builds

There are distinct differences between a debug build and a release build. As the names imply, the debug build is for debugging purposes, and the release build is for deployment to a production environment. VS .NET automatically creates the configurations for the debug and release build types and sets the appropriate default options and settings. The default settings for each build type are as follows:

- The debug configuration of the project or solution is compiled with full symbolic debug information.

- The release configuration of the project or solution is fully optimized and contains no symbolic debug information. Debug information is still generated in separate Programmer Database (*.pdb) files, although they are not linked to the project.

Build configurations change throughout the development lifecycle as the application moves between different environments, including the development, test, and production environments. Each build environment has its own purpose and requires differences in the way that you compile the build. The build configuration for each environment addresses these variations. Figure 8-1 shows the typical environments and build characteristics for each build configuration.

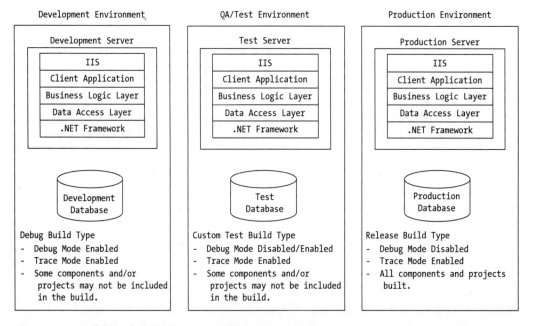

Figure 8-1. Build configurations for application environments

While the project or solution is in development, the debug build is often used to compile and test the project or solution. Debug builds are compiled repeatedly throughout the development lifecycle as new functionality is added and as bugs and exceptions are fixed. The build configuration at this stage is constantly changing to incorporate new components and to troubleshoot and finalize the build configuration. Exception resolution in the application at this stage usually involves two steps. First, compilation exceptions such as incorrect syntax, misspelled keywords, and type mismatches are corrected as they are encountered during the build process. Modern compilers and IDEs catch most of these exceptions up front and prevent the build from completing successfully until they are resolved. Second, debugging tools find and correct exceptions caused by logical and semantic issues in the code. These exceptions may make it into the build and then turn up at runtime during unit testing (or worse, in production, if the exception is not caught).

In the development environment, the build type is called the *debug build*. This build type is compiled with debug symbols and typically includes strategically located tracing information. The debug build usually has the following characteristics:

- Debug mode is enabled.

- Trace mode is enabled.

- Some components are excluded from the build so that the developer can focus on testing a more limited section of the application.

Debug builds are often not used when the project or solution is ready for formal QA testing. In this environment, the compilations errors have already been resolved and developers have tested the components within the project or application. The exceptions encountered in this environment are usually integration errors and logical program flow exceptions unforeseen by the developer. To troubleshoot and resolve these exceptions, it is common to have trace mode enabled, and optionally have debug mode enabled also. Whether you enable debug mode depends on what the goals are for the formal testing. Typically, unit testing is focused on identifying exceptions, and on gathering as much information as possible when exceptions do occur. The goal of unit testing is to communicate back to the developer what the exceptions are, and what is known about them, so that the developer can resolve the problems. Debug information has an important role to play in this effort.

If performance measurement is one of the testing goals, then you will not compile the project in debug mode, since this mode creates bigger, slower builds that have an adverse effect on performance. In this case, you will want to mirror the build that will go into production, so you would want to compile the project in Release mode. The release build type uses the same build configuration as will be used for the production-ready release build.

The *custom* build type is a compromise between the standard debug and release build types. A custom build configuration can be based off either the default debug build or release build configuration. It is useful for creating a test build in development for testing a variety of issues and features. The custom build type selectively excludes components and files that are not ready-for the build. The custom build type usually has the following characteristics:

- Debug mode is either enabled or disabled

- Trace mode is enabled

- Some components and files are excluded from the build

An important factor in configuring a custom build is to identify the interactions between components within the project or application. Care must be used to make sure the exclusion of components does not adversely affect or negate the testing performed on the components included in the build.

Once the project or solution is fully developed and sufficiently debugged to pass unit testing, you are ready to compile the application into a release build. The release build is characterized by the following:

- Debug mode is disabled

- Trace mode is enabled

- All application components and files are included in the build

Release builds are smaller and faster than debug builds, because they are compiled with optimizations and without debugging symbols. Optimizations are typically excluded from debug builds, because they complicate the relationship between source code and generated instructions. Debug builds, on the other hand, use a simpler compilation algorithm. Release builds may contain tracing information that can be conditionally activated to diagnose issues in the production environment that are not readily observed in the development and test environments.

Setting the Build Configuration

The settings for each build type reside in the project and solution configurations. Because there can be multiple projects in a solution, there can be multiple project configurations associated with a solution configuration.

You manage the relationships between solution and project configurations through the Configuration Manager in VS .NET. You access the Configuration Manager from three locations within VS .NET: the Build menu; the Solution Configurations drop-down list in the main toolbar; or the solution's property pages (discussed in the "Managing Solution Configurations" section). Figure 8-2 shows the Configuration Manager dialog box for the AspNetChap8 and AspNetChap8A sample projects that accompany this chapter.

Table 8-1 describes each element in the dialog box.

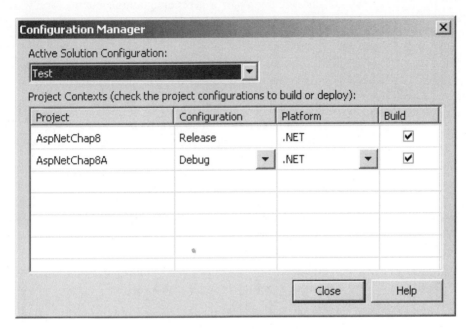

Figure 8-2. The Configuration Manager dialog box

Table 8-1. Configuration Manager Elements

ELEMENT NAME	DESCRIPTION
Active Solution Configuration	Displays the solution build configurations defined in VS .NET. You can change the solution build configuration here or in the Solution Configurations drop-down list on the main toolbar. The drop-down list gives the option to create a new solution configuration with the New menu item or edit an existing configuration with the Edit menu item.

Table 8-1. Configuration Manager Elements (continued)

(continued)

ELEMENT NAME	DESCRIPTION
Project Contexts	Project Contexts displays the project name, a drop-down list of project configurations and platforms, and check boxes for selecting the projects to be built and (if enabled) deployed. Each combination of project configuration and platform chosen determines the project configuration that will be used. You can sort the columns by clicking the column names.
Project	Displays the project names found in the current solution.
Configuration	Displays the project build configurations available. The drop-down list gives the option to create a new project build configuration or rename an existing build configuration using New or Edit.
Platform	Displays the platforms available for the project. The drop-down list gives the option to add a new platform or edit an existing one using New or Edit. The type of project determines what platforms are available. There is a one-to-one correspondence between project configurations and platforms. When you add a new platform to the project, it creates a new project configuration.
Build	Specifies whether to build this project. An unchecked project will not be built, even if there are project dependencies on the project.

The Configuration Manager allows you to manage the specific solution build configurations and project configurations you want set up at any specific time. For solutions with multiple projects, this is a useful tool to manage the project configurations as it relates to the solution configuration. As Figure 8-2 shows, you can assign different project configurations to a solution configuration. In the sample, the scenario could be that AspNetChap8 is ready for testing, but AspNetChap8A is still in development. In this case, you can assign a solution configuration called "Test," which consists of a release build of AspNetChap8 project and a debug build of AspNetChap8A.

Managing Solution Configurations

You manage the solution configuration using the solution's property pages. You can open these property pages in two ways:

- Right-click the VS .NET solution file in the Solution Explorer window. Select Properties from the pop-up menu.

- Highlight the solution file in the Solutions Explorer window, and then select Properties from the Project menu.

The solution's property pages, which has different properties from the project's property pages, offer the ability to do the following tasks:

- Determine in what order projects run in the debugger

- Determine in what order projects build using dependencies

- Define and edit solution and project build configurations

Figure 8-3 shows the sample property pages for the AspNetChap8 solution. The solution contains two projects, AspNetChap8 and AspNetChap8A. Table 8-2 describes each tag.

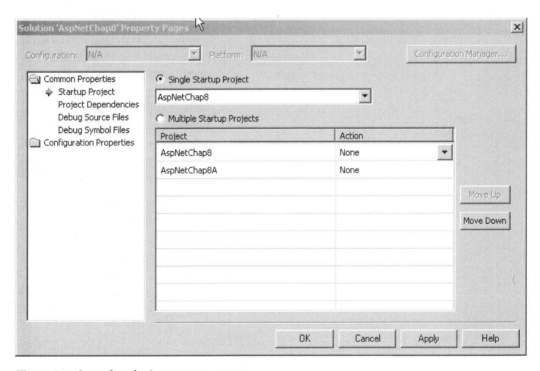

Figure 8-3. Sample solution property pages

Table 8-2. Elements of the Solution Property Pages

OPTION NAME	DESCRIPTION
Startup Project	Assigns the startup project to run when the debugger is started. It can be specified as a Single Startup Project, where only one project is started, or as Multiple Startup Projects, where more than one project is run when you start the debugger. If you select Multiple Startup Projects, then each project can be assigned one of the following actions from the pull-down list: **Start**: Run the project when the debugger is started. **Start without Debugging**: Run the project when the debugger is started, but do not debug this project. None: Do not run this project when you start the debugger.
Project Dependencies	Sets the project dependencies, if any, for the projects in the solution. The dependency is defined as "Project AspNetChap8A depends on Project AspNetChap8." Setting project dependencies determines the build order for the projects; in this case, AspNetChap8 would be built before AspNetChap8A.
Configuration Properties ➤ Configuration	Function and layout are similar to the Configuration Manager. Here you can set how different versions of solutions and their projects will be built.

Managing Project Configurations

You define the project configurations using the property pages. The project configurations are sets of properties for each supported combination of build and platform (for example, Debug .NET or Release Win32). For ASP.NET applications, the only supported platform option is .NET. In this dialog box, you can manage the project's Common Properties and Configuration Properties. The properties are saved in the project's `.vbproj` file.

The Common Properties contain the following groups of parameters:

- **General**: Sets the relevant information about the current project including the assembly name, output type, startup object, and root namespace.

- **Build (Common Properties)**: Sets the compilation defaults including the compiler options and the application icon

- **Designer Defaults**: Sets the page layout, the target schema, and the client-side script language

- **Imports**: Sets the namespaces for this application

- **Reference Path**: Sets where the reference files are to be stored

- **Web Settings**: Sets the defaults for Web projects, including offline behavior and Web access method

The Configuration properties contain the following groups of parameters:

- **Debugging**: Sets the start project, sets the start options including command-line arguments, and sets the debugger to enable for this build

- **Optimization**: Sets the types of optimization including removing integer overflow checks, enabling optimizations, and enabling incremental builds

- **Build (Configuration Properties)**: Sets the output path, specifies whether to emit debugging information, and controls whether warnings will be raised

- **Deployment**: Specifies the configuration override file (if any) to use during compilation

To open the project's property pages, select the desired project or projects in Solution Explorer. On the Project menu, select Properties. Figure 8-4 shows the sample project's property pages for the AspNetChap8 project.

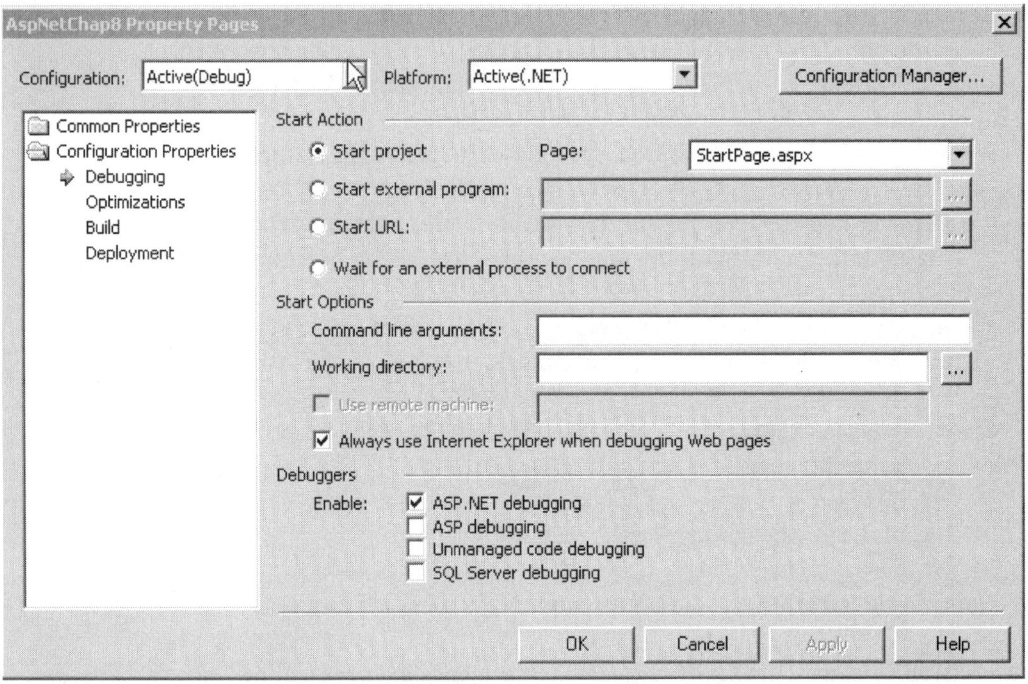

Figure 8-4. Sample project's property pages

To create a new project configuration, click the Configuration Manager button on the upper-right corner of the dialog box. Within the Configuration Manager, select New from the Configuration pull-down list, enter a configuration name, select whether you want to create a separate solution for the new configuration, and click OK. The new configuration will then be available from the pull-down list in the property pages.

The Debugging Tab

The Debugging tab allows you to specify additional actions when the project goes into run mode. You can take these two actions:

- **Start Action**: Indicates the item to start when the application is debugged: the project, a custom program, a Uniform Resource Locator (URL), or nothing. By default, the Start Project option is enabled.

- **ASP.NET Debugging**: Determines if the debugger should attach to the server to enable debugging of ASP.NET pages.

The Build Tab

The Build tab allows you to set the attributes for the project's executable or build output. You can set these properties:

- **Generate Debugging Information**: Specifies whether the application should enable debugging information. By default, debug information is enabled for the Debug configuration and disabled for the Release configuration.

- **Register for COM Interop**: Specifies the compilation output to be a COM Callable wrapper for your class library and registers it with the operating system similar to RegSvr32.exe. The option is only available if the Output Type property of this application is a class library and if the class library assembly is strongly named.

- **Warnings**: Specifies whether warnings are enabled during compilation and how they will be handled.

- **Enable build warnings**: Directs the build warnings to the Task List. The developer can utilize the Task List to track the warnings.

- **Treat warnings as errors**: Directs the compiler to treat build warnings as errors. If a warning occurs, the compiler will not produce an application output file.

- **Define DEBUG constant**: Defines and passes the DEBUG=1 constant to the compiler. Debug class statements are compiled in the output.

- **Define TRACE constant**: Defines and passes the TRACE=1 constant to the compiler. Trace class statements are compiled in the output.

The Deployment Tab

The Deployment tab contains one property, Configuration Override File. It specifies a Web configuration file with which to build and deploy the project. The selected *.config file will be renamed to Web.config when the project is deployed. You should maintain separate Web.config files for each environment you will be building for, such as the development server or the production server. This property applies only to ASP.NET applications.

Executing Compilation and Conditional Compilation

Both the trace and debug modes have associated conditional attributes. You can enable or disable the trace and debug modes independently. Thus, there are four possible cases: debug, trace, both, or neither. The release build in production does not have to enable tracing, but it is often useful to do so. Debug builds typically enables both debugging and tracing.

You can set the conditional attributes in the compiler settings in several ways:

- The project's property pages

- The command line

- #CONST (for Visual Basic) and #define (for C#)

The conditional attributes for debugging and tracing are in the Build (Configuration Properties) tag in the project's property pages.

- In VB .NET, select the check boxes to enable the two properties: Define TRACE constant and Define DEBUG constant.

- In C#, type the name of the setting you want to enable into the Conditional Compilation Constants field. Because C# is case sensitive, the names must be uppercase. For example, to define both debugging and tracing, you must enter the following text into the field: DEBUG;TRACE (note the use of a semicolon as the delimiter between the constants).

To set the debugging and tracing attributes from the command-line compiler, use the conditional compiler constants specific to the language—in this case, /d or /define. Enter the following switches in the command line:

- **VB .NET**: /d:TRACE=TRUE /d:DEBUG=FALSE

- **C#**: /d:TRACE /d:DEBUG=FALSE

Likewise, you can execute conditional compilation within the code using the specific language directive, #CONST or #define. Type the suitable statement at the top of the source code file before any class or function code blocks.

In VB .NET, enter the following:

```
#CONST <ATTRIBUTE> = <true.false>
where ATTRIBUTE = TRACE or DEBUG and true = enable
```

In C#, enter the following:

```
#<define/undefine> <ATTRIBUTE>
where ATTRIBUTE = TRACE or DEBUG and define = true
```

Using Debugging Tools in Visual Studio .NET

Debugging an ASP.NET Web application with VS .NET is similar to debugging a Windows application. The integrated VS .NET debugger provides powerful tools for debugging both types of applications. In this section we describe some of the debugging tools provided by VS .NET for debugging ASP.NET applications both locally and on a remote server. Debugging involves discovering and correcting logical and semantic errors within the application. To meet these needs, the debugger allows you to inspect and modify the runtime behavior and state of the application through a set of server-side debugging tools integrated into VS .NET.

Using the Task List Window to Resolve Build Errors

VS .NET provides good support to help troubleshoot and resolve build and syntax errors. When a project is built in VS .NET, build errors will be written to a Task List window, with a text description of the error, and the file and line number on which the error occurred. Figure 8-5 shows a Task List window with a build error. The window shows an "Argument not specified" error, which is caused by calling a function without the correct number of arguments.

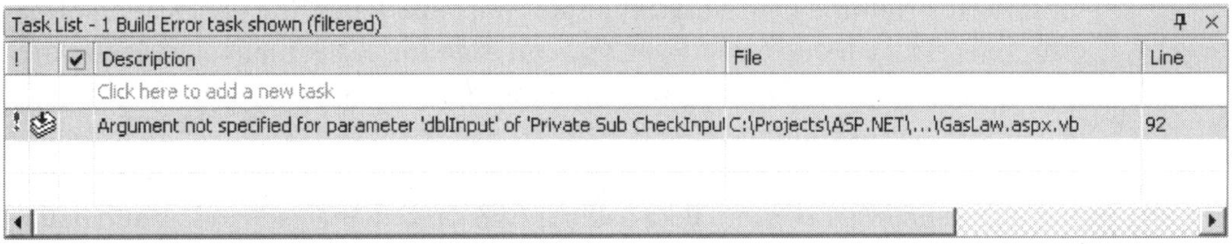

!	☑	Description	File	Line
		Click here to add a new task		
! 🗂		Argument not specified for parameter 'dblInput' of 'Private Sub CheckInpu	C:\Projects\ASP.NET\...\GasLaw.aspx.vb	92

Task List - 1 Build Error task shown (filtered)

Figure 8-5. Task List window

You can click the error in the Task List and VS .NET will open the file and highlight the specific code within the file that causes the build error. A useful feature of the Task List window is the ability to keep track of the outstanding build errors since the last build. When you fix an error, it disappears from the Task List.

Setting the Debug Mode

To debug an ASP.NET application, you must first create a debug build using the debug build type. Then you must instruct the application to use the debug symbols. Debug mode tells ASP.NET to generate symbols for dynamically generated files and enables the debugger to attach to the ASP.NET application. You set the debug configuration attribute in the Web.config file in the <compilation> section. To enable debug mode, set the debug attribute to "true":

```
<compilation defaultLanguage="vb" debug="true" />
```

Because attributes are case sensitive, make sure the attribute name is "debug," not "Debug" or "DEBUG." ASP.NET automatically detects any changes to the Web.config file and applies the new configuration settings. You do not need to recompile the application after changing this setting because the setting simply instructs ASP.NET to attach the application to the existing debug symbols. ASP.NET applications inherit settings from Web.config files at higher levels in the URL path. The highest-level file, named Machine.config, is at the machine level and is located in the systemroot\Microsoft.NET\Framework\versionNumber\CONFIG directory. All ASP.NET applications inherit the base settings from this file. These hierarchical configuration files allow you to change settings for several ASP.NET applications simultaneously. Chapter 2, "Introducing ASP.NET Applications," provides a detailed discussion of ASP.NET application configuration.

Working in Debugger Windows and Dialog Boxes

Debugging involves the use of a debugger, a powerful tool that allows you to observe the runtime behavior of your program and determine the location of semantic errors. Using a debugger, you can examine the content of variables in your program without having to insert additional calls to output the values. You can insert a *breakpoint* in your code to halt execution at a certain point. When your program stops (in other words, enters break mode), you can examine local variables and other relevant data using the VS .NET debugger window and dialog boxes. Some windows allow you to execute statements, and others simply allow you to monitor current, in-scope variables. Table 8-3 summarizes the debugger window and its corresponding functionality.

Table 8-3. Debugger Window Functionality

WINDOW	FUNCTIONALITY
Autos	Displays variables used in the current statement and the previous statement. The current statement is the statement at the current execution location.
Breakpoints	Lists all breakpoints currently set in your program and displays their properties. You can use this window to set (create) new breakpoints, delete breakpoints, enable or disable breakpoints, edit a breakpoint's properties, and find the source or disassembly code corresponding to a breakpoint.
Call Stack	Displays the function or procedure calls currently on the stack.
Command	Either issues commands or debugs and evaluates expressions in the IDE.
Disassembly	Shows assembly code corresponding to the instructions created by the compiler. These assembly instructions correspond to the native code created by the JIT compiler, not the intermediate language generated by the VS .NET compiler.
Locals	Displays variables local to the function containing the current execution location.
Memory	Displays large buffers, strings, and other data that do not display well in the Watch or Variables window.
Modules	Lists the modules (DLLs and EXEs) used by your program and shows relevant information for each.
Output	Displays status messages for various features in the IDE. These include build errors that occur when a project is compiled and the results when Transact-SQL syntax in a stored procedure is checked against a target database.
QuickWatch	Evaluates a variable or expression and edits the value of a variable or register.
Registers	Displays register contents. Values that have changed recently appear in red.
Running Documents	Helps debug scripts, especially scripts generated by code on the server. It displays a list of documents currently loaded into the process you are running.

(continued)

Table 8-3. Debugger Window Functionality (continued)

WINDOW	FUNCTIONALITY
This (Me)	Examines the data members of the object associated with the current method.
Threads	Examines and controls threads in the program you are debugging. A *thread* is a sequence of executable instructions created by a program.
Watch	Evaluates variables and expressions and keeps the results. You can also use this window to edit the value of a variable or register.

Most of the time, you will not need to use all these windows while debugging an ASP.NET application. You enable the debug windows through their respective tool menu. You can drag and anchor each window anywhere on the development window within VS .NET. When you are not using a window, you can hide it by selecting the Auto Hide icon or close it by clicking the Close icon. Let's discuss some of the most commonly used debug windows in further detail.

Some of the main functions provided by the debug windows are the ability to evaluate variables and expressions and to set or edit the value of a variable. Several windows support this set of functions, notably the Autos, Locals, QuickWatch, This (Me), and Watch windows. The only difference between these windows is the scope of the variables within the window's control. Many of the windows are available only when the application is in break mode. One of the common methods to enter break mode is to set breakpoints in the application. To set a breakpoint, right-click on the left sidebar of the code window next to the line of code in question, or press F9 to set a breakpoint on the line where the cursor is located. Figure 8-6 shows a breakpoint set within the DebugWindows2.aspx file in the sample project.

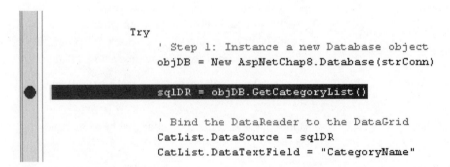

```
Try
    ' Step 1: Instance a new Database object
    objDB = New AspNetChap8.Database(strConn)

    sqlDR = objDB.GetCategoryList()

    ' Bind the DataReader to the DataGrid
    CatList.DataSource = sqlDR
    CatList.DataTextField = "CategoryName"
```

Figure 8-6. Setting a breakpoint

Using the Autos Window

The simplest way to check the variables in the current and previous statements is to use the Autos window. This window provides the smallest scope among the windows. To display the Autos window, choose Debug ➤ Windows ➤ Autos. (The debugger must be running or in break mode.) The window automatically identifies and displays the variables in the current and previous statement—hence the name *Autos*.

In the DebugWindow2.aspxfile, you return an array by using the Select() method within the Tables collection:

```
sortExp = "ProductName ASC"
drarray = myDS.Tables(0).Select(filterExp, sortExp,
DataViewRowState.CurrentRows)
```

The easiest way to check whether the input parameters to the Select() method are correct is to use the Autos window. Figure 8-7 shows the Autos window in VS .NET. If you wanted to change the value of a listed variable in a debug window, you would select the variable value to edit by double-clicking it or by pressing the Tab key. Then type in the new value and press the Enter key. In Figure 8-7, the sortExp variable is selected and is in the process of being edited.

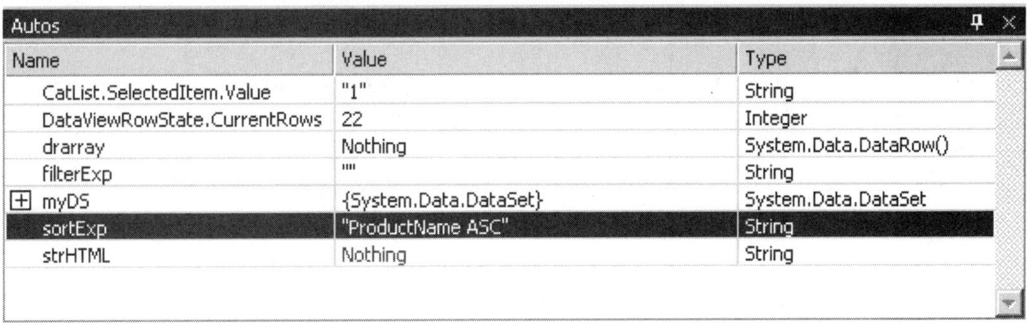

Autos		
Name	Value	Type
CatList.SelectedItem.Value	"1"	String
DataViewRowState.CurrentRows	22	Integer
drarray	Nothing	System.Data.DataRow()
filterExp	""	String
⊞ myDS	{System.Data.DataSet}	System.Data.DataSet
sortExp	"ProductName ASC"	String
strHTML	Nothing	String

Figure 8-7. The Autos window

Using the Locals Window

The Locals window provides the ability to view and update variables local to a function. To display the Locals window, choose Debug ➤ Windows ➤ Locals. (The debugger must be running or in break mode.) The Locals window is similar to the Autos window. Instead of merely listing the variables from the current and previous statements, the scope of the variables within the Locals window is the function of the current execution location. As an example, Figure 8-8 shows the Locals window displaying the variables found in the Autos window as well as other variables local to the function `Button1_Click`.

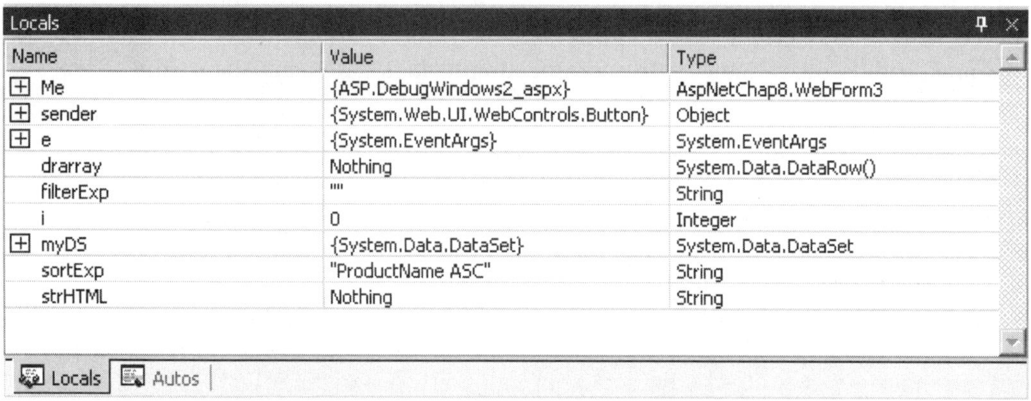

Name	Value	Type
⊞ Me	{ASP.DebugWindows2_aspx}	AspNetChap8.WebForm3
⊞ sender	{System.Web.UI.WebControls.Button}	Object
⊞ e	{System.EventArgs}	System.EventArgs
drarray	Nothing	System.Data.DataRow()
filterExp	""	String
i	0	Integer
⊞ myDS	{System.Data.DataSet}	System.Data.DataSet
sortExp	"ProductName ASC"	String
strHTML	Nothing	String

Figure 8-8. The Locals window

You can change the scope of the Locals window by doing one of the following:

- Using the Debug Location toolbar to select the desired function, thread, or program

- Double-clicking an item in the Call Stack or Threads window

You can change a variable the same way as in the Autos window. Select the value by double-clicking it, type the new value, and press Enter.

Using the Watch Window

The Watch window enables you to evaluate variables and expressions and edit the value of a variable or register. To display the Watch window, choose Debug ➤ Windows ➤ Watch and then click Watch1, Watch2, Watch3, or Watch4, depending on which one you want. (The debugger must be running or in break mode and supports a maximum of four Watch windows.) The behavior of the Watch window is similar to the other debug windows discussed, with the exception that the user specifies the variables listed in the Watch window. Figure 8-9 shows the Watch window with two variables, `drarray` and `sortExp`.

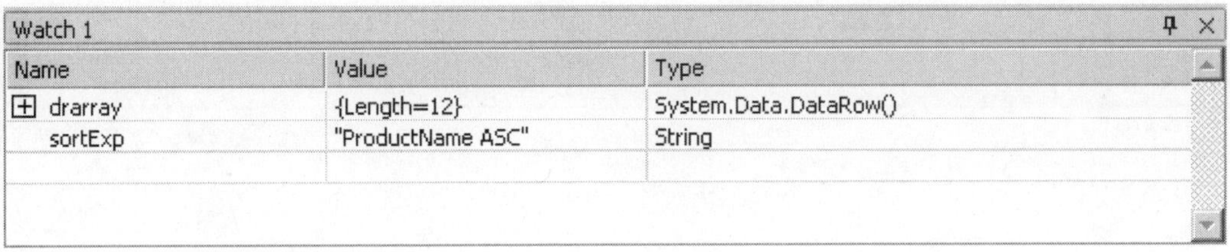

Watch 1			🔲 ✕
Name	Value	Type	
⊞ drarray	{Length=12}	System.Data.DataRow()	
sortExp	"ProductName ASC"	String	

Figure 8-9. The Watch window

To add a new variable to the Watch window, select a row within the window and type the variable in the Name column. Once you add a variable to the Watch window, you can continue to monitor its value as you step through your program execution.

Using the QuickWatch Dialog Box

You can use the QuickWatch dialog box to quickly view a variable, expression, or register. The two ways to open the QuickWatch dialog box are as follows:

- From the Debug menu, choose QuickWatch. (The debugger must be in break mode.)

- In a source window, right-click a variable name and choose QuickWatch from the shortcut menu. This automatically places the variable into the QuickWatch dialog box. (The debugger must be in break mode.)

Because QuickWatch is a modal dialog box, you cannot leave it open like the Watch window to watch a variable or expression while you step through your program. If you need to do that, you can add the variable or expression to the Watch window by selecting the variable in the QuickWatch window and clicking the Add Watch button. Figure 8-10 shows the QuickWatch dialog box with the variable drarray, which holds the DataRow object that is returned from the Select() method of the DataSet using this code:

```
filterExp = ""
sortExp = "ProductName ASC"
drarray = myDS.Tables(0).Select(filterExp, sortExp,
DataViewRowState.CurrentRows)
```

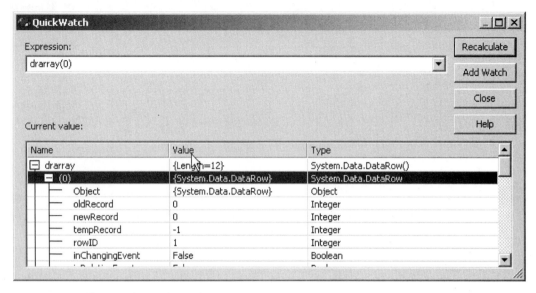

Figure 8-10. The QuickWatch window

Using the Breakpoints Window

The Breakpoints window lists all breakpoints currently set in your program and displays their properties. In the Breakpoints window, you can set (create) new breakpoints, delete breakpoints, enable or disable breakpoints, edit a breakpoint's properties, or find the source or disassembly code corresponding to a breakpoint. To display the Breakpoints window, select Debug ➤ Windows ➤ Breakpoints. Figure 8-11 shows an example of the Breakpoints window.

Name	Condition	Hit Count	Data	Program
☑ ● DebugWindows.aspx.vb, line 26 character 9	(no condition)	break always (currently 0)		[2092]...
☑ ● DebugWindows2.aspx.vb, line 95 character 9	(no condition)	when hit count is equal to 2 (currently 0)		[2092]...
☑ ● DebugWindows2.aspx.vb, line 116 character 9	when 'strHTML = "" is true	break always (currently 0)		[2092]...

Figure 8-11. The Breakpoints window

To view or edit the properties of the breakpoint, right-click a breakpoint and select Properties to show the Breakpoint Properties dialog box (see Figure 8-12). Note that the Breakpoints Properties dialog box displays the condition and hit count parameters for each breakpoint. The condition parameter allows you to

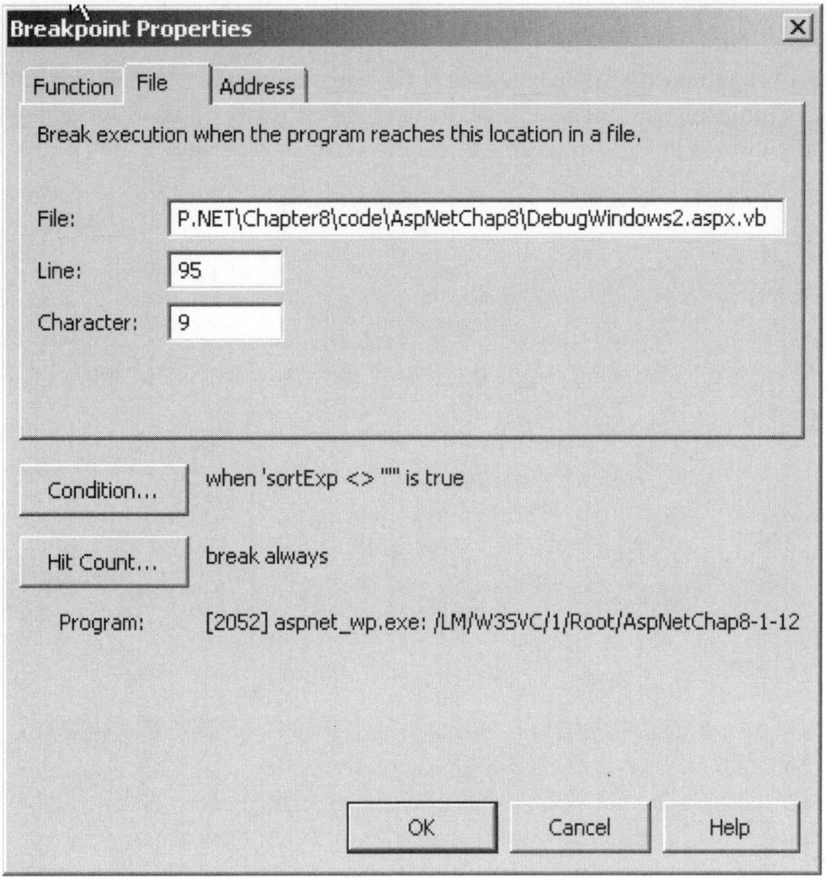

Figure 8-12. The Breakpoint Properties dialog box

set a conditional expression to control when the breakpoint takes effect. The hit count parameter allows you to set one of four conditions:

- Break always

- When hit count is equal to n (where *n* is an editable numeric parameter)

- When hit count is a multiple of n

- When hit count is greater than or equal to n

So, a question arises while discussing breakpoints: Can you edit code while in break mode? VS .NET does provide an option to do this under Tools ➤ Options ➤ Debugging ➤ Edit and Continue. The command actually behaves differently based on the type of language used in your program. VS .NET does not support Edit and Continue for Visual Basic or C# code. You can use the command for C/C++ programs only. In Visual Basic or C#, you cannot edit the code and continue debugging with the new code. Instead, the program behaves according to the selection in the Edit and Continue options window, as shown in Figure 8-13.

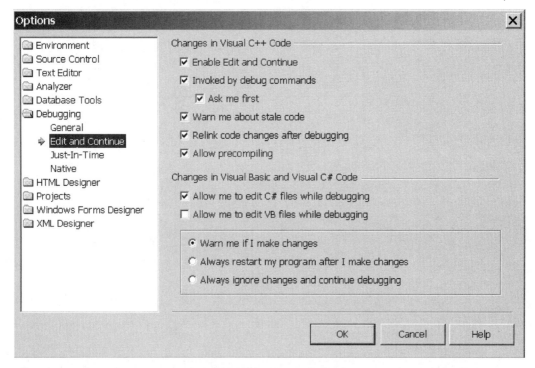

Figure 8-13. The Edit and Continue options window for Visual Basic, Visual C#, and Visual C++

Using the Command Window

The Command window allows you to issue commands or to debug and evaluate variables expressions in the debugger. To display the Command window, choose View ➤ Other Windows ➤ Command Window. The command has two modes: the command mode and the immediate mode.

Working in Command Mode

The > prompt within the Command window indicates the window is in command mode. The command mode executes VS .NET commands or commands not found within the menu system. VS .NET commands allow the user to display—and in some cases, execute—dialog boxes, windows, and other items within the IDE through a keyboard command. For example, you can add the selected variable within the code window to the QuickWatch window by typing the following while in command mode:

```
Debug.QuickWatch
```

The command mode supports IntelliSense, so you can view the list of available commands within the window. The command mode also supports aliases, which can be custom defined using the alias command. VS comes with a set of predefined aliases for your convenience. To view the list of existing aliases, type alias while in command mode. A predefined alias commonly used is ?, an alias for Debug.Print.

Working in Immediate Mode

You use the immediate mode for evaluating expressions, executing statements, and printing variable values. To open a Command window in immediate mode, press Ctrl+Alt+I. To change from command mode to immediate mode, enter debug.immediate or use the alias immed. There is no prompt within the Command window when in immediate mode. Instead, the window title will display "Command Window—Immediate." To switch back to command mode from immediate mode, enter cmd or press Ctrl+Alt+A.

You can evaluate and execute expressions during the debug process while in immediate mode. You can also execute a single command while in immediate mode by prefacing the command with a greater-than sign (>).

Using Programmatic Debug Tools

An integral part of development is the ability to programmatically output relevant information during an application's execution. You can debug application flow by strategically placing several debug statements throughout the code and writing information out to a specific window. The Output window displays text output from the various IDE tools, including debug statements. The debug windows allow you to do much the same thing, so you rarely need to insert debug statements into code just to check values. One method of debugging is to check for conditions within the application to make sure the logic is correct. An *assertion* is a statement placed within an application that evaluates to "true" when the condition in the argument to the assertion evaluates to "true." By defining the assertion arguments to correspond to the application logic, you can use assertions to determine if the application is functioning properly. The .NET Framework provides a Debug class, which you can use to print debugging information and emit assertions.

Using the Debug Class

The Debug class provides write and assert methods to help debug applications during development. The Debug class is part of the System.Diagnostics namespace and must be imported into the code to be used. With the Debug class, you can record information about errors and application execution to logs, text files, or other devices for later analysis. The compilation configuration drives the availability of the Debug class. By default, a debug build compiles the procedures and functions of the Debug class, whereas a release build does not. Therefore, debug statements do not affect the size and performance of an application's release version.

Table 8-4 describes the Debug class's methods.

Table 8-4. Debug Class Methods

METHOD	DESCRIPTION
Assert()	Checks a condition and writes a message to the Listeners collection if the condition is "false."
Fail()	Writes an error message to the trace listeners in the Listeners collection. The message will include the passed-in message string and a dump of the call stack indicating where the Fail() method was called.
Write()	Writes information to the trace listeners in the Listeners collection.
WriteLine()	Same as Write() except this method includes a carriage return.
WriteIf()	Writes information to the trace listeners in the Listeners collection if a condition is "true."
WriteLineIf()	Same as WriteIf() except this method includes a carriage return.

By default, the Debug class writes all messages in the Output window by passing the messages to the set of listeners within the Listeners collection. You can write the debug messages to other destinations by adding other types of listeners to the Listeners collection. This will be covered in more detail in the section "Adding Listeners to the Trace.Listeners Collection."

Debugging with Assertions

There are many times during development when you need to check for logic errors within the application. Certain application flows and conditions may generate unforeseen errors caused by logic errors. Assertions help you pinpoint these problem areas in the application.

You can use an assertion to test conditions within the application that should hold true if the application is functioning correctly. An assertion raises if the condition of the specified argument to the assertion evaluates to false. If the condition evaluates to true, then the assertion has no effect on the application. For example, a mathematical application may have assertions to make sure the divisor is not equal to zero. If it is equal to zero, then the condition would be false, and an assertion would raise. This would help the programmer debug what condition caused the divisor to be set to zero.

The `Debug.Assert()` method evaluates a condition and, if the result is false, sends diagnostic messages to the Listeners collection. The `Assert()` method outputs the call stack with file and line numbers for each line in the call stack. The default behavior of the `Assert()` method outputs the message to the default trace output, when the application is run in user-interface mode, and also displays the message in a message box. You can customize this behavior by adding a listener to, or removing one from, the Listeners collection.

The `GasLaw.aspx` page of the AspNetChap8 project includes an example of the `Debug.Assert()` method. The page calculates a value of the Ideal Gas Law, $PV=nRT$, provided the other three parameters are entered. Figure 8-14 shows this page.

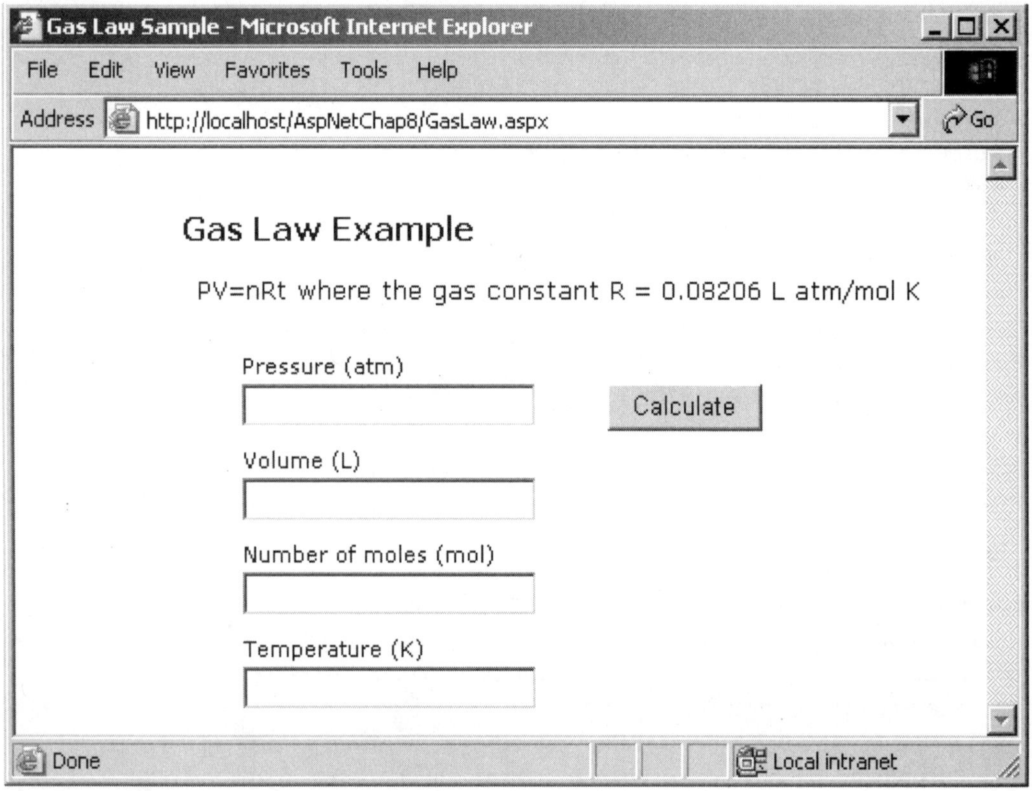

Figure 8-14. The Gas Law example page for illustrating debugging

The page includes a subroutine that tests to make sure the input values are not zero. You must import the System.Diagnostics namespace to use the Debug class:

```
Imports System.Diagnostics
Private Shared debugSwitch As New BooleanSwitch("debugLevelSwitch", _
        "Debug Boolean Switch")
Private Sub CheckInput(ByVal dblInput As Double)
    If debugSwitch.Enabled Then
        Debug.Assert((dblInput <> 0), "Error:  Input cannot be zero.", _
            "Details to follow.")
    End If
End Sub
```

The subroutine does not automatically assume that debugging is enabled. Instead, it uses the BooleanSwitch class to read a flag from the Web.config file. You can use a simple configuration setting to dynamically enable or disable debug code from executing:

```
<system.diagnostics>
      <switches>
              <add name="debugLevelSwitch" value="1" />
      </switches>
  </system.diagnostics>
```

The assertion statement will be evaluated only if the debug switch is enabled. Whenever the input is equal to zero, the condition will be false and the assertion will take effect, writing the assertion message to the Listeners collection. The `Assert()` method has two optional string arguments for the short message and the long message. They are outputted with the assertion, if available. In this case, because no additional listeners were added to the Listeners collection, the default listener will output the message to the Output window as follows:

```
-- DEBUG ASSERTION FAILED --
-- Assert Short Message --
Error:  Input cannot be zero.
-- Assert Long Message --
Details to follow.
    at GasLaw.CheckInput(Double dblInput)
    C:\Projects\ASP.NET\Chapter8\code\AspNetChap8\GasLaw.aspx.vb(46)
...
```

When an application is compiled in a release configuration, `Debug.Assert()` statements are not included in the compilation. Thus, it is important when using `Debug.Assert()` statements to make sure that the logic and functionality of the application does not change when the assertion is removed. Otherwise, you may introduce a bug that only exists in the release build. Also, it is a good idea to avoid procedure or function calls within the `Assert()` method call. The reason is that other procedures and functions may change the state or value of variables and have an adverse effect on the application.

Debugging Client-Side Script Using Visual Studio .NET and Internet Explorer 6

VS .NET supports the debugging of client-side scripts, including JavaScript, VBScript, and JScript. VS .NET provides debugging services in conjunction with a script host such as Internet Explorer (IE). Script debugging works differently from server-side debugging in that you must specify the exact process you want to debug. Once you load the script into the script host, you can attach the VS .NET script debugger directly to the script host process and set breakpoints throughout the script.

Follow these steps to set up client-side script debugging using VS .NET and IE 6.0 (these software versions represent the minimum required versions for script debugging, in large part because VS .NET must have IE 6.0 installed on the same machine.):

1. Open IE and enable script debugging for your machine by selecting Tools ➤ Internet Options and switching to the Advanced tab. Scroll down to the Browsing category and uncheck the Disable Script Debugging box.

2. Next, load the script in the script host. Using IE, browse to the script that you want to debug. The script may be embedded within an `*.html` or `*.aspx` page as an include file. You should have only one IE window open to make it easier to locate the process to which you need to attach.

3. Now, open VS .NET and load the project for debugging. You open the project that contains the script you want to debug and then open the script in a code window.

4. Attach the debugger to the script host process. In other words, in VS .NET, open the Processes window, as shown in Figure 8-15, by selecting Debug ➤ Processes.

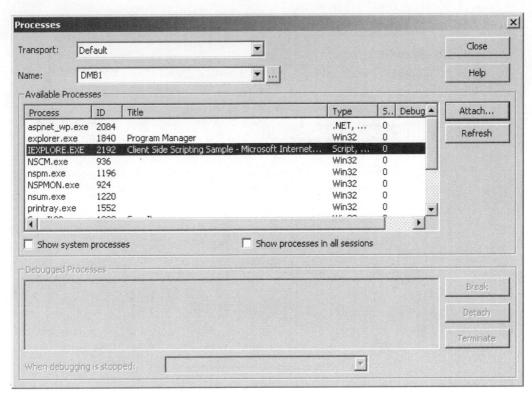

Figure 8-15. The Processes dialog box

5.   Locate the IEXPLORER.EXE process from the Available Process list and
     highlight it. Next, click the Attach button. You will see a pop-up window,
     shown in Figure 8-16.

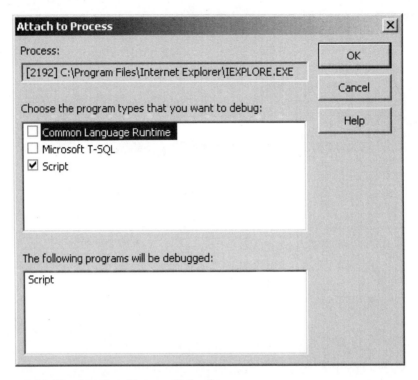

Figure 8-16. The Attach to Process dialog box

6. Check the Script check box and click OK, which returns you to
    the Processes dialog box. The Processes window should now show the
    IEXPLORER.EXE script host process in the Debugged Processes window
    (see Figure 8-17). The process has been assigned a Process ID that
    uniquely identifies the process thread. Below this window is a combo
    box that indicates the action to take when debugging is stopped. You
    may choose to either detach the debugger from the process or to termi-
    nate the script host process completely.

7. Click the Close button, and the VS .NET project will now be in
    break mode.

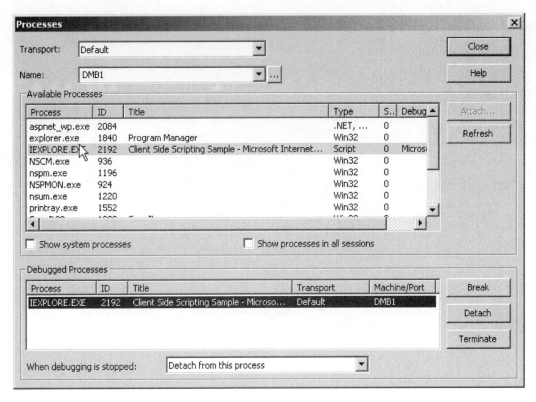

Figure 8-17. The debugged Processes window

8. Now you can set your breakpoints. Switch to the code pane that contains
    the debugged script and set breakpoints. You cannot set a breakpoint
    directly on the JavaScript function declaration. Instead, you must set the
    breakpoint just inside the function. You can set the breakpoint on a vari-
    able declaration as long as the declaration also initializes the variable in
    the same line (see Figure 8-18).

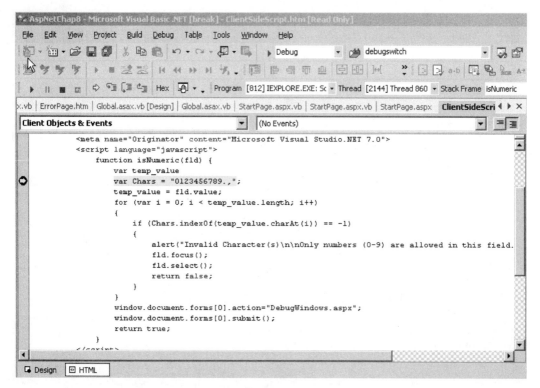

Figure 8-18. Client-side script debugging process

9. Finally, detach or terminate the debugged process: You can stop debug-
    ging anytime from within VS.NET or by manually closing the IE browser
    window. If you close the process from within VS.NET, the debug window
    shows a message like the following:

```
The program '[1588] IEXPLORE.EXE: Script program'
    has exited with code 0 (0x0).
```

This concludes the discussion of debugging tools and technologies in
VS .NET.

Using Tracing Tools in ASP.NET

Tracing documents the execution path of an application and allows you to write
trace statements and run assertions without interrupting the execution flow. By

contrast, debugging enables you to interact with the code during execution and affect its outcome. There are two distinct programmatic tracing tools available for ASP.NET applications:

- **The TraceContext class**: This is a special class only available to ASP.NET that allows tracing at the page level.

- **The Trace class**: This is a robust class defined in System.Diagnostics.Trace that provides methods and properties to trace the execution of an application.

Using the TraceContext Class

The TraceContext class captures and presents execution details about a Web request. Specifically designed as a tracing tool for ASP.NET applications, the TraceContext class is available through the System.Web namespace in the Page.Trace property. When you use the Trace property in an ASP.NET page, it is important to understand that you are using an instance of the TraceContext class, not the more robust Trace class defined in the System.Diagnostics.Trace namespace.

In addition to showing user-provided trace content, the TraceContext class automatically includes performance data, control-tree structure information, and state management content. Trace information may also include some of the lifecycle stages of a page request. The TraceContext class is useful as a quick way to view the state of a page and the events within the rendering of the page. It is purely a method to show the state information for a page. Output of the TraceContext class is appended to the page and does not provide support output to another resource.

Using the TraceContext Class Methods and Properties

The TraceContext class provides two methods to write to the trace log: Warn() and Write(). Each method supports up to three arguments, a tracing category, a text message, and optional error information. If only one argument is passed, then it will be treated as the text message. If two arguments are passed, then the first argument will be treated as the category and the second argument as the text message. The only difference between the two methods is that the text from the Warn() method is displayed in red.

The TraceContext class has two properties:

- **IsEnabled**: Indicates whether tracing is enabled for the current Web request

- **TraceMode**: Gets or sets the sorted order in which trace messages should be output to a requesting browser

You can use these properties programmatically to control the tracing characteristics of a page.

Enabling the TraceContext Class

Whether the statements using the TraceContext class take effect on the page depends on whether page-level tracing is enabled or disabled. Similar to the Debug class statements discussed earlier, if page-level tracing is disabled, then the TraceContext class statements do not output to the page. You can control page-level tracing either at the page level or at the application level. Enabling page-level tracing directs ASP.NET to append a series of diagnostic information tables to the output of the page and to display any custom diagnostic messages from the TraceContext class to the trace information table. The information and tracing messages are appended to the output of the page and sent to the requesting browser. The information is also available using a separate trace viewer (discussed in the "Enabling Application Trace in Web.config" section).

Enabling Page-Level Tracing with the @ Page Directive

You control page-level tracing with the Trace attribute of the @ Page directive. To enable tracing for a page, add the Trace attribute to the @ Page directive at the beginning of the *.aspx file and set its value to "true."

```
<%@ Page Trace="true" TraceMode="SortByCategory" %>
```

As an example, the following code enables page-level tracing in GasLaw.aspx and adds Trace.Warn() statements to trace the logical flow of the page based on different inputs:

```
Private Sub WriteTrace(ByVal strMsg As String)
    Trace.Warn(strMsg)
End Sub
```

The trace output appears as shown in Figure 8-19 for an input with a zero value.

Request Details

Request Details

Session Id:	kdpo525540mi2pboccmden55	**Request Type:**	POST
Time of Request:	7/16/2002 8:57:33 PM	**Status Code:**	200
Request Encoding:	Unicode (UTF-8)	**Response Encoding:**	Unicode (UTF-8)

Trace Information

Category	Message	From First(s)	From Last(s)
aspx.page	Begin Init		
aspx.page	End Init	0.000139	0.000139
aspx.page	Begin LoadViewState	0.000210	0.000071
aspx.page	End LoadViewState	0.000576	0.000366
aspx.page	Begin ProcessPostData	0.000644	0.000068
aspx.page	End ProcessPostData	0.000823	0.000179
aspx.page	Begin ProcessPostData Second Try	0.000894	0.000071
aspx.page	End ProcessPostData Second Try	0.000953	0.000060
aspx.page	Begin Raise ChangedEvents	0.001012	0.000059
aspx.page	End Raise ChangedEvents	0.001076	0.000064
aspx.page	Begin Raise PostBackEvent	0.001135	0.000059
	Pressure entered is 0.97	0.010739	0.009605
	Volumn entered is 1.23	0.015835	0.005096
Error: Input cannot be zero.	Details to follow.	0.037443	0.021608
	Number of moles entered is 0	0.037594	0.000151
aspx.page	End Raise PostBackEvent	0.039228	0.001634
aspx.page	Begin PreRender	0.039339	0.000111
aspx.page	End PreRender	0.039446	0.000107
aspx.page	Begin SaveViewState	0.041290	0.001844
aspx.page	End SaveViewState	0.041501	0.000211
aspx.page	Begin Render	0.041564	0.000063
aspx.page	End Render	0.044154	0.002591

Figure 8-19. Trace outputs using the Warn() *and* Write() *methods*

Interpreting the Page-Level Trace Output

Page-level tracing output provides six sections of detail, as described in Table 8-5.

Table 8-5. Trace Output Sections

OUTPUT SECTIONS	DESCRIPTION
Control Tree	The Control Tree section displays information about server controls within the page. It displays the ID, type, render size, and view state size of the control. The information gives an idea of the controls being used, as well as the associated cost (render size and view state).

(continued)

Table 8-5. Trace Output Sections (continued)

OUTPUT SECTIONS	DESCRIPTION
Cookies Collection	The Cookies Collection section displays the names, values, and sizes of the cookies that the client sends in the request headers.
Headers Collection	This section provides the HTTP headers presented by the client to the server. It is a simple table that lists name-value pairs.
Request Details	The Request Details section displays basic request information, such as the session ID, time of the request, HTTP request type, and HTTP response status code.
Server Variables	The Server Variables section displays a name-value pair table of server variables.
Trace Information	The Trace Information section displays a table view of categories and messages, including messages from the TraceContext.Warn() and Write() methods. This section also provides the time from first to last byte.

Enabling Application Trace in Web.config

You can enable tracing for the whole application by setting the <trace> section values in the Web.config file, under the System.Web node. To enable application trace, set the enabled attribute in the trace node to "true" and set the other optional attributes. This has the same effect as setting the page-level Trace attribute to "true" on each page within the application:

```
<configuration>
  <system.web>
    <trace enabled="true" requestLimit="10" pageOutput="true"
           traceMode="SortByCategory" localOnly="true" />
  </system.web>
</configuration>
```

The trace configuration in Web.config has five trace attributes that control the tracing characteristics (see Table 8-6).

Table 8-6. ASP.NET Trace Attributes

PROPERTY	DEFAULT	DESCRIPTION
enabled	"false"	Sets the ASP.NET page- or application-level trace.
localOnly	"true"	Set to "true" if you want the trace viewer (`trace.axd`) to function only on the host Web server; otherwise set to "false."
pageOutput	"false"	Set to "true" to display the trace information both on an application's pages and in the trace viewer (`trace.axd`); otherwise set to "false" to only display in the trace viewer.
requestLimit	"10"	Number of page requests to store on the server.
traceMode	"SortByTime"	Indicates whether trace information is displayed in the order it was processed, "SortByTime," or alphabetically by user-defined category, "SortByCategory."

These attributes are scoped at the application level, but they are overridden at the page level by any attributes defined in the @ Page directive.

Using the Trace.axd HttpHandler

With the Web.config file, you can enable application tracing but disable the output from displaying directly on the Web page:

```
<system.web>
    <trace enabled="true" pageOutput="false" requestLimit="10" localOnly="true" />
</system.web>
```

In this case you would use the Trace.axd handler to read the trace output from the page. Trace.axd is an HttpHandler, which is a specialized class for handling HTTP Requests (HTTP handlers are discussed in great detail in Chapter 2, "Introducing ASP.NET Applications"). The trace.axd handler displays the trace output from an ASP.NET page. When requested, the handler gives a trace log of the last n requests; *n* is determined by the value set by requestlimit="[int]" in the configuration file.

To use the `trace.axd` utility, simply request `trace.axd` from the root application directory. This brings up a listing of the last n requests in the application, as shown in Figure 8-20.

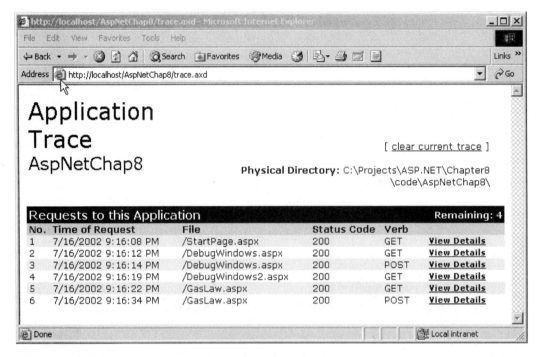

Figure 8-20. Trace output using the `trace.axd` *utility*

The View Details link brings up the trace information for each request. The only difference is `trace.axd` does not display the page outputs.

Using the Trace Class

The Trace class offers a robust set of methods that mirror the methods of the Debug class discussed earlier. The Trace class is in the `System.Diagnostics` namespace; you must import this namespace to use the class.

Enabling the Trace Class

You configure tracing with the Trace class as part of the project's property pages. By default, tracing is enabled in both debug and release builds. You can set the

trace mode in the project's property pages under Configuration Properties
➤ Build ➤ Define TRACE constant. When checked, the Trace class statements are
compiled into the build.

Understanding the Trace Class Methods

The Trace class has the same set of methods as the Debug class. Table 8-7
describes the methods available in the Trace class.

Table 8-7. Common Trace Class Methods

METHOD	DESCRIPTION
Assert()	Tests a specified condition and displays a message if the condition is "false."
Fail()	Sends a message to the Listeners collection. Message will include the customer message and a dump of the call stack.
Write()	Writes information to the trace listeners in the Listeners collection.
WriteIf()	If the condition is "true," writes information to the trace listeners in the Listeners collection.
WriteLine()	Same as Write() except this method includes a carriage return.
WriteLineIf()	Same as WriteIf() except this method includes a carriage return.

Adding Listeners to the Trace.Listeners Collection

As stated earlier, you can customize the target of the Debug class's assertion
message by adding listeners to the Debug.Listeners collection. The Trace class
behaves similarly. By default, the DefaultTraceListener is added to the Listeners
collection to provide the default output methods for the Trace class. The
DefaultTraceListener writes to the Output window, so you must add other listeners to output to other destinations if the Trace is to function outside the debug
environment. These other listeners inherit from the TraceListeners base class.

As an example, you can update the CheckInput subroutine in GasLaw.aspx to
write to the event log. Writing to the event log requires the EventLogTraceListener.
Here, you use the Add() method in the Listeners class to add your
EventLogTraceListener to the collection. You use the Contains() method to make
sure you do not add more than one listener. The updated code is as follows:

```
Private Sub CheckInput(ByVal dblInput As Double)
    Dim myTraceListener As New EventLogTraceListener("AspNetChap8")
    If traceSwitch.Enabled Then
        If Not System.Diagnostics.Trace.Listeners.Contains(myTraceListener) Then
            System.Diagnostics.Trace.Listeners.Add(myTraceListener)
        End If
        System.Diagnostics.Trace.Assert((dblInput <> 0), _
            "Error:  Input cannot be zero.",  "Details to follow.")
    End If
End Sub
```

When this code is executed, you will get the error in the event log, as shown in Figure 8-21.

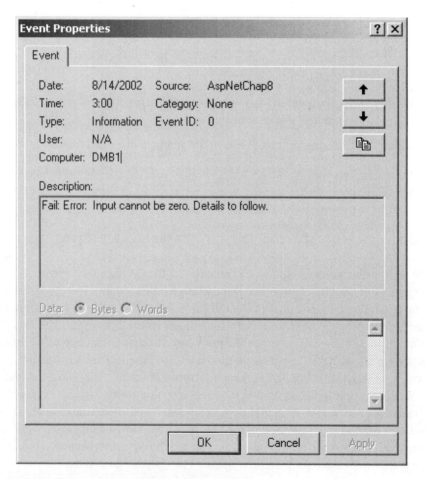

Figure 8-21. Trace error message in the event log

Trace Switching

You can control when information is written to the output target of a trace by using the features of the BooleanSwitch and TraceSwitch classes. The BooleanSwitch class provides a simple on/off activation switch, and the TraceSwitch provides a multilevel switch. To use a BooleanSwitch, first define the level of the BooleanSwitch in the Web.config file. The configuration in the file should be as follows:

```
<configuration>
<system.diagnostics>
    <switches>
        <!-- This switch controls data messages. In order to receive data
        trace messages, change value="0" to value="1" -->
        <add name="mySwitch" value="1" />
    </switches>
  </system.diagnostics>
...
</configuration>
```

You can find an example of using the BooleanSwitch in GasLaw.aspx. First create a new instance of the BooleanSwitch:

```
Private Shared myBoolSwitch As New BooleanSwitch("mySwitch", _
    "Trace Boolean Switch")
```

Then, you use the BooleanSwitch.Enabled property to determine whether to output trace information. The Enabled property returns "true" if the BooleanSwitch is enabled (set to 1) in Web.config. In this example, the WriteTrace() subroutine performs this task as follows:

```
Private Sub WriteTrace(ByVal strMsg As String)
    If myBoolSwitch.Enabled Then
        System.Diagnostics.Trace.WriteLine(strMsg)
    End If
End Sub
```

NOTE *In the preceding sample, you could achieve the same functionality with the following statement:* System.Diagnostics.Trace.WriteLineIf(myBoolSwitch. Enabled, strMsg). *However, you will usually get better performance by testing the BooleanSwitch before calling the debug (or trace) method. This saves the overhead of evaluating all the parameters in the* WriteLineIf *method.*

TraceSwitch provides a mechanism to define multiple trace levels within an application. To define the settings, add a TraceSwitch configuration in Web.config as follows:

```
<system.diagnostics>
    <switches>
        <!-- This switch controls general messages. In order to
        receive general trace messages change the value to the
        appropriate level. "1" gives error messages, "2" gives errors
        and warnings, "3" gives more detailed error information, and
        "4" gives verbose trace information -->
            <add name="TraceLevelSwitch" value="1" />
    </switches>
```

Previously, we have added a switch named "TraceLevelSwitch" and assigned it a value of 1. In code, you can read the value for TraceLevelSwitch by creating a Share member as follows:

```
Private Shared trSwitch As New BooleanSwitch("TraceLevelSwitch", "Trace Switch")
    ...
    If trSwitch.Level = TraceLevel.Error Then
        System.Diagnostics.Trace.WriteLine(strMsg)
End If
```

The TraceLevel is a predefined enumeration within .NET, as shown in Table 8-8.

Table 8-8. TraceLevel Enumerations

NAME	VALUE	DESCRIPTION
Off	0	No trace messages
Error	1	Output error handling messages
Warning	2	Output error handling messages and warnings
Info	3	Output error handling messages, warnings, and informational messages
Verbose	4	Output all messages

This concludes the discussion of tracing tools in VS .NET.

Exploring Strategies for Exception Management

A well-designed exception management strategy for an application provides valuable information to assist technical support and the development team with the information they need to identify and resolve issues in the production environment. The exception management strategy should do the following:

- Detect exceptions.

- Log information regarding the exception.

- Notify the appropriate agent.

Exceptions are caused by a breach of an implicit assumption made within code. Exceptions can be raised by a fault in an application's code, from code in a library outside of the application, or even from the common language runtime. They are not necessarily errors but are merely scenarios where an unexpected event has occurred. An exception can be thrown explicitly as a result of an anticipated event to bullet-proof an application from adversely affecting other applications or to provide a robust user experience.

Once a Web application is in production, exceptions must be logged in a meaningful way so that developers can analyze and troubleshoot the issues later, without having to witness the issues first-hand. Unattended monitoring exists to help monitor and track application issues and performance in the production environment. The following sections focus on how you can use unattended monitoring as part of an exception management strategy for the production environment.

Detecting Exceptions

The .NET Framework supports structured exception handling for all .NET languages. Structured exception handling provides a controlled structure to detect and handle exceptions raised during application execution. Using the try, catch, and finally code blocks can prevent exceptions in portions of the code from affecting other portions of the application. The structure of the code blocks is as follows:

```
Try
     'executable code with potential exceptions
Catch [Exception Class]
     'code to handle a specific exception.
     'there can be mulitple catch code blocks, each to handle a different exception
Finally
     'code used for cleanup, this code is always executed
 '   independent of whether or not an exception is thrown
```

You should not use exceptions to control the normal flow of an application. For example, the GasLaw.aspx page has the potential to have a divide by 0 exception. Because that is caused by an invalid user input, we have implemented code to check and handle this scenario without having to use exception handling. If exceptions are incorporated as part of the normal flow, the code will become unreadable and unmanageable.

It is good practice to catch exceptions as soon as possible. If the application cannot find a Catch block to handle the exception, then it checks the Catch statements in the outer exception handlers, progressing through the entire call stack until a match is found. If it cannot find any, it raises the exception all the way to the initial caller, usually the user interface application. In the case of ASP.NET, you can design robust error handling at the page or application level, but it is still good practice to avoid having unhandled exceptions migrate up the call stack.

Filtering Exceptions

You can filter exceptions based on the exception type with the `Catch` exception blocks. For example, the Database class in the AspNetChap8 project employs many methods from the SQL data provider. In the `GetProdList()` function, the exception handling handles SQL exceptions differently from other exceptions with the following code:

```
Catch SQLExp As SqlException
    Return (New DataSet())
Catch e As Exception
    Throw New Exception("Error: " & e.Source & ": " & e.Message)
Finally
    ' Close the SQL connection (DataSet is disconnected)
    If m_sqlConn.State = ConnectionState.Open Then m_sqlConn.Close()
End Try
```

Depending on the requirements of your application, each specific exception can have its own processing code.

You can filter SqlException, IOException, and other specific exceptions as part of your exception handling. This not only allows you to customize your handling for these specific exceptions, but it also allows you to display meaningful information about the type of exception encountered.

Best Practices for Throwing Exceptions

Throwing exceptions is always expensive (because so much information gets passed, and you are delegating). As such, you should throw an exception only when additional intervention is required and, even then, decide if you need to throw the whole exception or can raise an error with limited information.

If it is possible for your component to handle an exception internally, it should do so. Throwing unnecessary exceptions increases the chance that the calling component will not handle the exception and instead propagate the error up the call stack. You should not use exceptions as a means of communication between components. You should use events instead.

If, however, you do need to throw an exception up the call stack, then you have three ways to propagate the exception:

- **Automatic propagation**: Ignore the exception and allow it to move up the call stack until it reaches a Catch block that matches the exception.

- **Catch and rethrow the propagation**: Catch the exception and perform any tasks needed within the current method. Then throw the exception up the call stack.

- **Catch, wrap, and throw the wrapped exception**: Catch the exception and perform any tasks needed within the current method. Then wrap the exception inside another exception with more meaning to the caller and throw the wrapped exception to the caller.

If you choose to generate custom exceptions within your component, be sure to document them so that developers using your component will best be able to handle them. The documentation should include a description of the exception, the conditions in which the exception will likely occur, suggested ways for resolving the error condition, and any error codes or additional information that the exception returns.

Managing Unhandled Exceptions in ASP.NET

In an ASP.NET application, an unhandled exception can propagate to the Web page itself. When this occurs, ASP.NET employs two events to handle exceptions that reach the boundary of the application.

- **Page_Error**: Page-level event to handle exceptions on an individual page

- **Application_Error**: Application-level event to handle exceptions propagated from any page in the application

At the page level, the Page base class exposes a `Page_Error()` event handler, which you can override in your pages. This handler is called whenever an unhandled exception is thrown at runtime. To override the `Page_Error()` handler, simply add a `Page_Error()` subroutine to the page's code-behind file:

```
Sub Page_Error(ByVal Source As Object, ByVal E As EventArgs)
    ......
End Sub
```

The application-level event handler for unhandled exceptions is the `Application_Error()` subroutine, which is located in the `Global.asax` file. This handler is a last resort destination for unhandled exceptions. For this reason, the handler code should log the exception information, send notifications, and perform any other necessary actions before gracefully returning an error message to the user:

```
Sub Application_Error(ByVal sender As Object, ByVal e As EventArgs)
    ' Fires when an error occurs
    ......
End Sub
```

Logging Exception Information

Exception information must be properly logged to be useful to the developer and support services. If it is not properly logged, it becomes difficult to track down the source of the exception or to extract any relevant data and trends from the information. You can log exception information and report it to one of three destinations:

- Windows event log

- Relational database

- Custom log file

Each destination has its advantages and disadvantages.
The advantages of the Windows event log as a destination are as follows:

- It is reliable.

- It is available in Windows NT and Windows 2000.

- It has built-in log file size management.

- It is easy to use.

- It is supported by most monitoring tools.

- You can easily analyze the sequence of events within a system.

The disadvantages of the Windows event log as a destination are as follows:

- The event log is tied to a server, so the data is not centralized if more than one server is used. An application can log to a remote server's event log, but the chance of failure is high and should be avoided.

- Logged information can be overwritten depending on the event log configuration.

- Improper configuration can cause log blocking if the event log is full.

The advantages of a relational database as a destination are as follows:

- Data is centralized and accessible from multiple servers.

- Database tools support queries and reporting.

- You can define the structure of the log data to best meet the needs of the application.

The disadvantages of a relational database as a destination are as follows:

- Dependent on a database, which introduces additional risk of connectivity and database health.

- It is difficult to sync up database-logged data and application logs in the Event Viewer.

- Most monitoring tools do not support interaction with a database.

The advantage of a custom log file as a destination is that you have flexibility in choosing the format of the log file. The disadvantages of a custom log file as a destination are as follows:

- You have to deal with issues relating to concurrent access.

- You have to design a method of managing log file size.

- You must develop tools to read and administer the log file.

- You must configure monitoring tools to read the log format.

.NET supports event logs through the `System.Diagnostics` namespace. To illustrate how to create a unique event log and insert logs, add the code to write to the event viewer in the application error event in `Global.asax` as follows:

```
Imports System.Diagnostics
Sub Application_Error(ByVal sender As Object, ByVal e As EventArgs)
        ' Fires when an error occurs
        Dim ErrorDescription As String = Server.GetLastError.ToString
```

```
'Creation of event log if it does not exist
Dim EventLogName As String = "AspNetChap8"
If (Not EventLog.SourceExists(EventLogName)) Then
    EventLog.CreateEventSource(EventLogName, EventLogName)
End If

' Inserting into event log
Dim Log As New EventLog()
Log.Source = EventLogName
Log.WriteEntry(ErrorDescription, EventLogEntryType.Error)

End Sub
```

In the application-level event handler, a log named "AspNetChap8" is created if it does not exist in the event log. If it already exists, the error entry is added to the existing list of events. When you test the `ErrorSample.aspx` page and get the "Resource not found" error as before, the `Application_Error()` event handler gets invoked and the resultant event is logged to the viewer. Figure 8-22 shows an example of a logged event as it appears in the Event Viewer utility. If the resultant event is not logged, it is likely caused by a permissions issue. Recall that Web application code is run in an ASP.NET worker process. By default, the identity of this process is a local ASPNET account. For this sample to work, the process identity must have write permissions to the event log.

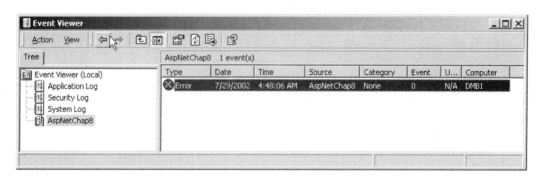

Figure 8-22. Event logged to the Event Viewer

Selecting the event will display the Event Properties dialog box that will display the exception type and description as in Figure 8-23.

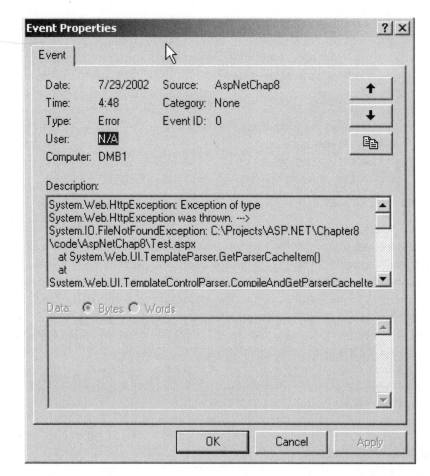

Figure 8-23. Event properties

Understanding Exception Notification

It is important to log exceptions to understand what caused them and how to resolve them. However, it is also important to notify support staff of exceptions in a timely manner. Exception information is not helpful unless it is provided to the person or group that is capable of interpreting and resolving the exception.

A common notification method is to send an email to the appropriate parties when an exception occurs. Many third-party application monitoring and log scraping tools exist that also include email and alert features to notify developers of application issues. However, it is relatively simple to implement this feature in ASP.NET. Again, you can set this up to function within the page-level error event or the application-level error event. For this example, add the email functionality to the application-level error event as follows:

```
Sub Application_Error(ByVal sender As Object, ByVal e As EventArgs)
    ' Fires when an error occurs
    ' event log code here
    Dim mail As New MailMessage()
    Dim ErrorMessage As String
    Dim strSubject As String
    strSubject = Request.Url.ToString & " Site Error"
    ErrorMessage = "Error encountered in page " & Request.Url.ToString & ": " & _
            Server.GetLastError.ToString
    mail.To = "administrator@domain.com"
    mail.Subject = strSubject
    mail.Priority = MailPriority.High
    mail.BodyFormat = MailFormat.Text
    mail.Body = ErrorMessage
    SmtpMail.Send(mail)
End Sub
```

Writing Custom Error Pages

In addition to the exception management common to all languages in the .NET Framework, ASP.NET provides some functionality to manage how an exception should be displayed to the user. If an error occurs in an ASP.NET application, a default error page is displayed. The page displays the error message, a description of the error encountered, and the requested URL. For example, the ErrorSample.aspx page generates an error by requesting an unavailable resource (see Figure 8-24).

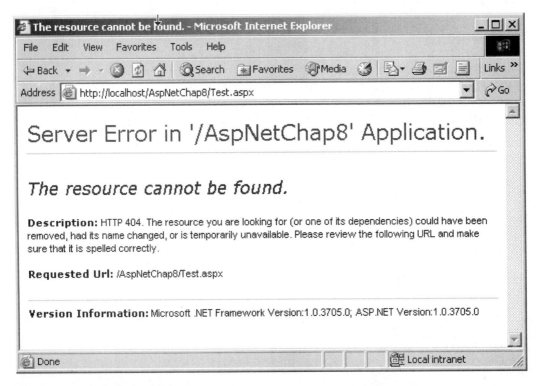

Figure 8-24. Default error page

If you wanted to display a more user-friendly error page, you can customize a default error page for your ASP.NET application. To set up the custom error page, follow these steps:

1. Create an error page (in our example, ErrorPage.htm).

2. Update the Web.config file to set the defaultRedirect parameter in the <customErrors> directive within <system.web>.

3. If necessary, you can also specify pages for certain HTTP error codes by using the statuscode attribute:

```
<customErrors defaultRedirect="ErrorPage.htm" mode="On" />
    <error statuscode="500" redirect="/errorpages/ServerError.htm" />
```

Besides the defaultRedirect parameter that stores the name of the custom error page, you can set the mode parameter with one of three values:

- **Off Mode**: Sets ASP.NET to use its default error page for both local and remote users in case of an error.

- **On Mode**: Sets ASP.NET to use the user-defined custom error page instead of its default error page for both local and remote users. If a custom error page is not specified, ASP.Net shows the error page describing how to enable remote viewing of errors.

- **RemoteOnly**: The default ASP.NET error page is shown only to local users. Remote requests will first check the configuration settings for the custom error page or finally show an IIS error.

Having updated Web.config and deployed ErrorPage.htm to the Web server, going through the same test generates the page shown in Figure 8-25.

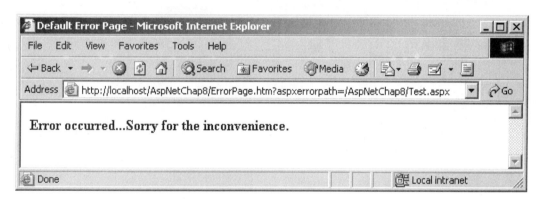

Figure 8-25. Custom error page

This concludes the section on unattended monitoring. Central to the concept of unattended monitoring in a deployed application is the exception management strategy. In addition, applications should take advantage of the specific exception management features provided by ASP.NET.

Summary

The .NET Framework SDK and VS .NET provide an excellent set of tools for diagnosing and resolving application exceptions. In this chapter we discussed how to use debugging and tracing tools to diagnose known issues and perform application monitoring in ASP.NET applications. We discussed the concept of build configurations to define build types. Applications go through several build types during the development process, from debug builds to release builds. VS .NET makes it easy to manage build configurations, and it also provides a number of integrated debug windows that allow you to step through an application and examine its state. The .NET Framework SDK provides specialized Debug and Trace classes for implementing programmatic debugging and tracing. In addition, ASP.NET provides a specialized TraceContext class for tracing ASP.NET Web applications. Finally, we discussed the importance of an exception management strategy for deployed applications, which includes unattended monitoring. We provided examples of the exception management features provided by ASP.NET.

Index

About Apress

Apress, located in Berkeley, CA, is a fast-growing, innovative publishing company devoted to meeting the needs of existing and potential programming professionals. Simply put, the "A" in Apress stands for *The Author's Press™*. Apress' unique approach to publishing grew out of conversations between its founders, Gary Cornell and Dan Appleman, authors of numerous best-selling, highly regarded books for programming professionals. In 1998 they set out to create a publishing company that emphasized quality above all else. Gary and Dan's vision has resulted in the publication of over 70 titles by leading software professionals, all of which have *The Expert's Voice™*.

Do You Have What It Takes to Write for Apress?

Apress is rapidly expanding its publishing program. If you can write and you refuse to compromise on the quality of your work, if you believe in doing more than rehashing existing documentation, and if you're looking for opportunities and rewards that go far beyond those offered by traditional publishing houses, we want to hear from you!

Consider these innovations that we offer all of our authors:

- **Top royalties with *no* hidden switch statements**
  Authors typically receive only half of their normal royalty rate on foreign sales. In contrast, Apress' royalty rate remains the same for both foreign and domestic sales.

- **Sharing the wealth**
  Most publishers keep authors on the same pay scale even after costs have been met. At Apress author royalties dramatically increase the more books are sold.

- **Serious treatment of the technical review process**
  Each Apress book is reviewed by a technical expert(s) whose remuneration depends in part on the success of the book since he or she too receives royalties.

Moreover, through a partnership with Springer-Verlag, New York, Inc., one of the world's major publishing houses, Apress has significant venture capital and distribution power behind it. Thus, we have the resources to produce the highest quality books *and* market them aggressively.

If you fit the model of the Apress author who can write a book that provides *What The Professional Needs To Know™*, then please contact us for more information:

editorial@apress.com